JOHN:

The Gospel of Belief

Careful and patient scholarship and a deep devotion to communicating the truths of the Christian faith have been the twin passions of Merrill C. Tenney's long and fruitful career as a minister, lecturer, writer, and teacher (most recently at Wheaton College, Wheaton, Illinois). Professor Tenney holds the doctorate in Biblical and Patristic Greek from Harvard University. As noted on the back panel, he is the author of several books, which have enjoyed a wide readership throughout the world.

In 1975 *Current Issues in Biblical and Patristic Interpretation,* a collection of essays by his former students, was presented as a well-deserved tribute to him on the occasion of his seventieth birthday.

JOHN:
The Gospel of Belief

An Analytic Study of the Text

by

MERRILL C. TENNEY, Ph.D.

Dean of the Graduate School,
Wheaton College, Wheaton, Illinois

WILLIAM B. EERDMANS PUBLISHING COMPANY
Grand Rapids, Michigan

TO MY WIFE
Helen J. Tenney
who labors with me
in the gospel

Foreword

Nearly three thousand years ago Solomon said that of the making of many books there was no end. If he thought that was true in his day, I wonder how he would express the idea today, when more new volumes are printed in one year, in Europe and America, than were probably to be found in the entire library of this wisest of all men. This statement of Solomon's, however, has in it a very serious admonition, which many people miss: If there is no end to the making of books, one thing is sure, we cannot, even if we would want to (and only a foolish man wants to) read all the books that are being published. In fact, a Christian cannot read all the books that are being published about the Bible and about the Christian faith, not even all the good ones. If, then, we cannot read all the books that have been and are now being published regarding our holy faith, it is necessary for us to exercise discrimination in the matter.

This necessity for separating the ordinary from the extraordinary, the good from the best, is particularly important in the matter of studies and commentaries on the various books of the Bible. Frankly, there are thousands of ordinary volumes about the Bible, and various parts of the Bible, that no one today need ever consult. I do not mean that these volumes which can be passed by do not contain some truth, and would not convey a blessing in reading, but I do mean that there are other volumes, on the same subjects, which are infinitely superior and these are the ones, when life is so short and the Word of God so important, that we ought to seek out.

I suppose that more volumes have been written about John's Gospel, and parts of this Gospel, and the author, than about any other one portion of the Word of God, with the possible exceptions of the book of Genesis and the book of Revelation. Of these, some important, I have no hesitancy at all in strongly recommending to Bible students, teachers, and ministers everywhere this new volume on the Gospel of John by my beloved friend, Professor Tenney of Wheaton College.

To begin with, the author has had a thorough discipline in New Testament Greek, and inasmuch as this is the language in which John wrote his Gospel, it is important to know something of this language if one is to determine, with absolute accuracy, the meaning of John's profound sentences. I do not mean a man cannot get great spiritual blessing from this Gospel without a knowledge of Greek, but such a knowledge certainly does help him to determine the finer shades of meaning, and this Professor Tenney has done for us in these rich pages. In the second place, Dr. Tenney knows the best literature that has arisen around this Gospel, and his conclusions are so much the more dependable. He has wrestled with the writings and conclusions of the best scholars, and his own convictions are the result of prolonged study. In the third place, Dr. Tenney has written this volume with painstaking care; in fact, I happen to know that some parts have been rewritten four and five times, and all at least three times. Too many religious books today are carelessly thrown off, in a few weeks of seclusion in some mountain resort, or in a bedroom on a train as one hurries about the country. Finally, the truths that Dr. Tenney has here brought forth have been tested both in the classroom and in the pulpit. Dr. Tenney is recognized as one of the ablest New Testament teachers in this country today.

There are many things to commend in this volume which will reveal themselves as a student turns these pages. We should emphasize the word *student*. This volume is for those who really wish to make a study of John's Gospel, to know the deeper veins of its great message, and to understand more thoroughly the conflict between belief and unbelief which it sets forth. Not the least of the assets of this book are the splendid outlines which Professor Tenney has worked out with distinct originality. In fact, I think his outline of the resurrection narrative in John's Gospel—and this is a favorite subject of mine—is about the finest outline on this great passage that I have seen anywhere. I commend him for breaking away from the frequently-repeated, erroneous emphasis concerning the Greek words for love in 21:15-17, and for his remarkable charts analyzing certain portions of the Gospel.

Three results certainly will accrue to any Christian who seriously gives himself to the study of these pages. First of all, he will have a deeper understanding of this inexhaustible book in which the only begotten Son of God is revealed so uniquely and triumphantly. Secondly, he will be stimulated to further study, and will have in his hands keys for unlocking additional treasures deposited in John's strangely glowing pages. Finally, he will discover in his own heart an increasing love for the Lord Jesus, a deeper appreciation of His divine person, and of the work which He did during His incarnation. I congratulate Professor Tenney on the thoroughness of this study, and wish to heartily recommend it as one of the most helpful books for Bible study to be published in this country.

WILBUR M. SMITH

Fuller Theological Seminary,
Pasadena, California

Preface

Many excellent critical commentaries on the Fourth Gospel already have been published which can never be superseded. There is, however, a dearth of study books which treat the Gospel as a unit, and which unfold its structure in such a way that the average Christian who is not trained in theology can master its thought. JOHN: THE GOSPEL OF BELIEF is prepared for a reader to use with his Bible as an aid to private study. The book is not intended to be read independently of the Biblical text, nor should it be regarded as a substitute for personal research. It is designed as a guide by which the individual may make his own analysis of JOHN, and so derive from the Gospel the particular message that it may have for him.

The analytical method which is illustrated in the exposition of the Prologue and of chapter twenty of JOHN is the basis for the outlines in the book. The topical studies are purposely incomplete, but are samples of the kind of investigation that may be pursued in the doctrine and vocabulary of any part of Scripture. The reader should try the methods for himself, and should add the results of his original study to whatever he finds in these pages.

Acknowledgments are due to the Macmillan Company, of New York, and to the Cambridge Press of Cambridge, England, for permission to quote from E. A. Abbott's *Johannine Grammar;* to John Murray of London, England, for the use of numerous short extracts from Brooke Foss Westcott's *The Gospel According to St. John;* and to the *Sunday School Times* for the use of four of the author's articles on "The Keys to

11

John's Gospel," which were published in the January issues of the *Times* of 1947.

The author is indebted also to Miss Mildred Cook of Los Angeles, California, for her expert editorial counsel, and to his colleague, Dr. C. Raymond Ludwigson of Wheaton College, who graciously lent his skill in preparing the map that accompanies the text.

M. C. T.

Wheaton College
Wheaton, Illinois

Table of Contents

13

List of Charts and Diagrams

JOHN: THE GOSPEL OF BELIEF

INTRODUCTION

Introduction

The Christian public of today has come into possession of a vast body of expository literature which has gradually been produced during the last nineteen centuries through an intensive study of the Biblical text. Much of this literature has proved useful in that it has clarified the meaning of the Scripture. Some of this writing, of course, has been misinterpretation which has ranged from harmless vagaries to pernicious error. Modern Christians are the heirs of all the ages, and have much in the way of aids to study and thinking provided by the scholars and commentators of the past.

However, the possession of this body of literary aids constitutes a real peril. There is danger of substituting the explanation for the text itself. Men read what Dr. X and Professor Y have to say about the text rather than let the text talk to them.

A little reflection will reveal that when the Fourth Gospel was first written no such procedure was followed. Its writer did not append to it a commentary in order that his readers might understand what he meant. He felt that the work would interpret itself. It was written as a piece of direct evangelistic propaganda, and its avowed purpose was to arouse faith, not to befog intelligence. It was designed to stand on its own merits, and to convey clearly its own message.

Of course, allowance must be made for the fact that the Christians who first read this Gospel or listened to it while it was read to them were not handicapped by having to use a translation. They did not have to stop every now and then to discuss what the portion meant "in the Greek"; they read

the Greek. Modern readers do have that handicap; and since
the thoughts of one language are never completely translatable
into another, some comment may be necessary to bring out all
the shades of meaning which the Greek possesses and which
the English cannot always reproduce. Nevertheless the general excellence and variety of modern translations reduce the
handicap to a minimum of importance. Certainly the Christians of the first century and those of the twentieth century
both can understand the substance of the Gospel of John sufficiently well to profit by its main teachings and to grasp its
spiritual significance.

One other concession must be made for the modern reader.
He lives at a time so remote from that of the Fourth Gospel
that he may often despair of understanding the book's allusions without aid. Indeed some explanations are necessary in
order to bridge the gulf, formed by the changes of the passing
years, between the custom and thought of the first century and
those of the twentieth century.

Granting, then, that the differences both in language and
customs between readers of the first century and those of the
modern day constitute a difficulty to overcome, it is still true
that the first century Christian has much to teach men today.
Though he could not take from his book shelf a commentary
to enable him to understand this Gospel (and, indeed, he experienced no need for such assistance), he must have been able
to draw from the Scripture what it was intended to teach. The
book must have had some key to self-interpretation which
would enable the casual recipient to benefit by its truth. What
was the key?

The clue to this interpretation lies in the literary structure
of the book. If the author was an intelligent person, he must
have had some goal in view when he wrote his work and some
definable method of making the contents crystal clear to his
audience. If the writing were to be read publicly, it must be

divisible into units, each of which would make a suitable lesson for unlearned hearers. If it were to be read privately, it must be so planned that the reader would progress steadily toward a definite objective in thinking. In neither case could the author afford to confuse obscurity with profundity.

This study operates, therefore, on the thesis that a straightforward analysis of the text of JOHN is the only proper approach to an understanding of its meaning. While other methods of study are undoubtedly legitimate and fruitful, the analytic study based on the natural structure of the book is most likely to reveal the author's intention in writing.

The purpose of this present treatise, consequently, is to analyze the Fourth Gospel in such fashion that the author's main aim, theme, and developed teaching shall be clearly revealed. This work is intended to be a seed-bed for thought rather than a granary. The reader should be prepared to think for himself, and to do his own harvesting from the use of the suggestions proffered here.

The method followed in the prosecution of this purpose is threefold: first, an attempt is made to discover what the author of the Fourth Gospel has to say about his own purpose and plan in writing the Gospel; second, a glimpse is given into the unfolding of his method of procedure in dealing with his stated theme; third, a consecutive analysis is offered of each of the component sections of the treatise as they advance the theme. This method is applicable to almost any book of the Bible; and if the reader will master and use it, he will be able to uncover new and startling treasures in the Book of God.

Critical questions of authorship, integrity, genuineness, sequence of text, historical value of the narrative, etc., will not be treated extensively in ·this volume, since the casual reader is not usually interested in technical minutiae and since JOHN is generally used as it stands in the most widely accepted version. Many of these questions are recognized as being of great importance; but they have already been given consideration by other writers. The chief purpose of this book is to treat analytically the existing structure of JOHN rather than to produce a critical introduction to it.

The analysis of JOHN will be taken up in three parts. Part I, The Structure of the Gospel, will deal with a general consideration of the methods of outlining the Gospel, subsequent to a careful interpretation of the key which the Gospel itself provides. Part II, The Textual Analysis of the Gospel, will consist of an exposition of the text, divided into periods representing the various stages of the career of Jesus as presented by JOHN. Part III, The Topical Analysis of the Gospel, will furnish a topical summary of the content of the Gospel under various headings supplied by the phraseology of the Gospel itself.

Part I

THE STRUCTURE OF THE GOSPEL

CHAPTER I

The Internal Evidence of Structure

GRANTING that the existing text of the Fourth Gospel is substantially identical in content and arrangement with that which its author originally committed to manuscript, the chief clue to the interpretation of the book is its structure. This structure is discernible from three angles: (1) a formal statement of purpose and method made by the author; (2) the patent divisions of the book, whether logical, chronological, or geographical; and (3) the use of repeated terms in the vocabulary which may, by the frequency and distribution of their occurrence, reveal the shift of interest from one topic to another.

The Formal Statement of the Author

In John 20:30, 31 there is a clear declaration of the author's intention in writing the book. Following as it does the climactic confession of Thomas, this assertion closes the main narrative and makes the final appeal to the reader. A grammatical analysis of this section should, therefore, reveal what the author had in mind when he composed the work. This process of investigation is similar to the old-fashioned method of diagramming sentences. For example,

30 Many other signs therefore did Jesus
        | in the presence of the disciples,
        | which are not written
                      in this book:
31 But these are written,
        | that ye may believe
        | that Jesus is the Christ,
        | the Son of God;
        | and   believing
        | that./........ye may have life in his name.

The sentence divides naturally into two coordinate clauses, "many other signs did Jesus . . ." and "but these are written . . ." These clauses, each of which makes a main statement, are placed at the extreme left-hand margin of the page. Modifying phrases, such as "in the presence of the disciples," and subordinate clauses, such as "that ye may believe . . ." are written directly beneath the words which they modify or on which they depend. This purely mechanical arrangement reveals at a glance what are the main statements of the passage, and what are the secondary ones. A summary of the main statements yields the following at once : (1) Jesus performed many signs which are unrecorded in this book; (2) those that are recorded are written for a definite purpose. The two points give the information that the author knew more than he wrote, but that what he did write was intended to fulfill a particular purpose.

Furthermore, in these two main sentences there are three outstanding words: *signs, believe, life*. These three are pivots of thought, and deserve definition.

Signs is the English translation of the Greek *semeia*, the plural of *semeion*, which is the characteristic Johannine word for miracle. Three other words are used in the New Testament with much the same meaning. *Teras* appears in Acts 2:19 and elsewhere, is translated wonder, and emphasizes the character of the miracle as a portent or prodigy, something outside the usual course of events. *Dunamis* is the root of the English word dynamite, stresses the power revealed in the performance of the miracle, and implies the spiritual energy which produced it. It is frequently used by Matthew, as in 11:20, 21, 23, etc. *Paradoxon,* in English, paradox, pictures the contradictory nature of the miracle, its incongruity with the order of the natural world, and its strangeness to the usual current of thought. *Semeion,* however, when applied to a miracle, usually implies that the deed is an indication of some power or meaning behind it to which it is secondary in importance. For instance, in Luke 2:12, the angel said by way of instructing the shepherds: "And this *is* the sign unto you: Ye shall find a babe wrapped in swaddling clothes, and lying in a manger." The fact that the child was wrapped in a certain type of garment was proof that it was the one of which the angel had spoken, and was called *sign*.[1] While the use of this term as applied to a miracle is not confined to JOHN, it is the only word used for miracle in that Gospel. JOHN, then, presented the miracles not merely as supernatural deeds nor as manifestations of supernatural power, nor even as exceptions to the usual current of events, but definitely as material witnesses to underlying spiritual truth. The teaching attached to each miracle is designed to bring out its spiritual significance, and, conversely, the miracle is the concrete demonstration of the power discussed in the teaching.

If the initial sentence of this key be interpreted in the light of the given definition, the meaning becomes plain that the central events of the history of JOHN are certain signs which the author has selected from a larger group that Jesus performed. The casual way in which he stated that "many other signs therefore did Jesus" conveys the impression that he had

---

1. For a fuller discussion of the use of these terms in the vocabulary of the New Testament, see Richard C. Trench, *Synonyms of the New Testament* (Tenth edition, corrected and improved, Eerdmans, Grand Rapids, 1948, pp. 340-345).

no difficulty whatsoever in finding enough of them to make convincing evidence. He was careful to tell that they were performed "in the presence of his disciples." These occurrences were adequately attested by the witness of those who saw them performed. There was a tacit assumption that appeal could be made to these witnesses in case of doubt; or, if the witnesses were not surviving, at least there *were* witnesses. The signs were not the products of the writer's personal imagination. Certain deeds performed by Jesus of Nazareth were so startling that they deserved special notice, and called for explanation. Furthermore, these deeds bespoke something unusual in Christ's personality, and were themselves signposts pointing in the direction of something new.

What were these signs?

Since discussion of them will be undertaken in the main body of the exposition, no lengthy analysis will be attempted here. There are seven in all, exclusive of the resurrection and the draught of fishes recorded in the twenty-first chapter. The resurrection differs from the others because the act itself did not take place in public sight and because it was not performed on someone or something apart from Jesus Himself. The draught of fishes is in the Epilogue, which is not a part of the main body of the Gospel.

Each of these seven signs revealed some specific characteristic of Jesus' power and person. They are in order:

The Changing of Water into Wine 2:1-11
　In this first miracle of His ministry, Jesus revealed Himself as the master of *quality* by effecting instantaneously the change that the vine produces over a period of months.

The Healing of the Nobleman's Son 4:46-54
　By healing the boy who was more than twenty miles distant from Him, Jesus showed Himself the master of *distance,* or *space.*

The Healing of the Impotent Man 5:1-9
The longer a disease afflicts a man, the more difficult it is
to cure. Jesus, by curing instantly an affliction of thirty-
eight years' standing, became the master of *time*.

The Feeding of the Five Thousand 6:1-14
By multiplying the five flat loaves and two small fishes of
one boy's lunch into enough to feed five thousand men,
besides women and children, Jesus showed Himself to be
the master of *quantity*.

The Walking on the Water 6.16-21
This miracle demonstrated His mastery over *natural law*.

The Healing of the Man Born Blind 9:1-12 (41)
The point of this miracle is not so much the fact that
Jesus healed a difficult case as that He did so in answer to
the question as to why this man should have been so
afflicted. Thereby Christ showed that He was the master
of *misfortune*.

The Raising of Lazarus 11:1-46
This miracle indicated that Jesus incontrovertibly was the
master of *death*.

These seven miracles, then, are preeminently *signs* because
they point to those aspects of Jesus' ministry in which He
demonstrated His transcendent control over the factors of life
with which man is unable to cope. Quality, space, time, quantity, natural law, misfortune, and death circumscribe humanity's world. Daily existence is a struggle against their limitations. Christ's superiority over them as revealed by these
events called signs was proof of His deity and a clue to understanding what the writer desired to say about Him.

To return to the structure of this key, the writer was not
content only to describe his main approach, but he stated also
the purpose for it. "These [signs] are written that ye may
believe." Naturally, when signs are present, two reactions
are possible: acceptance, or rejection. The entire book is an

attempt to swing the reader to the side of acceptance, as embodied in the word *believe.* The underlying Greek word, *pisteuo,* is used no less than ninety-eight times in the Gospel and is customarily translated *believe,* though in a few instances it is rendered *trust* or *commit.*[2] Never does it mean a mere assent to a proposition. It usually means acknowledgement of some personal claim, or even a complete personal commitment to some ideal or person. John sought to lead his readers to a settled faith on the basis of actual signs which were historic episodes, and which connoted the spiritual reality behind them as well.

The third element in the structure of this key is the second subordinate clause which completes the definition of the purpose: "and that believing ye may have life in his name." Believing is not sufficient in itself as the fulfillment of the purpose; believing is the means to a greater end. This end is expressed in the word *life.* Life, *zoe,* in the Fourth Gospel, means more than animal vitality or the course of human existence. It was carefully defined by Jesus in John 17:3:

> And this is life eternal, that they should know thee the only true God, and him whom thou didst send, even Jesus Christ.

Life, so defined, possesses various elements. It implies *consciousness;* for there is no knowledge without conscious existence. Further, it signifies *contact,* for one cannot apprehend those things with which one has neither direct nor indirect contact. Again, it involves *continuity,* or duration, because knowledge of God presupposes coexistence with Him. And finally, it assumes *development,* since the knowledge of God must be a growing, not a static thing. Eternal life, man's full destiny, is the objective of the teaching of this Gospel.

When these three statements, centering in the words *signs, believe,* and *life,* are put together, the author's key to the Gospel

---

2. John 2:24, and elsewhere in Rom. 3:2, I Cor. 9:17. Gal. 2:7.

appears plainly. Around the *signs* are clustered the teachings which interpret these phenomena in terms of spiritual truth. In *belief*, and its opposite, *unbelief*, are seen the actions and reactions within the narration. Through *life*, and its opposite, *death*, is expressed the outcome of destiny determined by belief and unbelief.

There is a logic in this structure, too. Belief presupposes that which will produce it. The Scriptures never demand belief without furnishing adequate reason for committal to the person or proposition toward which belief should be directed. Even in John 11, where Jesus placed seeing after believing by saying to Martha, "Said I not unto thee, that, if thou believedst, thou shouldest see the glory of God?" Jesus had already given Martha a reason for believing through the presentation of His own person. Just so, the signs were intended to demonstrate the kind of person in whom the Gospel seeks to focus belief. All that Jesus is and all that He may require may not be known; but John's representation of Him in action and of His mastery of every situation demonstrated fully His adequacy for all human emergencies. Furthermore, the resurrection, which was the crowning sign of all, proved that He still lives to meet the needs of those generations that have extended beyond the time of the writing of the Gospel. He is not only an historic reality, but is man's eternal contemporary.

Belief, also, must issue in life, which in this passage does not mean chiefly conduct. It relates to what is received, not primarily to what is achieved. Negatively, life is the opposite of condemnation (3:17, 5:24), and, positively, it is the knowledge of God (17:3), satisfaction (6:35), preservation and enjoyment (10:10), and eternal duration (12:25). Life, according to the Gospel of John, is qualitative as well as quantitative. It is the natural consequence of a complete commitment of self to Christ.

These three words, *signs, belief, life,* provide logical organization of the Fourth Gospel. In the *signs* appear the revelation of God; in *belief,* the reaction that they ought to evoke; in *life,* the result that belief brings. They integrate the appeal of the entire Gospel. The language of these two verses (20:30, 31) affords a few more clues to an understanding of the content of the Gospel.

A Selective Gospel

Many other signs therefore did Jesus . . . which are not written in this book: but these are written . . .

A comparison of the Fourth Gospel with the Synoptics will show that JOHN records far fewer miracles than they; and that except for the episodes of the Feeding of the Five Thousand and the Walking on the Water the miracles are not identical with those of the Synoptic record. There is similarity in character between some of these remaining five and some of those in the Synoptics, but that is all. The same holds for the historical events. The inevitable conclusion is that the author purposely organized his record from existing materials with two general objectives in view: to concentrate his material on one purpose, and to avoid repetition of what had already been published or what was current in oral form.

An Attested Gospel

Many other signs therefore did Jesus *in the presence of the disciples* . . . (Italics ours)

Paul states in I Corinthians 15:6 that the disciples at the time of Jesus' death numbered not less than five hundred. There is no reason to assume that the signs recorded were all performed in the presence of that many disciples. Probably less than a dozen were present on most of the occasions mentioned; at the Feeding of the Five Thousand all five hundred might have been present, since it was the largest attendance of Jesus' ministry for which there are figures. The main point of the statement in this key is that the *signs* were not the products of a pious imagination. They were attested by credible witnesses. The writer is not asking his readers to accept these statements on his personal word.

An Apologetic Gospel

The use of the word *apologetic* does not mean a Gospel that is making an excuse for what it teaches. It rather connotes a defense of an established position. Plainly John sought to establish conviction: "these are written, that ye may believe." Nor does this apologetic purpose imply that the facts have been distorted in order to create a good impression. There is no defense so adequate as truth; and the simple recital of what actually took place is the surest method of confirming faith. Apologetic purpose may sometimes lead to willful perversion of the facts of the case, but it need not do so if the facts make their own case.

An Interpretative Gospel

". . . that Jesus is the Christ . . ."

The Fourth Gospel interprets the life of Jesus of Nazareth in terms of the Messiah predicted in the Old Testament and awaited by the Jewish nation. The Greek word *Christos* and its Hebrew counterpart *Messiah* both mean *Anointed*. Once a common adjective, applying to any official who was set apart for special service by the rite of anointing, this word became a technical term for the Deliverer who should come to release Israel from her enemies and to reign over the restored House of David. On this Messiah were focused the promises given to Abraham, to David, to the prophets—in short, all of the Old Testament hope. Thus, the Gospel links the Messiah of the Old Testament with the consciousness of the individual believer.

A Definitive Gospel

". . . the Son of God . . ."

It is noteworthy that nowhere in this Gospel did Jesus call God "our Father" in such a way as to imply that His disciples were of equal status with Him, or that they had the same relation to God that He had. On the contrary, He asserted that His relation to God was peculiar, and His enemies so understood Him as John 5:18 says:

> For this cause therefore the Jews sought the more to kill him, because he not only brake the sabbath, but also called God his own Father, making himself equal with God.

Preeminently, then, this Gospel defined Jesus of Nazareth as *the* Son of God.

An Effective Gospel

"And that . . . ye may have life . . ."

The purpose of this Gospel goes far beyond the mere creation of an opinion about its subject. The creation of a personal faith in Christ is the summit of its purpose; but this very faith has a still greater objective, *life*. The Gospel is intended to affect and transform the outlook and career of its reader. It is definitely planned with reference to his destiny. *Life* includes all of man's relations with God. If life is the complex of experience produced by contacts with the surrounding world, this Gospel aims to make God, incarnate in Christ, an historical and actual part of that personal complex. Real life begins with Him.

The Divisions of Action

In common with the three Synoptic Gospels, JOHN sets forth an orderly account of the events of the life of Jesus. The order is indicated by the stages of action, marked off by development in the narrative. The stages are as follows:

Prologue	1:1-18
The Period of Consideration	1:19-4:54
The Period of Controversy	5:1-6:71
The Period of Conflict	7:1-11:53
The Period of Crisis	11:54-12:36a
The Period of Conference	12:36b-17:26
The Period of Consummation	18:1-20:31
Epilogue	21:1-25

The Prologue comprising the first eighteen verses of the first chapter is introductory to the rest of the book. It stands by itself, for it gives only the background for the historical narrative that follows. It states the nature of the principal character, introduces His forerunner, and clarifies His mission and its intended effect.

The Period of Consideration offers the person of the Son to men for their consideration and evaluation. The effect of the forerunner's work as described in 1:19-51 caused several of his disciples to transfer their allegiance to the new prophet, and collectively to believe in Him as a result of the first miracle. Following this initial acceptance by the first disciples, He was presented to Judaism in Jerusalem, particularly in the person of Nicodemus, to the Samaritans through the Samaritan woman, and to the world at large as represented by the nobleman from Capernaum.

In each of these cases there was a different human need. The disciples of John had followed to the best of their ability the light available to them, but they desired fuller religious certainty. Nicodemus represented intellectual need; for he asked questions presupposing considerable thought. The Samaritan woman was emotionally unstable, and needed emotional adjustment. The nobleman's problem was physical. In each of these typical human situations, Jesus revealed Himself as the master of men and of their personal problems. The reader is informed of His sufficiency for each of these needs, and is shown how He and His works produced belief in the lives of those concerned.

The Period of Controversy begins with chapter 5. The miracle recorded was in many respects no different from that given in chapter 4. Both were miracles of physical healing, and both were performed under extraordinary circumstances. The point of the two is quite different, however. The healing of the nobleman's son (4:46-54) was an illustration of Jesus' appeal to the world on the basis of power made visible. The miracle of the man at the pool was cited as the beginning of controversy. From this point on to the end of chapter 6, Jesus was the storm center of argument between Himself and those who disbelieved His claims. The climax of the section was reached in the confession of Peter (6:67-69), which emphasized the faith of the Twelve in contrast to the general decline of belief on the part of many other disciples and of the populace at large.

Controversy inevitably resolves itself into conflict. The Period of Conflict, 7:1 to 11:53, records events which illustrate definite hostility between Jesus and His critics which had sharpened to bitter hatred. No less than four times was it stated that the Jews sought to kill Jesus (7:19, 25, 8:37, 11:53). The mind of the multitude was divided. Each fresh presentation of Jesus aroused new questioning on the part of many, belief on the part of some, and an increasing intensity of hatred on the part of others, until after the raising of Lazarus, the heads of the nation took official action for His removal (11:53). The leaders of organized Jewry realized that the time had come when the issue must be decided without delay.

The Period of Crisis, 11:54 to 12:36a, comprises the series of episodes just preceding the Passover week and the first few days of that week. Jesus, in spite of the threats against His life, returned to Jerusalem for the Passover, and publicly offered Himself to the people for their final choice. Five groups of people, portraying five distinct reactions to Him, were involved in this closing complex of events. The priests and Jewish officials, who had already made up their minds about Him, were plotting His death. His intimate friends, centering in the family at Bethany, gave Him their parting gift. The masses were moved by curiosity or by temporary interest. The Greeks, possibly proselytes, showed a genuine spirit of inquiry, though they probably knew less about Him than any of the others did. The disciples were bewildered, and while loyal in intent, except for Judas, seem to have had no clear concept of what to do or say next. The combination of the attitudes of these groups produced a situation out of which anything might come; the conflicting tensions appeared plainly in the ensuing action and in the divergent results.

The Period of Conference, 12:36b to 17:26, is, in a sense, a parenthesis in the action of the Gospel. It records Jesus' conference with the disciples for the purpose of preparing their minds for His death, and with the Father that He might make His final report on His commission and intercede for the disciples whom He had won. Since the permanent interest of the Gospel is in the work that was done within the circle of believers rather than in the historical currents of the outside world, this section, though parenthetical to the narrative, is of the highest importance to its meaning.

The main action of the Gospel as embodying the plot reaches its peak in the Period of Consummation, 18:1 to 20:31. The crucifixion and death of Jesus terminated the historical career as far as the world was concerned. Jesus' predictions concerning Himself, the priests' design against His life, the divine demonstration of love and sacrifice were consummated at this point. As human biographies go, the life of Jesus ended in pathetic tragedy.

The Fourth Gospel, however, does not consider the tragedy to be final. Its emphatic declaration of the resurrection of Jesus, treated in terms of its effects upon human personality, showed how the incarnate Word conquered death and all its powers. Thus, in the concluding sentence of this section, tragedy is turned into triumphant faith: "Because thou hast seen me, thou hast believed: blessed are they that have not seen, and yet have believed" (20:29).

Verses 30 and 31, already discussed as the key to the Gospel, add nothing to the narrative, but emphasize its purpose. The twenty-first chapter, or Epilogue, lies outside the main body of the narrative and plot, though related to it. As the main body of the Gospel was directed to the purpose of creating belief, the Epilogue is directed to the purpose of using belief. The word *believe* does not once occur in this passage; rather, the keynote is *follow*. The Epilogue is evidently an attempt to concentrate the result of the reader's thinking upon his own faith and service.

The logical sequence of these divisions is apparent, but one question might legitimately be raised: Are these divisions natural to the text, or arbitrary? A fair criterion of their accuracy may be obtained by comparing them with the chronological and geographical divisions of the text, which are apparent and which are not susceptible of arbitrary alteration. If the majority of the division points agree within the three outlines, one may be reasonably sure of the accuracy of the results; if there is a marked divergence, a reconsideration of outline would be advisable. An examination of the chronological and geographical divisions, then, may prove fruitful in confirming the validity of the initial outline.

THE STRUCTURE OF THE GOSPEL OF JOHN BY DIVISIONS

ACTION	CHRONOLOGICAL		GEOGRAPHICAL	
Prologue 1:1-18				
Period of Consideration 1:19-4:54	Day One	1:19-28	Bethany beyond Jordan	1:28
	"On the morrow"	1:29-34		
	"On the morrow"	1:35-42		
	"On the morrow"	1:43-51		
	Day Three	2:1-11	Cana of Galilee	2:1-11
	"After this"	2:12	Capernaum	2:12
	"Abode not many days"			
	The *Passover* at hand	2:13-22	Jerusalem	2:13-3:21
	During *Passover*	2:23-3:21		
	"After these things"	3:22-36	Land of Judaea	3:22-36
			Aenon near Salim	3:23
	During activity of John	4:1	Samaria	4:1-42
	"After two days"	4:43		
			Galilee	4:43
			Cana	4:46

Period of Controversy 5:1-6:71	"After these things" 5:1-47	Jerusalem	5:1
	A Feast "After these things" 6:1-21	Other side of Galilee	6:1
	Passover at hand 6:4	Proceeded to Capernaum 6:16, 17	
	"On the morrow" 6:22-59	Synagogue at Capernaum 6:59	
Period of Conflict 7:1-11:53	"After these things" 7:1-13	Galilee	7:1-13
	Feast of Tabernacles at hand 7:2 "The midst of the *Feast*" 7:14	Jerusalem Jerusalem	7:14-10:39 7:53-8:11
	Feast of Dedication 10:22-39	Aenon (?) Bethany	10:40-11:16 11:17-53
Period of Crisis 11:54-12:36a	*Passover* at hand 11:54-57 "Six days, before the *Passover*" 12:1 11	Ephraim Bethany	11:54-57 12:1-11
	"On the morrow" 12:12-36a	Jerusalem	12:12
Period of Conference 12:36b-17:26	"Before the *Feast of the Passover*" 13:1	Room in city 13:1-14:31a Removal 14:31b-17:26	
Period of Consummation 18:1-20:31		Crossing Kidron 18:1-11 Garden House of Annas 18:12-14 Court of Caiaphas (?) 18:15-27	
	"Sixth hour" 19:14	Praetorium 18:28-19:16 Golgotha 19:17-30	
	"Preparation" 19:31	Garden burial 19:31-42	
	First Day 20:1-18	Garden tomb 20:1-18	
	Evening 20:19-25	Upper room 20:19-25	
	Eighth Day 20:26-29	Upper room 20:26-29	
Epilogue 21:1-25	"After these things" 21:1-23	Sea of Tiberias	21:1-23

The Chronological Divisions

The Fourth Gospel is more thoroughly chronological in its organization than are the Synoptics. The Gospel of Mark makes no pretense of attempting chronological order, though it does take note of the sequence of events in the Passion Week. Matthew is generally topical in its arrangement. Luke provides careful dating for the birth of John the Baptist (Luke 1:5), for the birth of Jesus (2:1), and for the ministry of John the Baptist, which opens the main portion of the narrative (3:1). Luke's interest is that of the historian who seeks to locate the general setting of his narrative rather than that of the chronicler who desires to date each item of the sequence. John is interested more in the internal coherence of his own story. His datings have a religious rather than a political significance, for he centers his thought around the Jewish feasts.

These chronological references in JOHN can be arranged by groups or blocks. The Prologue stands by itself; "In the beginning" is the keynote as far as chronology is concerned. The entire content of the Prologue is timeless, and so the element of dating does not enter into it at all.

Actual chronology begins with John 1:19. From this beginning of the ministry of John the Baptist to the close of the marriage at Cana there is one group of events tied together by a single chronological thread. Three times in this text the phrase "on the morrow" occurs. Whether the three sections of the text introduced by this phrase refer to the action of three successive days or whether they refer to three separate acts,[3] all of which took place on the day after the action of John the Baptist as recorded in 1:19-25 is a question that may be debated. One thing is clear: they unite the sections into one consecutive line of thought which is continued by 2:1-11, opening with the phrase "on the third day." This group of five units, totaling three to five days' time, incorporates the initial presentation of Jesus to the men who became His disciples, and

---

3. H. A. W. Meyer, in his *Critical and Exegetical Handbook to the Gospel of John*, (New York: Funk and Wagnalls, 1884), p. 89, takes the view that these days are successive. If so, it is difficult to explain "the third day" (2:1) unless it is assumed that it means the third day after leaving Judea (1:43). In that case, there must have been a blank day between the calling of Nathanael and the arrival at Cana.

records their reactions to Him. Chronologically and topically the units coincide.

In 2:12 the phrase "after this" introduces a new chronological division. No specific interval is mentioned; the words imply only succession. They mark an advance in time, not always a distinctive period of any length. Similar phraseology occurs at 3:22, 5:1, 6:1, 7:1 and 21:1. Where it occurs, it generally makes a break of sense as well as of time. On the other hand, 2:12 need not suggest a long residence in Cana. Probably a longer time elapsed between 2:12 and 2:13 than between 2:11 and 2:12. The content of 2:12 is not given. The paragraph is transitional between the introduction of Jesus to the disciples and the larger Judean ministry which commences with 2:13.

There are at least three observances of the Passover given in JOHN. The first one appears in 2:13, the second, midway of the ministry, in 6:4, and the final one in 11:55. The unnamed feast of 5:1 also may be a Passover. If so, it constitutes a fourth, and fixes the length of Jesus' ministry at three and one half years.

In addition to the Passovers, two other feasts are mentioned, the Feast of Tabernacles, which usually was celebrated in the last week of September,[4] and the Feast of Dedication, which came in the winter, in the later part of December.[5] Around these feasts are grouped the bulk of the narrative so that it almost becomes an intermittent series of glimpses of Jesus as He attended the feasts or as He taught following them.

The largest block of material centers around the last Passover. In common with the Synoptists, John devotes the largest single section of his narrative to the events of the Passion.

4. David Smith, *Commentary on the Four Gospels*, (Garden City, New York: Doubleday, Doran and Company, Inc., 1928), III, p. 128.
5. *Ibid.*, p. 181.

The accompanying chart does not show any close chronological order in the Gospel of John. Major topical divisions coincide with changes of time. For instance, the final period of Jesus' life began just before the last Passover, and extended a week beyond it. It opened in 11:54, 55, where it is stated that the Passover of the Jews is "at hand," and closed with 20: 26-29, which can be dated "after eight days," subsequent to the crucifixion. Though it is subdivided into small periods of days and hours, it constitutes a unit. Topically, however, it is subdivided into the Period of Crisis, the Period of Conference, and the Period of Consummation. Each of these may be separated justifiably from the others because of a change in subject matter, though they are by no means unrelated. On the other hand, the major chronological divisions coincide with the topical divisions.

The reason for the grouping of these divisions is not perfectly clear. As already indicated, the text of JOHN is divided into several large blocks. The first centers around the days beginning with the Baptist's recognition of Jesus and terminating with the wedding at Cana (1:19-2:11). After a transitional paragraph (2:12), the second block is introduced, centering in the first Passover in Jerusalem, and the interviews with Nicodemus, the Samaritan woman, and the nobleman of Capernaum. No exact length of time is stated, but these events seem to have occurred in close succession. The third block begins at 5:1 with the healing of the man at the pool; the fourth mentions a Passover, and the fifth block of text commences with chapter 7, with its allusion to the Feast of Tabernacles, and probably includes the entire body of text through 10:21, since the latter verse contains an allusion to the healing of the blind man recorded in chapter 9. The sixth block is the account of the events at the Feast of Dedication in 10:22-39. The episode of the raising of Lazarus is not definitely connected with any special incident, and so cannot be located chronologically. Probably it was not long before the final Passover. The last block of text, aside from the Epilogue, is that of the Passion period, from 11:54-20:29.

No special motive for selecting these blocks of events rather than others can be assigned. The writer was interested in the Jewish feasts, and apparently believed that Jesus' utterances on these occasions were especially significant. No hint is given as to why His discourses should have been confined so largely to these periods. Perhaps the best explanation is that the author recalled events by groupings that were attached to a definite place and to a definite time, since they fitted the plan of his presentation in that order.

The Geographical Divisions

The three major geographical divisions in JOHN are the three major units of Palestine in the time of Jesus: Galilee, Samaria, and Judea. In these areas the larger part of the action took place, and the motion of the narrative alternated between Galilee and Judea. One exception might be noted: the events which marked the introduction of Jesus in 1:19-51. These probably took place on the east side of the Jordan near one of the fords north of the Dead Sea, and accessible both to Jerusalem and to the cities of Galilee by connecting roads.

Unit One centers in Galilee around Capernaum and Cana. The sites of both are disputed. Probably Capernaum is to be identified with Tell Hum on the north shore of the sea of Galilee, two and one half miles west of the mouth of the Jordan.[6,7] It was the scene of much of Jesus' ministry, though John gives much less prominence to it than do the Synoptists. Cana was located near Nazareth, about four and one half miles to the northeast. Three blocks of text belong to this geographical unit: 2:1-12, 4:43-54, and 6:1 to 7:13. In Galilee

---

6. W. Ewing, "Capernaum" in *The International Standard Bible Encyclopedia*, I, pp. 566b-567.

7. Brooke Foss Westcott, *The Gospel According to John*, (London: John Murray, 1908), I, pp. 87, 88. Westcott agrees with Ewing.

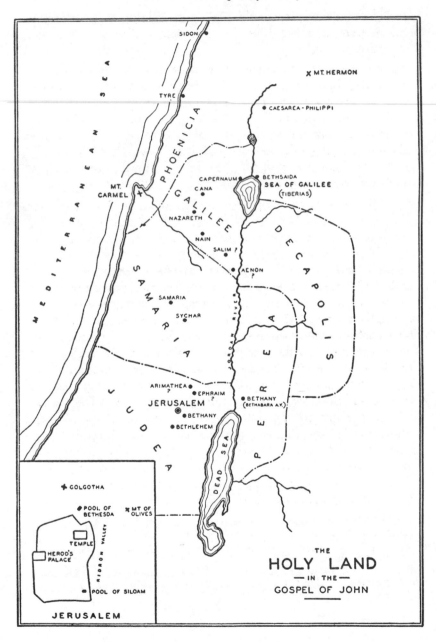

THE
HOLY LAND
— IN THE —
GOSPEL OF JOHN

Jesus' popularity reached its greatest height, culminating in the attempt to make Him king; and in Galilee also the final defection began.

Unit Two, which relates to Samaria, comprises only one block of Johannine text, 4:1-42. Its sole content is the interview with the woman of Samaria. John shows that he is familiar with the topography and history of Samaria by his allusions to Sychar and to the piece of ground that Jacob gave to his son Joseph (4:5) where Jacob's well was located. The sojourn in Samaria was not of long duration, for Jesus was merely passing through enroute from Jerusalem to Galilee.

Unit Three deals with Jerusalem and Judea. In the Fourth Gospel Jerusalem is more prominent than the cities of Galilee. No less than four visits to Jerusalem are recorded (2:13-3: 21, 5:1-47, 7:14 to 10:39), including the visit of the Passion Week (12:2 to 20:29). If the two feasts mentioned in 7:14 and 10:22 mark two separate visits to the city, Jesus must have made five trips to Jerusalem. The atmosphere of the city is normally represented as hostile to Him. His appearance there was usually the occasion for a disturbance or for a plot of some kind. The two signs that took place in Jerusalem, the healings of the man at the pool and the blind man, and the great discourses that followed them were important in the history of the controversy concerning Jesus' person. The former miracle precipitated the controversy, the second was used as an illustration of the alignment of the parties that disagreed over Him. If the raising of Lazarus be considered as connected with Jerusalem, for it took place in Bethany less than two miles from the city, the concluding controversial miracle of Christ's career also occurred there.

The various natural and architectural features of Jerusalem are mentioned in some detail. The sheep gate (5:2), the pool of Bethesda (5:2), the temple (2:14, 7:28, 8:2, 59) with its treasury (8:20) and porches (10:23), the pool of Siloam (9:7), the brook Kidron (18:1), the garden of Gethsemane

(18:2), the residences of Annas and Caiaphas (18:15), the Praetorium (18:28, 33), Golgotha (19:17), the garden of burial (19:41), the place of the gathering of the disciples (20:19) were all familiar to the author.

The blocks of text which comprise these geographical units agree fairly well with the chronological and logical divisions previously noted. With every major change of topic there is a change of location, though the division is not always clear-cut. For instance, the last large geographical unit, 12:12 to 20:29, concerns action in Jerusalem during the fortnight before and after the Passion. In it are three main periods of action, Crisis, Conference, and Consummation. The first of these includes also the retirement to Ephraim and a brief stay in Bethany, which are, however, introductory to the last week in Jerusalem.

No geographical location can be assigned to the Prologue, and the Epilogue relates wholly to Galilee. It is noteworthy that only the Fourth Gospel alludes to the lake of Galilee as "the sea of Tiberias" (6:1, 21:1).

CHAPTER II

The Significance of the Structure

THE foregoing treatment of the content of the Gospel of John has demonstrated that it possesses a definite structure. The declaration of purpose, the progress of action, and the chronological and geographical divisions indicate clearly that the author had an extensive knowledge of the career of Jesus, and that his arrangement of the narrative is both intelligent and purposeful. It is equally plain that his story was not written as a biography, for there are gaps in it which he did not pretend to fill. It is not primarily history, for his chronology is incomplete, though he is more detailed in his datings than are the Synoptists. Neither does the account pretend to cover all of Jesus' tours, for there is some generalizing,[8] and a lack of uniformity in giving details concerning the places Jesus visited. While all these facts afford clues to the divisions of the book, the real purpose of this Gospel is moral. It deals with actual events, but only as they are related to a spiritual conflict.

This is not the same as saying that JOHN has no literal historical significance or that it should be interpreted allegorically. On the contrary, the book should be regarded as a piece of history which is utilized not as a chronicle, but as an historical apologetic. It is a popular presentation of spiritual truth for an audience which either had been influenced by the philosophical currents of the day, or was likely to be so influenced.

According to the traditional view, supported by the earliest external evidence, JOHN was written in Ephesus for the use of

---

8. Cf. "after this," 2:12; "after these things," 5:1, 6:1, 7:1; "and he went away again," 10:40; "Jesus . . . departed thence," 11:54.

the churches of Asia Minor.[9] Other theories have been advanced, which have attributed its origin to Alexandria [10] or to Palestine,[11] or possibly to Syrian Antioch;[12] but none has been thoroughly substantiated. Most of these theories agree that it was written to combat the pagan philosophies of its day that· tended in the divergent directions of materialism and of mysticism. In contrast to these tendencies, the Person that JOHN presents is neither a forlorn and misunderstood prophet, nor a divine apparition or ideal with no real human substance. He is the Word made flesh (1:14), and as such is truly man and truly God. His advent brought a new element into man's life, and has rendered incomplete all systems of thought that do not take ample cognizance of Himself and of His claims. The profound truth of this new revelation is presented in simple language that a child can understand, but with a wealth of meaning that the learned cannot exhaust.

The express purpose of the Gospel is to create belief. Faith is a necessary element in all progressive human life, and in some measure it is prerequisite to all relationships. JOHN enlarges upon this principle by inculcating an active and aggressive faith in Christ as the directive force in all spiritual life.

Furthermore, the Gospel provides a clear demonstration of the meaning and effects of faith. If faith eventuates in life, the prospective believer has a right to know what that life is. It is vigorous, growing, and expanding, revealed by its conflict with the opposing forces in the environment around it. In fact, the conflict in JOHN, rather than its events, is significant, for in the plot as worked out in the person of Jesus the real meaning of the book becomes apparent.

---

9. Irenaeus, *Against Heresies*, III, i. Cf. Eusebius, HE, III, xxxix, pp. 1-7.

10. Alfred M. Perry, "Is John an Alexandrian Gospel?," *Journal of Biblical Literature*, LXIII, (1944), pp. 99-106.

11. C. F. Burney, *The Aramaic Origin of the Fourth Gospel*, (Oxford: Clarendon Press, 1922), p. 127.

12. *Ibid.*, pp. 127-131.

A plot, as may be ascertained from any good novel, is the pattern of conflict between two opposing forces of human life in which one force triumphs over the other. The plot of JOHN reveals the perennial struggle between good and evil evinced in the contest of belief and unbelief directed toward the person of the Lord Jesus. Throughout all the sections of this Gospel there is a development of faith in Christ, beginning with the lowest and most rudimentary type of belief, and continuing to a lofty and intelligent worship which is contrasted with unbelief. This unbelief begins with an undefined emotional hostility and ends in a deliberate rejection of His person. The causes and results of both belief and unbelief are illustrated by historical events, and the words of Jesus Himself are utilized to make the applications as the narrative progresses.

The conflict of the plot appears in the *vocabulary*. The contrasting terms of light and darkness, love and hate, life and death, flesh and spirit, slavery and liberty, illustrate various aspects and stages of the development of this conflict.

The plot is built by the *characters*. On almost every page of the Gospel there appear contrasting types, some who believed and some who did not. They are not "wooden soldiers," either utterly believing or utterly faithless, created by a literary imagination "to point a moral or adorn a tale." Development in both directions appears. An initially unbelieving Thomas finally rises to a peak of magnificent faith; a Pilate lapses through compromise into ultimate indifference.

The plot is expressed in the *action*, for the vocabulary and the characters are only a part of the action. In some of the characters such as the Samaritan woman and the man born blind the development of belief is completely portrayed; in other instances, as in the contacts with the disciples in chapter 1, or in the case of the nobleman in chapter 4, the individual case represents only one phase of that development. In any case, the direction of the appeal is always toward belief.

There are two aspects of this plot because there are two aspects of the person of Christ—the human and the divine.

As a portrayal of human struggle the Gospel of John is a deep tragedy. All the worst of human passions and behaviors, all the utmost of human suffering and failure are adequately set forth. Jealousy, avarice, hatred, envy, lust, duplicity, disloyalty, ingratitude, stupidity, brutality, hypocrisy, spite, and every other evil motive or quality are illustrated in the action of this drama. Conversely, unselfishness, generosity, kindliness, purity, honesty, sincerity, and self-sacrifice may also be found. Apart from divine intervention, as in all great tragic literature, the evil triumphs, and in the crucifixion the tale ends sadly and disappointingly.

More than this, the tragedy is ironical. The more humanity struggles against evil, the more deeply it is involved. For instance, Peter avowed that he would never forsake his Lord, but would lay down his life for Him (13:37). The exact opposite occurred. In the life of Jesus Himself irony is apparent. Although He was virtuous, He suffered all possible indignities; majestic, He died in ignominy; powerful, He expired in weakness. Particularly is this fact illustrated by His claims, as they contrast with His end. He claimed to possess the water of life, and He died thirsting. He claimed to be the light of the world, and He died in darkness. He claimed to be the good shepherd, and He died in the fangs of the wolves. He claimed to be the truth, and He was crucified as an impostor. He claimed to be the resurrection and the life, and He expired sooner than most victims of crucifixion usually did, so that Pilate was amazed. Strangely enough, the culmination of His career seemed to give the lie to its intended meaning. If the greatest examplar of righteousness that the world has seen became a helpless victim of evil, then supreme tragedy is the burden of JOHN.

From the divine viewpoint, the Fourth Gospel is not tragedy, but triumph. The plot reveals the victory of life over **death**, of love over hate, of light over darkness, and of spirit over flesh. The true culmination is not in the crucifixion, but in the resurrection. Unbelief does its worst at the cross, and halts there; faith holds to the resurrection, and so becomes victorious. The divine Word has not triumphed by being revealed in contrast to the world as a mystic vision untouched by the sordid realities of life, but rather by undergoing the worst that life could do and by rising above it unscathed. Nor is this vision splendid only a dream by which men delude themselves into thinking that they triumph over the world though actually they do not. Its call to faith produces a new practical reality for daily living.

Part II

THE TEXTUAL ANALYSIS
OF THE GOSPEL

THE PROLOGUE

THE PROLOGUE

CHAPTER III

The Prologue

1 : 1-18

ANALYSIS

1   In the beginning was the Word,
    and
    the Word was with God,
    and
    the Word was God.

2   The same was in the beginning with God.

3   All things were made through him;
    and
    without him was not anything made
                    that hath been made.

4   In him was life;
    and
    the life was the light of men.

5   And
    the light shineth in the darkness;
    and
    the darkness overcame[1] it not.

---

6   There came a man,
             sent from God,
             whose name was John.

7   The same came for witness,
             that he might bear witness of the light,
             that all might believe through him.

8   He was not the light,
      but *came*
             that he might bear witness of the light.

---

1. R. V. marginal reading for *katelaben*.

9   There was the true light[2]
                 which lighteth every man,
                 coming into the world.

10   He was in the world,
     and
     the world was made through him,
     and
     the world knew him not.

11   He came unto his own [things],
     and
     they that were his own received him not.

12   But
     . . . he gave the right to become children of God,
                 to them
                       as many as received him,
                 [2]to them that believe on his name:

13   who were born,
                         not of bloods,[3]
                         nor of the will of the flesh,
                         nor of the will of man,
                         but of God.

14   And the Word became flesh,
     and
     dwelt among us,
     and
     we beheld his glory,
                 glory as of an only begotten from a[3] Father,
           full of grace and truth.

15 | John beareth witness of him,
     | and crieth, saying,
     | This was he of whom I said,
     | He . . . is come before me:
     | that cometh after me
     | for he was before[4] me.

---

2. Italicized text omitted; not in original.
3. R. V. marginal reading.
4. R. V. margin reads, "first in regard of me." A different word from
the preceding word that is translated "before."

16　For of his fulness we all received,
　　　and
　　　[we have received] grace for[5] grace.
17　For the law was given through Moses;
　　　grace and truth came through Jesus Christ.
18　No man hath seen God at any time;
　　　the only begotten Son,[6]. . . he hath declared him.
　　　　　who is in the bosom of the Father.

THE first eighteen verses of the Fourth Gospel constitute a division technically known as the Prologue. This section sets the action and its interpretation in a framework of thought by means of which the average Christian may gain an understanding of the whole plot and its significance.

The mechanical analysis of this Prologue (see accompanying chart) divides its text first of all into two sections of unequal size which deal with the two persons mentioned in them: the LOGOS, or Word, and John the Baptist. The former is the name assigned to the Lord Jesus Christ, who is the subject of the main discussion. The latter is treated only in relation to the former, and is of subordinate importance. By so dividing the text, two lines of thought appear. Verses 1 to 5, 9 to 14, 16 to 18 concern the Word; verses 6 to 8 and 15 concern John the Baptist.

By placing in parentheses the sections relative to John the Baptist, one finds that the remaining text becomes a description of the Word, which divides generally into strophes of three lines each. For instance, verse one reads:

　　　　　In the beginning was the Word
　　　　　and
　　　　　The Word was with God
　　　　　and
　　　　　The Word was God.

---

5. Greek *anti;* literally, "in exchange for."
6. R. V. margin: "God only begotten." So read some of the best Greek MSS.

The structure is poetic: a three line stanza containing three distinct yet related statements, the second of which marks a logical advance in thought beyond the first, and the third beyond the second; yet all of which make a unit of thought. A few of these strophes contain four lines, marked out by coordinate conjunctions, but the triads or quaternions of lines each represent some one aspect of the Word in His relation to the universe.

The term LOGOS, which occurs four times, includes more than its English translation, "word." A word is an idea expressed through a combination of sounds or of letters. Without the idea or concept behind it, the medium would be meaningless. KXBZ might represent a radio station; but as a combination of letters or sounds, if it could be pronounced, it has no meaning whatsoever because no concept is attached to it. Just so the term LOGOS implies the intelligence behind the idea, the idea itself, and the transmissible expression of it. The term was used technically in the Greek philosophy of this period, particularly by the Stoics, to denote the controlling Reason of the universe, the all-pervasive Mind which ruled and gave meaning to all things. LOGOS was one of the purest and most general concepts of that ultimate Intelligence, Reason, or Will that is called God.

At this point it might be wise to distinguish between the use of a common term to express a truth and the wholesale borrowing of a concept by the use of the term customarily employed to represent it. The writer of the Fourth Gospel doubtless used LOGOS with full knowledge of its general meaning in the religious and philosophical vocabulary of his day. How could he do otherwise than adapt to his purpose the vocabulary of his time? If he refused to use it because it had connotations contrary to his meaning, he would be forced to remain silent for lack of media of expression. His usage should be understood in terms of his own definition. LOGOS is to be received in the light of the Person whom it denotes rather than as a concept of Greek religion which the author arbitrarily foisted upon Jesus of Nazareth. John's teaching is the starting point of a new philosophy based on the Risen Christ and expressed in a current term, rather than an attempt to absorb into paganism the teaching of and about Jesus by enveloping Him with a pagan concept.

The structure of the Prologue divides naturally into seven sections, each of which deals with some aspect of the LOGOS. These divisions contain the gist of the message of the Gospel, couched in abstract terms. The narrative which follows develops and implements it by means of historical illustration.

The Prologue, therefore, commences a presentation of the person of Christ which is quite different from that of the other Gospels. It is theological rather than biographical or historical in its approach. Of its biographical or historical accuracy there can be no legitimate doubt; but it is not primarily a chronicle, it is interpretation. It asserts that Jesus, the historic personage known to man, is the Ultimate Fact of the universe.

> A. The Word and Deity (1)
>   1. Eternity
>   2. Personality
>   3. Nature
>
> B. The Word and Creation (2, 3)
>   1. Antiquity
>   2. Agency
>   3. Activity
>
> C. The Word and Life (4, 5, 9)
>   1. The Fount of Life
>   2. The Effect of Life on Men
>   3. The Power of Life
>   4. The Scope of Life
>
> D. The Word and the World (10)
>   1. The Word Present
>   2. The Word Active
>   3. The Word Ignored

E. The Word and Men (11-13)
   1. Contact
   2. Rejection
   3. Reception
      a. Method
      b. Effects

F. The Word Incarnate (14)
   1. Act
   2. Process
   3. Revelation

G. The Word Revealing (16-18)
   1. Fullness
   2. Grace
   3. God

The Word and Deity (1)

The first predicate of the LOGOS is *eternity*. The phrase, "In the beginning," is essentially the same as that of Genesis 1:1, "In the beginning God created the heavens and the earth." The expression does not refer to the beginning of some particular process, a definite localized point of time, but rather to the indefinite eternity which preceded all time, the immeasurable past. The LOGOS cannot be said to have come into being at any given moment; He always was.

The second affirmation is that of eternal *personality*. The preposition *pros* translated "with" is the same one that is employed in Mark 6:3, where the inhabitants of Nazareth expressed their astonishment about Jesus by saying, "Is not this the carpenter, the son of Mary, and brother of James, and Joses, and Judas, and Simon? and are not his sisters here with us?" It implies association in the sense of free mingling with the others of a community on terms of equality. In John 1:1, then, it implies being on a level with and in communication with God. The LOGOS is not an impersonal principle, but is to be regarded as living, intelligent, active personality.

The third step is the assertion of *deity*. The Greek word *theos*, translated God, is employed here without the article. In the second clause the article is used: "The Logos was with the God."[7] When the article is used, the emphasis of the word is on individuality, God as a person; without the article the emphasis is on quality, God as a kind of being. The use of the word "divine" would be a fair translation, were not its modern connotation considerably weaker than the intended meaning of the text. "Deity" is a better rendering. "The Word was deity" clearly asserts that the LOGOS possessed and eternally manifested the very nature of God.

The Word and Creation (2, 3)

Having thus established the position of the LOGOS in the world of concept, the writer revealed His position in the world of action. The first sentence of the second triad is transitional. "This one was in the beginning with God."[7] It is little more than resumptive of the content of the first triad, and yet it is more, for it states that the LOGOS shared with God His place at the beginning of all things. Genesis 1:1 prepared the way for the description of His partnership with God in world activity which appears in the next clause: "All things came into being through Him."[7]

"All things" relates to the universe, its elements and its systems of law. "Came into being" implies a crisis, a transition from what was not to what is. The tense of the verb (aorist) implies occurrence without relation to elapsed time, an event, not a process. By the use of this tense the interest is not centered in the method of creation so much as in the fact of creation. It contrasts with the word *was*[8] in the first triad,

---

7. Original translation.
8. J. H. Bernard, *A Critical and Exegetical Commentary on the Gospel According to St. John*, (New York: Charles Scribner's Sons, 1929), I, p. 2: "The imperfect is used in three clauses of this verse and is expressive in each case of continual timeless existence."

which presupposes duration. The LOGOS exists eternally; the material universe, temporally.

Furthermore, the material creation is the product of the LOGOS. The same idea appears in Colossians 1:16 and in Hebrews 1:2[9] to convey the thought that the Son is the agent in creation as the contractor is the agent of the owner who builds a house. Christ is the medium through whom deity expresses itself.

The third line teaches the activity of the LOGOS. In the translation of this line the punctuation of the American Revised Version, which divides the verse after "hath been made" rather than before it, is deemed preferable to the marginal reading. The change in the tense of the underlying verb is what makes this last statement meaningful: "And apart from him there came into being not one thing which has come into being and still exists." The Greek word *gegonen* rendered above by the last six words of the paraphrase, is in the perfect tense, which denotes the present state as the continuing result of a previous act. The world in its entirety owes its origin to God through the agency of the LOGOS.

The Word and Life (4, 5, 9)

The third triad, relating to the LOGOS and spiritual life, expresses the dynamic behind creation. *Life* as a noun occurs no less than thirty-six times in this Gospel and eleven of these are in conjunction with the adjective *eternal*. Its connotation is not merely that of conscious existence, but of the life of God as a principle, expressed in human experience. This first use of the term is defined by connecting it with the LOGOS as its source and embodiment.

In the second line of the triad, life is described in terms of *light* which is the effect of life in the universe. The word is used in JOHN in a figurative sense as referring to the clear manifestation of the righteousness of God (3:19, 20, 21;

---

9. *di'autou*—through him.

12:35). Probably this is a reference to the account of creation which says that light was the first result of God's creative activity (Gen. 1:3). The life of the LOGOS in its manifestation brings illumination.

At this point in the Prologue the plot is introduced. The effect of the divine life is manifest in the world through the LOGOS, but the world is not readily receptive. On the contrary, the world cannot extinguish the light, but can dim it. Both the conflict and the outcome of it are implied in *apprehended*. The marginal rendering, *overcome*, is preferable;[10] for the word means to capture, overwhelm, overpower, achieve, rather than to understand, or grasp in a figurative sense. The continual resistance of the light to darkness and the inability of darkness to triumph in spite of the utmost that hatred and unbelief can do is the chief theme of JOHN.

Omitting the parenthesis, one more statement is added to the foregoing three: "The true [real] light, which lighteth every man, was coming into the world."[11] The word *true* (*alethinos*) means true in contrast to secondary rather than in contrast to false, original rather than correct. It is used of God in 17:3, where the stress lies on the ultimate character of God's being, not upon the essential truthfulness of His personality. This is the original light of which all others are feeble copies; the real, in contrast to the illusory. From the LOGOS proceeds all spiritual illumination. The claims of Christ which are discussed in the body of the Gospel are a detailed development of the principle that He is the source of all light.

The Word and the World (10)

World, used seventy-seven times in the Gospel of John, is one of the distinctive Johannine terms. Here it applies to the material and spiritual environment in which men live. The

---

10. Per contra, see John Scott, "Review of the *New Testament, Revised Standard Version*" in *Classical Weekly*, 40 (1947) 9, p. 70.
11. Original translation.

Word is not separated from their needs and surroundings by an impassable gulf; the spiritual and the material are not totally incapable of contact, as a false system would lead one to believe. The immanence of the LOGOS is asserted in that He has entered into the framework of life and has taken an active part in it, but the Word is not identical with the world. He is more than the soul of the universe, for the next statement says, "And the world came into being through him." It could not have come into being through His agency had He not been independent of it and prior to it. Again, as in the contrast of verses one and two, He *was* (denoting an enduring process of existence) ; the world *became* (denoting a crisis of creation). The transcendence of the Word as well as His presence in the world is thus stated.

"And the world knew him not." "Realized him not" might be an even better translation. The world as a system had no comprehension of the manifested Word, and no place for Him. The Synoptic Gospels show that the majority of the people had only a superficial comprehension of Him, and even His own disciples did not understand clearly His words, His personality, or His mission. This ignorance was the basis of the conflict, for what the world did not appreciate it rejected, and what it rejected, it hated.

The Word and Men (11-13)

Verses 11 through 13 develop further the statements of verse 10. "World" is a broad and collective term, speaking of humanity and its environment as one system. Verses 11 to 13 individualize and personalize the matter, showing how *contact* was established. The idiom "unto his own" really means "He came home." "His own" refers to property or to those things that make one's peculiar surroundings. The same expression is used in 16:32 referring to the disciples' departure, each man to his own home; and in 19:27 where it states that the beloved disciple took Jesus' mother to his own home. Because the world was His creation, He had come to visit His own property, thus asserting inherent right and ownership.

Rejection is the theme of the second line: "And his own people did not receive him." The neat Greek idiom which uses the neuter for "his own things" and the masculine for "his own people" cannot easily be rendered into English. It conveys the idea that those who were His own peculiar people connected with His proper surroundings did not accept Him as they might logically be expected to do. It is the expression of the same principle which Jesus uttered in the Synoptic parable of the wicked husbandmen (Matt. 21:33-46, Mark 12:1-12, Luke 20:9-16). In the body of the Fourth Gospel the rejection is amply illustrated by the attitude and action of "the Jews" in contrast to others. Christ was accepted by the Samaritans (chap. 4), was sought by the Greek Gentiles (12:20), but was spurned by the official representatives of His own people.

Rejection, however, has as its counterpart *reception.* John states that some did receive Him, and hastens to discuss the reception in terms of its effects. The redundant grammatical construction of this sentence serves to make all the clearer the fact that receiving and believing are equivalent terms. *Believe* is used here for the first time in the main sequence of thought, though it has occurred once before in 1:7 where it expresses the main objective of the teaching of the Baptist. Believing on His name is thus the key to receiving the revelation of the Word that has come into the world.

The effect of receiving the Word is a new relationship, the obtaining of the right of entrance into the family of God. The word rendered *power* by the King James Version and *right* by the American Standard Version means delegated authority, power, or privilege which is exercised by the consent of or on the appointment of another. It was used by Pilate when he asserted that he had authority to release or to crucify (19:10). This authority is more than a potentiality; the family relationship is made actual through a birth which is more than physical. The believers are given the life of God not by the biological process which imparted physical life, but by a divine impartation.

The Word Incarnate (14)

This verse is the pivotal statement of the Prologue. How was the Word "in the world"? What made deity manifest to humanity and available for its need? The incarnation is the answer. The recurrence of LOGOS in this fourteenth verse connects it directly with verses one and two. The change in verb is striking. Verse one speaks of the eternal nature and relation of the LOGOS to God; verse fourteen, of a change of relation to the world of men. First is the *act,* "the Word became flesh." He expressed Himself in a human personality that was visible, audible, and tangible. He partook of flesh and blood with its limitations of space and time, and with its physical handicaps of fatigue, hunger, and susceptibility to suffering, so that He belongs to humanity as well as to God.

Second, He "dwelt among us." "Dwelt" (*eskenosen*) really means "to pitch tent." "He camped among us." His stay was temporary, but not illusory. This verb is used only five times in the New Testament: in this passage, and four times in the Apocalypse (Rev. 7:15, 12:12, 13:6, 21:3). Two of these instances refer to God. In the Greek Old Testament the word is largely confined to use with reference to the Tabernacle where the presence of God "dwelt." Perhaps John assumed that the reader's knowledge of the Septuagint would connect this statement with the Old Testament doctrine of the presence of God which guided the Israelite, and "dwelt among them" by day and by night. The cognate noun (*skene*) which is almost wholly used to refer to the Tabernacle appears in connection with this verb in Revelation 13:6. The invisible, indefinable God has been brought down into daily life through the incarnation.

Third, the effect of this incarnation was revelatory. "We beheld his glory." "Beheld" (*etheasametha*) means "observed."

The verb contains the root of the word "theater" and connotes more than a casual glance. It involves a careful scrutiny of what is before one in order to understand its significance. The incarnate LOGOS was studied under all possible conditions, favorable and unfavorable. All the information that human investigation could produce was made available by His willingness to be questioned and observed. The conclusion of the disciples is finely expressed by the "we" clause, the first in the Prologue. The "we" may be general for all humanity; but it seems to be particular as expressing the feelings of the disciples, which can no longer be contained even in the elevated and impersonal style of the Prologue. The Incarnate Word evoked a reaction from those who received Him that could not be reduced to a philosophical proposition—the personal declaration must appear. Thus in the Prologue as well as at the close of the argument of the body of the Gospel, the element of personal confession revealed the heart of a loyal disciple.

Nor is this experience limited to observation. "Of his fulness have we all received, and grace in exchange for grace."[12] Between the observation and the confession is a personal appropriation of truth. The divine grace was exhibited by Christ and was transmitted experientially to His disciples. The progressive nature of this experience of grace is affirmed by the use of the preposition *anti,* translated "for" in the Revised Version. It means "in exchange for," "as a substitute for," so that as one blessing is used, a fresh one is substituted to take its place. Consequently the knowledge of Christ never becomes purely historic in the sense that one contact, limited to one event, is all there is of it. The growing realization of Christ in His contacts with men is convincing evidence of His illimitable fullness.

The Word Revealing (16-18)

The final and climactic statement of the Prologue concerning the LOGOS is found in verse 18. "No man hath seen deity at

12. Original translation.

any time; the only begotten Son [God], who is in the bosom
of the Father, he hath explained (him)."[12]
There is in the Greek text of this verse a very interesting
and startling variant. A number of the oldest and most reliable
manuscripts read *God* instead of *Son*. If the term originally
were written as an abbreviation, a change of one letter would
make the difference.[13] Although the most recent English
versions do not adopt this reading, the Greek text of Westcott
and Hort,[14] which is still regarded as the standard critical text,
gives it the preference. Though the phrase "only begotten
God" is not used elsewhere in Johannine writings, while "only
begotten Son" does occur several times, it seems more likely
that the familiar reading should have been substituted for the
unfamiliar than that the reverse should have taken place.[15] At
any rate, the evidence for "only begotten God" is so strong as
to be practically conclusive. If this reading be accepted, "only
begotten God" makes an unequivocal affirmation of the deity
of Christ, though the term "Son" is hardly less strong.

The intent of the author is to make clear that while the un-
veiled essence of deity has never been given to mortal sight,
the real character of God can be seen in the Son who is the
fullest expression of the Father's life and love. "Only begotten" does not imply physical generation, but transcends the
idea of creation. The expression, "in the bosom of the Father,"
means perfect understanding and love. The nature of the invisible and mysterious God is thus interpreted by One who is
qualified to do so through kinship and understanding. In
biographical writing a man can best be interpreted to the public
by a sympathetic son who has within him the father's nature
and who speaks the language of a generation with which the

---

12. Original translation.
13. $\overline{YC}$ vs. $\overline{\Theta C}$ in uncial characters.
14. B. F. Westcott and F. J. A. Hort, *The New Testament in the Original Greek*, (New York: Macmillan & Co., 1889), *in loco*.
15. Cf. the discussion in A. T. Robertson, *An Introduction to the Textual Criticism of the New Testament*, (New York: George H. Doran Co., 1925), p. 209.

father did not have direct contact. So God, through a Son who is called God and who is one with the Father, is interpreted to men who have been alienated from Him by sin. The verb translated *declare*, which describes the method of this interpretation, "is the verb technically used in Greek literature of a declaration or exposition of divine mysteries."[16] It implies that the interpretation of God given by the Son is complete and final as far as the needs of men are concerned.

The blocks of material in the Prologue devoted to John the Baptist are not to be regarded as an interpolation. They are the opening of an historic connection between the independent revelation of God in the Son and the course of prophecy and religion as represented in the person of John the Baptist. Perhaps there is also present the intent of distinguishing between John and the Messiah. The existence of disciples at Ephesus in the sixth decade of the Christian century who knew only the baptism of John (Acts 19:1-6) indicates that there may have been a need for emphasizing the priority of Jesus as the Messiah and for clarifying the relation between Him and John.

In the two passages that speak directly of John (6-8, 15) three points are stressed:

> His human personality
> His capacity as a witness
> His subordinate relation to the LOGOS

John's human personality was emphasized by the term used in the Greek text: "There came A MAN"[17]—meaning a human being rather than some other kind of being. His divine commission was asserted, but he was not said to have a divine nature. In this respect he was contrasted with the LOGOS, who was called God.

---

16. J. H. Bernard, *op. cit.*, I, p. 33.
17. Greek-*anthropos*, capitals for emphasis.

The Baptist's capacity as a witness was stressed. He was "sent from God" (1:6); he "came for a witness" (1:7), "he witnesses and has cried aloud" (1:15).[18] His function was not to point to himself, but to Another; for "he was not that light, but [came] that he might bear witness" concerning it (1:8). It was his task to present the LOGOS to men and to prepare them for His coming. Detail concerning John's witness is presented in the first main section of this Gospel.

John's relation to the LOGOS was that of subordination. Jesus said, "Among them that are born of women there hath not arisen a greater than John the Baptist" (Matt. 11:11), yet he always appeared in a secondary role. His own testimony to the LOGOS is that He who followed him chronologically has taken precedence over him, because of His inherent preexistence and greatness. Coupling verse 15 with verse 17, the passage shows that in the revelation of God through the Lord Jesus Christ there is a new beginning greater than the law and the prophets, more than a refurbishing of the older revelation and far surpassing it. Grace and truth have finally been revealed to mankind in Him, and in the blaze of that Light which lighted every man as it came into the world, all lesser lights pale and disappear.

---

18. Original translation.

THE PERIOD OF CONSIDERATION

THE PERIOD OF CONSIDERATION

A. The Witness of John the Baptist
B. The Presentation of John's Disciples
C. The Wedding at Cana
D. The Appearance at Jerusalem
E. The Interview with Nicodemus
F. The Confession of John the Baptist
G. The Samaritan Woman
H. The Nobleman of Capernaum

Chapter IV

The Period of Consideration

1:19 to 4:54

THE first main section of the Gospel of John comprises the Period of Consideration, so named because it narrates certain events by means of which Jesus was presented to the public for their consideration and acceptance. These events or appearances of Jesus were selected as representative, in order that His method of appeal to various classes might be plainly seen, and that the reader might be influenced by at least one of them.

The episodes may be listed as follows:

The Witness of John the Baptist	1:19-34
The Presentation of John's Disciples	1:35-51
The Wedding at Cana	2:1-11
The Appearance at Jerusalem	2:12-22
The Interview with Nicodemus	2:23-3:21
The Confession of John the Baptist	3:22-36
The Samaritan Woman	4:1-42
The Nobleman of Capernaum	4:43-54

The Witness of John the Baptist (1:19-34)

John the Baptist was introduced in the Prologue by the statement of his commission, his objective, and his message. Beginning with the nineteenth verse of the first chapter his testimony was given in reply to a series of questions:

Who art thou?	22
What sayest thou of thyself?	22
Why then baptizest thou?	25

In answering the first of these questions John clarified his position with reference to the Messianic and theological concepts of Judaism by three negative assertions.

He denied that he was the Christ.

The title, Christ, is a translation of the Hebrew Messiah which means *anointed,* and which was applied to the Deliverer God had promised to the Jewish nation. His advent was expected at any time, and any unusual personality who appeared within the nation was likely to be regarded as a potential Messiah.

He denied that he was Elijah.

The last promise of the Old Testament in Malachi 4:5 says:

> Behold, I will send you Elijah the prophet before the great and terrible day of Jehovah come. And he shall turn the heart of the fathers to the children, and the heart of the children to their fathers; lest I come and smite the earth with a curse.

It was common Jewish belief that Elijah would precede the Messiah's coming. Hence, if John were not the Messiah, he might be His predecessor. This same belief was reflected in the utterance at the cross in response to Jesus' misunderstood cry, "Eli, Eli, lama sabachthani" (Matt. 27:46, 47). Some standing by, who did not understand Jesus' Aramaic, thought that He was calling for Elijah who was supposed to rescue God's favored ones when they were in peril.

He denied that he was "the prophet."

Probably the question, "Art thou the prophet?", was a reference to the promise in Deuteronomy 18:15, where Moses prophesied:

> Jehovah thy God will raise up unto thee a prophet from the midst of thee, of thy brethren, like unto me; unto him ye shall hearken.

The quotation implied that the Jews drew a distinction between the unnamed prophet and the Messiah. It was a prediction of the Christ, though it emphasized His prophetic calling rather than His kingly office, which was His usual representation.

Since John repudiated the foregoing identifications suggested by the Jews, they called for a positive declaration: "What sayest thou of thyself?" In reply, he connected himself with the forerunner cited in Isaiah 40, who was sent to prepare the way of Jehovah. The imagery was taken from the days when there were no paved roads, only tracks across the fields. If a king were to travel, the road must be built and smoothed out that the royal chariot might not find the traveling unduly rough, nor be swamped in the mire. John claimed that he was to make the road for a greater personage who was to represent Jehovah.

The third question of the Jewish leaders showed their bewilderment over John's answers. If he did not possess the authority of the Messiah or of Elijah, or of the unnamed prophet, why should he arrogate to himself the right to baptize? Baptism was a Jewish rite that was usually exercised upon proselytes. Since it was emblematic of the washing away of sins and of one's entrance into a new life, the performance of it evidently was regarded as a claim of authority. The Synoptics connect it with repentance (Matt. 3:11, Mark 1:4, Luke 3:3). John said the baptism was not an end in itself, nor final in its effectiveness. It remained for the One coming after him to make it effective by the enduement of the Holy Spirit.

Following the negative testimony of John to his questioners came the positive testimony to Jesus: "Behold, the Lamb of God, that taketh away the sin of the world!" (1:29) The word lamb (*amnos*) is used only four times in the New Testament: here in verses 29 and 36, in Acts 8:32 which is a quotation of Isaiah 53:7, and in I Peter 1:19. In the latter two instances it denotes a sacrificial lamb, which is its usual meaning in the Septuagint, especially in the Pentateuch. The con-

notation seems to be: "Behold the *sacrificial* lamb of God." If
so, John's announcement anticipated Jesus' prediction of the
cross and the whole significance of Calvary. In John's witness
to Christ's fulfillment of the sacrifice, and in his witness to the
bestowal of the Holy Spirit he laid the foundation for all
practical Christian theology. John's purpose was the direction
of his followers away from himself to Christ. He had revived
Judaism with his pungent message of confession of sin and
repentance. Now something more was needed, a forward step
into a more complete revelation and into a fuller experience.

The Presentation of John's Disciples (1:35-51)

Verses 35 to 51 record the reaction of five of John's disciples
to the message which he delivered. The initial pair were Andrew and probably the author himself, though no name is mentioned. They may be called the first believers, since they were
the first to follow Jesus (37). The development of their belief
followed a definite pattern. First came the testimony of John:
"Behold, the lamb of God." They were not fully satisfied,
however, with a belief built on hearsay, for when Jesus questioned them as to what they wanted, they asked, "Where
abidest thou?" This inquiry was more than a polite request
for His address. It was a desire for fellowship. They wanted
to find Him out for themselves, and to discover whether the
testimony of John could be true.

The gracious invitation, "Come, and ye shall see" (39),
was typical of the Lord. He welcomed them and put Himself
at their disposal. The burden of their conversation during the
hours that followed is not described; but if it can be inferred
from the subsequent statement of Andrew, who was one of the
two, it must have involved a presentation of Jesus' claims to
messiahship on the basis of the Scriptures. Andrew testified
to the success of John's mission as the forerunner when he
said of Jesus, "We have found the Messiah" (41). The per-

sonal interview made him a convinced believer, and presumably produced the same effect on his companion.

This conviction on the part of Andrew resulted in action. He brought his brother Simon to Jesus. In one sentence Jesus summarized his whole career: "Thou art Simon . . ." He was named for Simeon, the unreliable, of whom Jacob said, in conjunction with Levi,

> Simeon and Levi are brethren;
> . . . .
> Cursed be their anger, for it was fierce;
> And their wrath, for it was cruel.
>
> (Gen. 49:5, 7)

Simon was hot tempered and vindictive, volatile and violent in action. Jesus predicted a change in his unsteady personality. "Thou art . . ., thou shalt be . . ." Out of the wavering Simon He made a stable and rocklike Cephas. The very name, Cephas, means rock, as its Greek equivalent, Peter, shows.

The episode of Philip and Nathanael paralleled the account of Andrew and Peter to the extent that Philip, like Andrew, brought another to Christ by his testimony. In other respects the story was quite different. Andrew sought out Jesus; Jesus called Philip. Peter responded silently but willingly to Andrew's testimony; Nathanael reacted to Philip's announcement by saying derisively, "Can any good thing come out of Nazareth?" Evidently he felt Philip's declaration that the Messiah was Jesus of Nazareth was a distinct anticlimax, for it was inconceivable to him that the profligate caravan town of Nazareth should produce the Messiah. He possessed high spiritual standards and outspokenly maintained them.

Jesus' verdict upon him, "Behold, an Israelite indeed, in whom is no guile" (47) was prompted by knowledge of Nathanael's mind. Jesus had seen Nathanael sitting under a fig tree even before Philip introduced him. "Under the fig tree"

was a favorite place for meditation.[1] The phrase as used in the
Old Testament is applied to one's home or garden where rest
and meditation are possible. It may be that Nathanael had
withdrawn under its shelter and was reading the passage in
Genesis 28 which narrated the vision of Jacob. Perhaps, he
mused, if God could reveal Himself to a scoundrel like Jacob,
who neither sought nor desired His presence, He should reveal
Himself to one who craved to know Him. Certainly some
similar idea may have been in his mind, for Jesus' statement
fitted such a situation perfectly. Guile was Jacob's chief trait
of character; his very name meant "supplanter." What Jesus
really said was: "Behold, an Israelite indeed, such as Jacob
became after God's revelation to him, in whom there is no old
Jacob left." Nathanael's sudden acceptance of Jesus' person
and his acknowledgment of Him as Son of God and King of
Israel indicated that Jesus had overcome his objections at one
stroke.

Jesus, however, did not let him lapse into self-satisfaction
over what he might consider to be a greater revelation than
Jacob had. He challenged Nathanael with the progressive pos-
sibilities of belief. As Jacob had seen the angels of God ascending and descending on the ladder, so Jesus promised
Nathanael that he should see the angels of God ascending and
descending upon Him. He Himself was to be the new medium
of revelation, a surer link between heaven and earth than the
ladder which for the errant Jacob meant a way to God.

The Wedding at Cana (2:1-11)

The language of the story implies that Jesus and His disciples were invited to the wedding because of indirect obligation. Mary was there; Jesus and His disciples were "also"
invited to the marriage. The "also" carries a slight connota-

---

1. Cf. Micah 4:4, Zech. 3:10, Isa. 36:16.

tion that Jesus and His followers were extra guests, invited because of their connection with His mother.

Mary's request to Jesus was at once a testimony to her personal confidence in His powers and acknowledgment of the social disaster which threatened the young couple. Had the wine actually failed, the occurrence would have been regarded as an insult to those present, and would have banished the host and hostess to practical isolation. Perhaps the shortage was occasioned by the unexpected arrival of Jesus and His party, in which case Mary may have felt that He was responsible.

The combined capacity of the waterpots was about 150 gallons. Reckoning a half pint to a glass, these vessels would contain about 2400 servings of wine—certainly enough to supply a large number of people for several days. In quality and quantity the new-made wine more than satisfied the needs and taste of those who attended the feast.

The significance of the miracle lay in the result that it produced. John 2:11 says: "This beginning of his signs did Jesus in Cana of Galilee, and manifested his glory; *and his disciples believed on him*" (italics ours).

The belief prompted by the sign was not the fullest that Jesus desired. Nevertheless it was an advance step beyond the initial belief that was only theoretical. The people had seen the miracle with their own eyes, and were able to draw the conclusion that a superior being was among them who had substantiated His claims by His deed of mercy and power.

The First Appearance at Jerusalem (2:12-22)

From Galilee Jesus went to Jerusalem at the season of the Passover. There He encountered a public different from that of Galilee. The disciples of John the Baptist, Jesus' first followers, were predisposed to belief in Him. The "Jews" of Jerusalem, whom the writer of this Gospel represented as a hostile group, were suspicious of His claims and jealous of His prowess.

Their suspicion and jealousy were revealed through His cleansing of the temple,[2] which was Jesus' protest against the commercialization of the spiritual heritage of Judaism. Since the temple was His Father's house (16), He resented its degradation to the level of a market. He had come to assert the claims of God upon His own nation, and He felt keenly the spiritual indifference which had turned worship into a means of profit.

Jesus' act in cleansing the temple presupposed authority as the representative of God. As He spoke of "my Father" He voiced His claim to a peculiar relation with God. His enemies took up the challenge immediately by asking for His credentials. In answer He declared the principle that the resurrection of His body would be the chief proof of His ministry. The Jews asked for a "sign" (18), and Jesus said, perhaps with a gesture toward Himself, "Destroy this temple, and in three days I will raise it up" (19). The crowd misunderstood Him completely, though the utterance was remembered for years afterward (Matt. 26:61), and the disciples did not understand His meaning until after the resurrection when it became an incentive to their faith. Although this truth was not fully developed at this time, the idea reappeared in the controversial discourses of chapters 5 and 6 (5:26, 6:38, 44, ff.), as well as in the consummating account of chapter 20.

The Interview with Nicodemus (2:23-3:21)

The opening ministry of Jesus in Jerusalem had attracted a great deal of attention, both favorable and unfavorable. Many of the people who had seen His signs "believed on his name"

---

2. This cleansing of the temple has been regarded as a chronological difficulty, for John placed it at the first Passover of Jesus' ministry, while the Synoptists speak of a cleansing of the temple which took place in the week of His passion (Matt. 21:12-17, Mark 11:15-18, Luke 19:45-48). Either there were two cleansings of the temple, or one has been misplaced in the account. The former is probably true, since there are slight differences in the two accounts which indicate separate events.

(2:23). This phrase expressed saving faith, but the comment indicates that in this case their faith was superficial. It was vested only in the signs and did not extend to a full acceptance of His claims and commands. The Greek text has the same word for "believe" in verse 23 and for "trust" in verse 24. The people believed on Christ, but He did not believe them. He knew their hearts and could evaluate their faith exactly. Although the statement is negative in that its main import is Jesus' reason for not trusting Himself to the crowds in Jerusalem, it conveys also the positive truth that He knew the human heart thoroughly. Consequently the three main interviews that follow exhibit His method of dealing skillfully with three different types of personality with the purpose of bringing them to belief.

The first of these personalities was Nicodemus. As a Pharisee he was zealous for the law and scrupulous in his observance of it. He was called "a ruler of the Jews" (1), which indicated that he had achieved a position of leadership in his nation. His coming by night might be attributable to any one of a number of motives: to fear of criticism, to a desire for uninterrupted conversation, or to an urge to make a private investigation before committing himself publicly for or against Jesus. Three utterances of Nicodemus in the ensuing conversation are recorded:

"Rabbi, we know that thou art a teacher come from God; for no one can do these signs that thou doest, except God be with him" (2).

Nicodemus' declaration was both a polite concession and an initial step of faith. His greeting revealed him as a gentleman and a thinker: a gentleman, because he paid Jesus a sincere compliment; a thinker, because his words implied that he had observed carefully Jesus' works, and had concluded that only a heaven-sent person could perform them.

The reply of Jesus was startling because of its abruptness: "Except one be born anew, he cannot see the kingdom of God"

(3). At first the statement seemed almost irrelevant; yet it really was the expression of Jesus' discernment. Because He "knew what was in man," He saw through Nicodemus, and knew that his circuitous approach concealed a deeper need. Nicodemus, like many another of his time, was seeking the kingdom of God. Jesus bluntly answered his question before he could ask it, asserting that without a complete change, comparable only to rebirth, the natural man could not enter the spiritual kingdom. "Cannot" implies incapability rather than prohibition. The natural man is not arbitrarily debarred from the kingdom. He is inherently incapable of apprehending it, just as a blind man cannot enjoy a sunset. God's mysteries are not the heritage of the learned, the moral, or the religious simply because of learning, morality, or religion; they are the heritage of the spiritually transformed.

The figure of speech which Jesus employed was possibly familiar to Nicodemus. At any rate, its meaning was clear to him. Just as an infant, by the very occurrence of his birth, is fitted for a new life in a strange realm, so men must experience spiritual rebirth preparatory to their entrance into the kingdom of God.

Nicodemus' second utterance was a twofold query. "How can a man be born when he is old? He cannot enter a second time into his mother's womb and be born, can he?" (4)[3]

To assume that a man so astute as Nicodemus should have thought the new birth to be literally physical is absurd. The question rather meant: "I acknowledge that a new birth is necessary, but I am too old to change. My pattern of life is set. Physical birth is out of the question and psychological rebirth seems even less probable. Granting the truth of what you say, is not my case hopeless?"

The reply of Jesus was an appeal to Nicodemus' knowledge. "Except one be born of water and the Spirit, he cannot enter

---

3. Original translation.

into the kingdom of God" (5). "Water" would recall to the inquirer the ministry of John the Baptist, whose preaching of repentance and of baptism would be fresh in his mind. To a Jew, the idea of baptism would be repugnant since it connoted the ceremony by which an unclean Gentile became a member of the Jewish faith.[4] Such a step as this for Nicodemus would involve humiliation, a virtual acknowledgment that he, a Pharisee, needed to repent just as a Gentile outside the law needed repentance.

Furthermore, this birth must come through the Spirit. The statement presupposed the activity of the Holy Spirit within all who entered the kingdom. Nicodemus knew nothing of the Spirit experimentally. In Old Testament teaching, the Spirit came upon the prophets or other specially chosen men for unusual reasons, but nowhere in Judaism was taught the coming of the Spirit upon all men for their personal regeneration. The mystery and reality of the Spirit's work were both contained in Jesus' illustration of the wind whose origin was undiscoverable but whose presence was manifest. Nobody could deny its existence. Thus it was with those born of the Spirit. The origin of their life could not be defined, but its actuality could be seen by all.

Nicodemus posed a further question: "How can these things be?" (9) This query should be interpreted as an earnest plea for a method of fulfillment, not as an expression of amazement and incredulity. The seeker was eager to participate in the spiritual privileges of which Jesus spoke, and he pressed the point. "How can I experience this new birth?" would be a fair paraphrase of the passage.

Jesus' rejoinder reflected surprise. "Art thou the teacher of Israel, and understandest not these things?" (10) The definite article implied that Nicodemus must have been re-

---

4. Cf. Emil Schürer, *A History of the Jewish People in the Time of Christ,* (Second Edition. New York: Charles Scribner's Sons, 1891), II, ii, pp. 319-324.

garded as the outstanding teacher in Israel, yet he was ignorant
of a cardinal spiritual truth. Jesus was hesitant about telling
him more. If he were unable to comprehend matters illustrated by material experience, he would be incapable of grasp-
ing truth which had no earthly analogy. Beyond Jesus' own
word there could be no further explanation. He was the sole
link between heaven and earth.

For this reason Jesus approached the problem from the
standpoint of the Jewish Scriptures with which Nicodemus
undoubtedly was familiar. He selected the story of the brazen
serpent (Num. 21:8) and made a direct comparison between
the serpent and Himself. It was a startling simile, for the serpent was the emblem of sin under judgment, as Nicodemus
would recognize. The points of comparison were as follows:

The brazen serpent was prepared by the command of God.

It symbolized God's way of saving men who are under the
condemnation of sin and who are suffering from its effects.

It made curative power available on the basis of faith rather
than of works. The sufferers did nothing but *look* at the
serpent.

It was lifted up on a "standard."[5] "Banner staff" would be
an acceptable translation. A banner staff was frequently
formed like a cross, with the transverse pole holding the
banner. The word here translated "lifted up" (*hypsoo*) was
used by John only of the passion of Christ (8:28, 12:32, 34),
and the inference is clear that he intended an analogy between
the brazen serpent and the cross.

The serpent itself was a representation of God's judgment
on sin.

The destiny of the individual was determined by his response
to God's invitation.

---

5. The term used is variously translated *sign, ensign, standard,* and, in
one or two instances, *sail.* Ordinarily it refers to an ensign mounted on a
pole so that it can be used as a signal or a rallying point for a camp or an
army. In this case, the pole is meant rather than what was hung on it.

In effect, Jesus told Nicodemus that the new birth was a direct result of faith in His death and resurrection power.

Verses 16 to 21 have been regarded by some commentators as an editorial addition to Jesus' words on the part of the writer, or as a piece of explanatory comment.[6] Certainly the preceding remark about the brazen serpent fitted neatly into the conversation with Nicodemus, and the ensuing explanatory remarks can scarcely be separated from the comparison with the Old Testament. The words may be the author's condensation of Jesus' utterance, but were doubtless based on what He said on this occasion. Possibly he was present at the interview, though he was not mentioned as being included in it.

The appeal was a summary of the teaching given in the implications of the conversation with Nicodemus. It contained God's attitude and purpose toward the world, and the double reaction of the believer and of the unbeliever. God's attitude is love. The word translated "love" is the noblest and strongest in Greek. It connotes an act of the will rather than an emotion, whim, or infatuation, and its measure is defined in terms of the result. "He gave his only begotten Son" (16). God's positive purpose in Christ is the salvation of the unbeliever. Although judgment is the inevitable consequence of disbelief, it is not God's primary desire for men. The breadth of the invitation is revealed by the "whosoever," which is as inclusive

---

6. B. F. Westcott, *op. cit.*, I. pp. 118, 119. "This section is a commentary on the nature of the mission of the Son . . . It is therefore likely (from its secondary character, apart from all other considerations) that it contains reflections of the Evangelist, and is not a continuation of the words of the Lord."
Per contra—F. Godet. *Commentary on the Gospel of St. John,* translated from the last edition by M. D. Cusin, (Third edition, Edinburgh: T. & T. Clark, 1890), II, pp. 68, 69. "Several theologians, with Erasmus (Neander, Tholuck, Olshausen, Baumlein), have supposed that the conversation between Jesus and Nicodemus closes with ver. 15, and that from ver. 16 it is the evangelist who speaks, commenting by his own reflections on his Master's sayings . . . On the other hand, would the *for,* ver. 16, indicate sufficiently a transition from the teaching of Jesus to the disciple's commentary? Would not the author have required to mark this important transition more distinctly? . . . "

and indefinite as possible. Salvation is not restricted to any race, color, or class, but is the heritage of all who will truly believe.

Judgment is the logical consequence of unbelief. As the man who turns his back to the sun deepens by his own shadow the darkness in which he walks, so the unbeliever intensifies the darkness of his own soul by his unbelief. His unbelief is in itself an admission of sin, since he will not come to the light to have his deeds made manifest and evaluated.

By this paragraph the author clinched the impression created by the interview with Nicodemus. Curiously enough, no statement is made concerning Nicodemus' decision. The appeal was directed to the reader that he might avail himself of the approach which God had provided, and so might profit from the directions which Jesus gave to Nicodemus about the new birth.

The Confession of John the Baptist (3:22-36)

John the Baptist was reintroduced to explain his relation to Jesus. In a day well advanced in the life of the Church he was still regarded as an authority who had not been displaced by Christ. The Fourth Gospel was presumably written to the Asian churches among whom, according to Acts 19, the tradition of John the Baptist's teaching on repentance and baptism had persisted. His declining influence among the populace of Judea in comparison with the rising influence of Jesus had caused comment among his disciples. They were jealous for him and said so. John's consciousness of the subordinate and temporary character of his mission was expressed in the single sentence: "He must increase, but I must decrease" (30). Thus John's self-abdication was made the answer to those who still placed him on an equal plane with Jesus.

The explanation in verses 31 to 36, where the author's hand is unmistakably seen, carried still further the appeal of verses 16 to 21. The antithesis of the heavenly and the earthly witness was asserted, and the authority of the former was stressed. The consequences of belief and unbelief in the witness were reiterated in stronger terms, for they were given with regard to the present rather than to the future. For the believer, eternal life is a present possession, not a reward bestowed at the gates of death. Wrath is the present lot of the unbeliever; he is already under condemnation. The contrast of *believe* and *obey* in verse 36 assists in defining the former term. Belief is obedience to the utterance of God; disobedience is unbelief. *Belief* is thus defined as commitment to authority rather than a passive opinion.

The Samaritan Woman (4:1-42)

The second of the great interviews of Jesus in the Period of Consideration was with the woman of Samaria. The occasion for the tour on which the interview took place was closely linked with the preceding paragraph on the witness of John the Baptist. Jesus realized that His success in winning disciples had created jealousy on the part of John's followers and that it had also brought about an attitude of questioning on the part of the Pharisees. He preferred to withdraw to Galilee, rather than to cause a rift among the potential believers and a premature antagonism to His own ministry. Judging by the fact that the Synoptics dated the beginning of His public ministry from the imprisonment of John, it seems probable that He felt the time had not come for open combat with His enemies.

A strange phrase introduces this episode: "He must needs pass through Samaria." The word "must" implies logical necessity rather than personal obligation. It is the term one would use in saying, "A triangle *must* have three sides." Why it should be used here is not immediately clear, since there were other roads that Jesus could have taken to Galilee. In the light of the general tenor of the Gospel, the word suggested that His reason was not geographical necessity nor social pressure, but the underlying compulsion of the Divine Will that sought out the lost Samaritan sheep. That little phrase, "He must . . .," makes this interview to glow with the light of destiny.

The place of the interview was Sychar, or near it. The city stood at a fork of the road, one branch of which went toward Capernaum and the other branch to Nazareth. The well of Jacob was located about one half mile from the village.

The time is given as the sixth hour (6). Bernard[7] takes the view that time in John's Gospel is computed from sunrise to sunset, which would make the sixth hour to be twelve o'clock noon. In this narrative it would explain why Jesus sat down to rest, since He would be weary after the travel of the morning, and ready for the food which the disciples had gone to buy. Although noon was not the customary hour for women to visit the well, the presence of the Samaritan may be explained plausibly by supposing that she was in ill repute among the women of her village, and so preferred to come for water at a time when others would not be there.

The woman was an interesting character. As the second in the series of interviews, she was all that Nicodemus was not. He was a Jew; she was a Samaritan. He was a man; she was a woman. He was learned; she was ignorant. He was morally upright; she was sinful. He was wealthy and from the upper class of society; she was poor, and probably almost an outcast. He recognized Jesus' merits and sought Him out; she saw Him only as a curious traveler and was quite indifferent to Him. Nicodemus was serious and dignified; she was flippant and possibly boisterous. It is hard to imagine a greater contrast in personalities than that which existed between these two individuals.

The tact and persistence of Jesus was demonstrated in His appeals to her. He began on the ground of her kindness. "Give me to drink" is a request that would be granted to almost any-

7. J. H. Bernard, *op. cit.*, I, p. 136.

body. One would scarcely deny a cup of cold water to his worst enemy. Doubtless Jesus knew also that the surest way to win the friendship of another is to ask a favor. The sense of having another obligated for a favor given is much more pleasing than the sense of being obligated for a favor received. Jesus' indebtedness to the woman for the drink might serve to undermine the natural prejudice that she as a Samaritan would have toward Him a Jew.

Her reaction was that of raillery. Good-naturedly she gave Him what He asked, but could not resist the opportunity to have a little fun with it. "How is it that thou, being a Jew, askest drink of me, who am a Samaritan woman?" (9) In other words, "We Samaritans are to you the scum of the earth, but we will serve well enough when you are thirsty!" There was a sting hidden in her jest. She felt inferior to this thirsty stranger and so made her reply a bit tart.

Jesus took no offense but tried a different appeal, this time to her curiosity. His statement would invariably bring a quick response from any woman: "If thou knewest . . ." The mere hint that He knew something that she did not know was sufficient to change her attitude from badinage to serious inquiry.

Incredulity and curiosity appeared in her reply. "Sir, thou hast nothing to draw with, and the well is deep: whence then hast thou that living water? Art thou greater than our father Jacob, who gave us the well . . .?" (11, 12). Her understanding was limited, but the shell of reserve behind the bantering manner was broken and she was ready for serious conversation.

In order to insure more than idle inquiry, Jesus appealed to her desire. "Every one that drinketh of this water shall thirst again: but whosoever drinketh of the water that I shall give him shall never thirst; but the water that I shall give him shall become in him a well of water springing up unto eternal life" (13, 14).

The woman's comprehension of this statement was quite imperfect. She did not grasp the fact that Jesus was speaking of spiritual water. She was still thinking in terms of the material. To her, His promise was a gratification of common human laziness. "Give me this water," she replied, "that I thirst not, neither come all the way hither to draw" (15).

Upon the expression of a genuine desire, however elementary and mundane, Jesus made an appeal to her ambition: "Go, call thy husband, and come hither." If she wanted badly enough what He had to offer, she would be willing to exert herself to obtain it. His command, taken at face value, called for a walk of a mile in the hot sun with only the word of a stranger to make it worth while. In that sense it was an appeal to faith. But Jesus had an even deeper purpose than appealing to ambition. The command had a double edge for it cut sharply into her heart. If she obeyed, her action would necessitate the disclosure of her private life to this wayfarer, and she was not ready for that.

Her reaction was that of sullen withdrawal. The curt answer, "I have no husband," containing four words in English and three in Greek, was spoken probably with a tone of keen resentment. The reply was true, but was intended as a screen for her own falsity. She did not wish to be investigated, least of all by a Jew.

While she struggled with the conflicting emotions of desire and withdrawal, Jesus calmly proceeded to unmask her completely by an appeal to her moral sense. "Thou saidst well, I have no husband: for thou hast had five husbands; and he whom thou now hast is not thy husband . . ." (17, 18). By the exercise of His prophetic knowledge He turned her life inside out before her very eyes.

This disclosure of His knowledge shocked her and put her on the defensive. Like many others whose moral position is challenged, she took refuge in arguing impersonally about religion. Acknowledging Him as a prophet, she immediately sought to divert His inquiry by asking Him the question which for years had divided Jew from Samaritan. "Our fathers worshipped in this mountain; and ye say, that in Jerusalem is the place where men ought to worship" (20).

Skillfully Jesus replied both to the controversial issue which she raised and to the deeper personal need concealed behind it. His reply was blunt, and He made no concession to the Samaritan position, for He said, "Salvation is from the Jews" (22). On the other hand, He lifted the whole problem out of the categories of time and space and made it a matter of the heart. "God is a Spirit: and they that worship him must worship in spirit and truth" (24). He appealed directly to her religious sensibilities. In effect, He said, "If you really want to know the truth about worship, you will find it not in the formula of our fathers, but in the relation of your own heart with God. You must deal with Him through His Spirit, and on the basis of truth, which precludes the kind of a life that you are living now."

The woman's answer showed that there was a measure of sincerity in her heart. She could have gone away at this time, but did not. Instead, she said with wistful emphasis, "I know that Messiah cometh . . . when he is come, he will declare unto us all things" (25). The words were a confession both of ignorance and of hope. She was waiting for light, and, soiled as she was, she clung to the ancient promise of God that a Deliverer would come who would take away the darkness from her eyes.

To such elementary faith as this Jesus revealed Himself more openly than He did even to Nicodemus. "I that speak unto thee am he" (26). It was a direct challenge to her personal faith. Would she believe, or would she not?

Through the interview may be traced a rising estimate of Jesus in the woman's thinking. In verse 9 she called Him a Jew—just another traveler who happened to be visiting Samaria. In verse 12 she suggested the possibility that He might be greater than Jacob, though she did not entertain the thought seriously. At any rate, He was an unusual personage. In verse 19 she called Him a prophet because she could explain His insight into her life in no other way. Finally, in verse 29, among her own villagers, she said, "You don't suppose that this is the Messiah, do you?"[8] She was too cautious to assert definitely that her judgment was correct, but her language implied that there was no doubt in her mind.

The consequent belief of the Samaritans is noteworthy, as the type of reaction that follows personal investigation of Jesus. The woman's testimony, plus the Lord's word (41), brought the conviction that He was the Saviour of the world.

In this one instance Jesus had to overcome the obstacles of the woman's indifference, materialism, selfishness, moral turpitude, and religious prejudice, ignorance, and indefiniteness. Nevertheless in this sample conversation He led her straight to the beginning of an active faith. The interview was a superb example of His divine understanding and mastery of human nature.

The conversation with the disciples (27 to 38) was parenthetic to the main narrative but not unimportant. It was a disclosure of Jesus' consciousness of His mission and of His desire that the disciples should share in it. They were bound by routine and convention. They could not understand why He would not eat, since He had seemed so faint when they left Him, and since they had gone to the trouble of procuring food for Him. Neither could they comprehend how He could lower Himself to talk to a woman in public, and a Samaritan at that. He disclosed that His chief passion in life, stronger even than the appetite for food, was to do the Father's will. There was a task waiting to be finished which the Father had committed to Him, and in which He wanted the disciples to have a part. As He uttered the words of explanation, the Samaritans, led by the returning woman, were filing toward Him along the path

8. Original translation.

through the fields. Looking upon them as they came, He said, "Lift up your eyes, and look on the fields, that they are white already unto harvest" (35). The invitation was another outcropping of the missionary vision of Jesus that appeared so often in the Fourth Gospel.

The Nobleman of Capernaum (4:43-54)

The third interview of Jesus which closed the series of His public presentations took place in Galilee two days after the visit in Samaria. His reception there was the result of His ministry in Jerusalem. The Galileans who had made the pilgrimage to the feast had seen His signs, or at least had heard of them, and were quite ready to welcome Him. The reference connects with the narrative of 2:23. Their belief was grounded on the works that He did, not on their faith in His person. John echoed Jesus' utterance which is quoted in all the Synoptics,[9] that "a prophet hath no honor in his own country" (44), although the reception accorded to Jesus in Galilee was more friendly than in Judea.

The key to the healing of the nobleman's son is given in the word "again" in verse 46. The report of the first miracle in Cana, coupled with the rumors that had come back from Jerusalem, had established the reputation of Jesus as a healer and wonder worker. In 2:11, the emphasis is laid on His disciples as if they believed on Him whether anybody else did or not. The Galileans were incredulous until they saw the power of Jesus fully demonstrated.

The nobleman was possibly a courtier of Herod the Tetrarch. His interest in Jesus was prompted by the sickness of his son, who had been ailing for some time.[10] The gradual decline of the child's health, with a sudden turn for the worse, drove him to look for aid wherever he could find it. Desperate, he turned to Jesus, and persistently pressed the request[10] upon

---

9. Matt. 13:57, Mark 6:4, Luke 4:24.
10. Greek imperfect.

Him to go down to Capernaum and heal his child. Jesus was weary of being solicited for an exhibition of His powers, and His brusque reply was a protest against the popular feeling concerning Him. "Except ye see signs and wonders, ye will in no wise believe" (48). He did not want to be regarded only as a worker of miracles or marvels while the message of His person was rejected.

The rejoinder of the nobleman revealed that he was no trifler. The language is heartfelt and emphatic: "Sir, come down ere my child die" (49). The ability of Jesus to perform supernatural deeds was no academic question to the nobleman; it meant the difference between life and death for his son. He demanded action, not inquiry into the genuineness of his motives.

The brief answer of Jesus, "Go thy way; thy son liveth" (50), put the man in a dilemma. If he took Jesus at His word, he did so with no assurance beyond that word that Jesus would do anything for him. If he refused to take Jesus at His word, he would insult the very man upon whom all his hopes depended, and so forfeit whatever benefits He might confer. With short and simple command Jesus put the nobleman in the position where he would be compelled to show real faith if he had any to show. The laconic simplicity of this account gives no inkling of the conflict which must have taken place in the nobleman's mind at that moment. Should he turn back to Capernaum, or should he continue to entreat Jesus to go with him and thereby obtain a tangible guarantee of His willingness to heal? Slowly, perhaps, but decisively, he took Jesus at His word, and turned homeward. This act John called "believing." "The man believed the word that Jesus spake unto him, and he went his way" (50b).

The encounter with the servants on the road showed that the nobleman's faith was justified. Overjoyed that the boy had recovered, the father believed and his whole house (53). The difference between the use of "believe" in verses 50 and 53 is that the former depicted a reluctant faith, born of necessity, and consisting chiefly in accepting the naked word of Christ because no better alternative could be found. It was the faith of desperation evoked by the father's plight and by Jesus' seeming severity. The second use of the term was the voluntary faith in Jesus' person which was prompted by gratitude. The use of "believe" in the absolute sense without a direct or indirect object indicated that the nobleman had come to a genuine faith in Christ as a person. The episode thus described the growth of this belief, and its nature. It is not confined to one occasion nor to one type of work, but involves utter confidence in Christ as a person who can be trusted with the dearest treasures and the deepest problems. When the nobleman realized that Christ could be trusted with his son, he committed himself and his household wholeheartedly to Jesus.

No further events are recorded in this Galilean ministry. The author has presented in three main interviews three different types of faith. The first was the cautious and judicial venture of the learned inquirer, Nicodemus, who came to Christ because of his desire to fit Him into a rational framework of thought. No definite decision is recorded. One is left to surmise what the puzzled but sincere Pharisee may have done, but his participation in the burial of Jesus showed that he maintained a sympathetic interest in Him to the last of His life. The second type of faith was a wistful yearning brought to light only by Jesus' persistent probing of the Samaritan woman's heart. He broke through the encrustation of her flippancy, indifference, and materialism, and brought her to a hopeful if not completely positive confession. The third type was the result of desperation, which compelled the nobleman to exercise faith as the lesser difficulty of a hard choice. In all of these cases there is at least some assurance that the person concerned emerged with a real confidence in Christ. The meaning, power, and goal of belief were thus amply demonstrated.

THE PERIOD OF CONTROVERSY

THE PERIOD OF CONTROVERSY

A. The Man at the Pool
B. The Claims of Jesus
C. The Witnesses
D. The Feeding of the Five Thousand
E. The Walking on the Water
F. The Discourse on the Bread of Life

CHAPTER V

The Period of Controversy

5:1 to 6:71

THE first period in the life of Jesus recorded in this Gospel contained His claims. He Himself presented some of them through an explicit avowal of messiahship, some were implicit in the titles ascribed to Him by His friends, and still others were latent in the miracles that He performed. He claimed nothing less for Himself than deity. He demanded nothing less from His followers than obedient faith.

It was inevitable that such claims and demands as His should meet opposition, especially when they interfered with the prejudices and sins of His hearers. Chapters 5 and 6 show the development of this opposition in debate and controversy before it broke into deadly conflict. On the one side was Jesus, who claimed the allegiance of men on the basis of His divine rights, and those who believed on Him; on the other side were those who disbelieved His claims, and so regarded Him as an impostor. The subject matter was centered around two events: the healing of the impotent man at the pool of Bethesda and the feeding of the five thousand in Galilee. These two events differed in character, in scope, in locality, and in response. One was negative, for it removed the handicap of a long standing disease. The other was positive, for it provided nourishment for the healthy crowd. One pertained to an individual; the other affected more than five thousand people. One took place in Jerusalem, the other in Galilee. The former evoked the enmity of the Jews; the latter brought the acclamation of the multitude. Both produced controversy, and to each story John has added the report of the teaching which grew out of the event.

The Man at the Pool (5:1-18)

The time of this miracle cannot be fixed with certainty. A comparison of 3:22 and 6:4 reveals that this event took place at an unnamed feast between Jesus' visit to Judea and the second Passover of His ministry. The career of John the Baptist had closed and was already a memory. Westcott, though he states that "most modern commentators suppose it to be the Feast of Purim (March),"[1] thinks that the Feast of Trumpets, which came in September, is the most likely possibility. With this Edersheim[2] agrees. Smith[3] says that it was probably the Passover since the tradition of Irenaeus supports it, and since the Passover was the only feast that Israelites were required to attend.

Nor can the place of the miracle be located. The pool was by the sheep market and evidently was fed by an intermittent spring. Topographical changes in the city of Jerusalem have made identification impossible at the present day.

The importance of this miracle is attached to its consequences rather than to the case itself. Nevertheless, it was unusual in some respects. The long illness of the man was an outstanding feature, and the fact that John mentioned it implied that he regarded it as significant. Thirty-eight years of sickness would indicate hopelessness from the physical standpoint; but there was a hint that the man was even more hopeless psychologically. He had become resigned to his fate and had accepted the inevitable.

Jesus' introductory question was sudden and startling: "Wouldest thou be made whole?" (6) In modern vernacular,

---

1. B. F. Westcott, *op. cit.,* I, pp. 181, 204-207.
2. Alfred Edersheim, *The Life and Times of Jesus,* (Eerdmans, Grand Rapids, 1947), I, p. 460.
3. David Smith, *The Days of His Flesh,* (Eighth Edition. New York and London, Hodder and Stoughton, n. d.), Appendix V, pp. 532-533.

He meant, "Do you *want* to get well?" The approach at first appeared foolish. No sick person would choose to remain sick. In this particular instance the man was waiting in hope that somebody would take pity on him and help him into the pool when the water bubbled, in order that he might avail himself of its supposedly miraculous powers. A closer examination of Jesus' address to the victim shows that He was probing his inner heart, "Have you the will to be cured?" The reply revealed that the man was placing the blame for his condition on what somebody else had not done for him. He was bound by his circumstances and could rise no higher than a futile complaint. The paralysis of body was accompanied by a partial paralysis of will. Jesus' selection of this man from the large number of invalids at the pool indicated His interest in restoring those who have been reduced to utter helplessness both in body and spirit.

Jesus' command was as incisive as the question. "Arise, take up thy pallet (ARV mg.), and walk" (8). To a man who had just expressed his total inability to do anything for himself, the command must have seemed like mockery. These crisp words were a challenge to an enfeebled will as well as to a paralyzed body. Jesus presented him with immediate personal action as a new alternative to dull acceptance of the inevitable. The masterful presence of Jesus created faith in him, and he arose and walked.

The third remark of Jesus occurred on a later occasion when He met the man in the temple. Jesus thought enough of him to make a special point of warning him. "Sin no more" (14) implied that his former state was a direct result of sin, and that he stood in peril of a worse calamity if he continued in his evil ways. The man seems to have been lax and unthinking. He needed the stimulus of a warning to insure the completeness of his deliverance.

The representation of the Jewish authorities in connection with this miracle was unflattering. Their concern was not for the healing of the man, but for the Sabbath. They were a perfect example of the unspiritual heartlessness which results from barren institutionalism. The law was "holy and righteous and good" (Rom. 7:12), and its requirement of the observance of the Sabbath was intended to provide men with a pause in the week's exhausting toil. When the regulation became a barrier to the performance of that which was inherently right, revision was necessary.

The Claims of Jesus (5:19-29)

The reply of Jesus to the accusations of the Jews contained not only a new ethical concept of the Sabbath, but also a new theology. His first extensive treatment of His relationship to the Father began with 5:17. It is significant that in the Fourth Gospel Jesus said either "my Father," or "your Father," but never "our Father." God was His Father and also the Father of other men, but the Fatherhood of God meant more to Him than it did to others. His explanation of His action on the Sabbath, "My Father worketh even until now, and I work," indicated that He made the Father His pattern, and that He felt that the Father's work constituted sufficient precedent and reason for His. His enemies understood what He meant, for they sought to kill Him because He had assumed the prerogatives of deity in calling God "his own Father."[4] The term *his own* meant peculiarly his, in a way that could not be applied to anyone else.

The elaboration of this thought by Jesus explained the relation of the Father and the Son.

---

4. John 5:17, *idion*—his own peculiar possession. The term was often used loosely in Koine Greek, but the context of this passage calls for a stricter interpretation.

The Father	The Son
stands in a peculiar relation to the Son (17)	is dependent on the Father (19)
originated the works of the Son (19)	has perfect knowledge of the Father (20)
loved the Son (20)	possesses life (21)
showed the Son His works (20)	is equal in honor with the Father (23)
committed all judgment to the Son (22, 27)	will raise the dead (25, 28)
receives worship of men (23)	is the means of salvation (24)
possesses inherent life (26)	
endowed the Son with inherent life (26)	

The Father is the source of all life and power, and has bestowed Himself upon the Son in unstinted measure. To the Son He has revealed His purpose and has committed into His hands power in salvation and authority in judgment. The Son, on the other hand, follows carefully the model set by the Father, shares equal honor with Him, and asserts Himself as Lord of the dead and of the living.

These assertions went far beyond a profession of prophetic office. Jesus claimed authority to duplicate and continue the Father's works, to bestow life upon men and to execute judgment upon them, and to raise the dead in the last day.

The Witnesses (5:30-47)

The magnitude of Jesus' claims called for substantiation. Five witnesses were introduced by Jesus to validate His statements.

His witness concerning Himself (30, 31)

There is an apparent conflict between the statement in 5:31, "If I bear witness of myself, my witness is not true," and that in 8:14, "Even if I bear witness of myself, my witness is true." The former was a concession to the legal rule that a man's testimony about himself is inadmissible as evidence in court, since it might be assumed that his judgment would be prejudiced. The latter was an avowal of personal competency to speak concerning Himself since He knew more about Himself than anybody else did. The statement in 5:30 indicated that He considered Himself unprejudiced because He was not seeking His own will, but was carrying out the will of Another, who sent Him. Since Jesus knew that His own witness would not be received, He turned next to other proof more conclusive to His hearers.

The witness of John the Baptist (32-35)

The appeal to John the Baptist was really directed to popular opinion. Jesus' hearers had sent an accredited delegation to report on John's message, for Jesus said, "Ye have sent unto John, and he hath borne witness unto the truth" (33). They had recognized John as "the lamp that burneth and shineth," a true illuminator of darkness. Since Jesus' audience had accepted John as unquestionably truthful and accurate, the logic of the situation demanded that they should believe his verdict concerning Jesus. The substance of John's testimony already has been recorded in the latter part of the first chapter of this Gospel.

The witness of the works (36)

The third confirmation of Jesus' claims was found in His works, which, He said, were more cogent than the testimony of John. "Works," as used in the Fourth Gospel, always refer to action as illustrative of character. In particular, the word means the miracles which are outstanding in importance and samples of divine power. As already noted, they were selected to portray all aspects of the divine power of Jesus, and to establish His claims as the Son of God. The product was the recommendation for the person.[5] Only the man sent from God could do the works of God, as Nicodemus said (3:2).

---

5. Cf. the utterances of Jesus in 9:3,4 and 10:37.

The witness of the Father (37, 38)

In addition to the indirect witness of the works, Jesus adduced the direct testimony of the Father. It may be that He was referring to the voice from heaven, which is recorded as having spoken three times in Jesus' ministry: once at the baptism (Matt. 3:17, Mark 1:11, Luke 3:22), once at the transfiguration (Matt. 17:5, Mark 9:7, Luke 9:35), and once after the triumphal entry (John 12:28). The two former instances are not paralleled in JOHN, and in none of them was the voice understood by the populace. Perhaps the absence of any manifestation generally audible or visible was the reason for Jesus' saying: "Ye have neither heard his voice at any time, nor seen his form" (37). Nevertheless the manifestation was not wholly subjective, for according to the Johannine passage in 12:28 a sound was heard though its meaning was unrecognized.

There is an intimation that a subjective condition was essential for understanding the objective manifestation. Jesus' words, negative as they were, implied that it is possible for the Father to reveal Himself directly to men by His "word" which abides in them. Perhaps He was referring to the prophetic formula so often used in the Old Testament, "the word of Jehovah came to . . ." Without an inward preparation, there is little likelihood of any apprehension of a revelation from without, granting that it is given; nor can the voice of the Father carry much weight with a man who has rejected the Father's emissary. If the inward message truly were present, there would be response to the outward "Word" whom the Father had sent.

The witness of the Scriptures (39-47)

The plainest and most accessible witness to His claims was the body of Scripture to which Jesus alluded when He said, "Ye search the scriptures . . ." (39). The plural "scriptures" was applied to the existing body of collected writings.[6] Jesus used the expression to refer to the Old Testament as He knew it, particularly the writings of Moses. The verb "search" is an indicative, not an imperative. It is not a command to search the Scriptures, but is a statement of fact. Zealous application to the law was a duty for the Jew, and in this occupation he felt that he would achieve eternal life. Jesus was attempting to point out the inconsistency of professing to study the law and of rejecting Him, since the law spoke of Him. He made a definite claim to be the object of prophecy in the Old Testament.

Although the Fourth Gospel does not stress prophecy to the extent that Matthew does, there are numerous references to it. The following is a list of Old Testament passages quoted in John, with the appropriate Johannine references.

    John 1:23..Isa. 40:3
         1:41..Dan. 9:25 (?), Hab. 3:13 (?), Exact reference
               uncertain.
         1:51..Gen. 28:12
         2:17..Ps. 69:9
         3:14..Num. 21:9
         6:31..Ex. 16:4, Neh. 9:15
         6:45..Isa. 54:13
         7:38..Isa. 44:3, 55:1, 58:11 (?)
         7:42..Mic. 5:2
        10:34..Ps. 82:6
        12:15..Zech. 9:9
        12:38..Isa. 53:1
        12:40..Isa. 6:10
        13:18..Ps. 41:9
        19:24..Ps. 22:18
        19:28..Ps. 69:21
        19:36..Ps. 34:20
        20:9 ..No definite passage, but reference to Scripture
              is explicit.

------

6. J. H. Bernard, *op. cit.*, I, p. 252.

No less than eighteen unmistakable references to the Old Testament occur in the text of JOHN, most of which are given a direct application to Christ, and there are other allusions in addition. If Moses (and the others) wrote of Him, then the testimony would have to be admitted by His enemies as incontrovertible.

Two other witnesses to His claims appear in the Gospel, but are not mentioned here because they were not available at this time. One was the Holy Spirit (15:26), who had not yet come upon believers because Jesus had not finished His work (7:39). The other was that of the individual disciples (15: 27), who would be ready to speak in His behalf only after being empowered by the Spirit (Acts 1:8).

This sevenfold witness is the foundation for faith found in the Johannine writings. As the various elements are illustrated and developed in the text, they provide a rational ground for confidence in the living Christ, and an appeal to the reader for self-committal.

The second aspect of the Period of Controversy is contained in John 6. Geographically and chronologically it is separate from the events of chapter 5. The phrase "after these things" introduces an indefinite interval between the argument with the Jews in Jerusalem and the contact with the populace in Galilee. The unity of the two sections lies in the effect produced. Both resulted in controversy which distinguished the trends of belief and unbelief with increasing definiteness.

The Feeding of the Five Thousand (6:1-15)

The narrative on which the discourse on the bread of life depends is common to all four Gospels. Since it is the only miracle recorded by all of them, it must have been regarded as possessing singular importance. There are several reasons which make it outstanding in JOHN.

*It was the occasion for testing the personal reactions of the
disciples.*

John did not record the retirement to Caesarea Philippi,
which in the Synoptics was the occasion for Peter's confession
voicing the decision of the Twelve (Matthew 16:13-20, Mark
8:27-29, Luke 9:18-20). He made the feeding of the five
thousand, usually connected chronologically with the retirement, the pivot at which popular favor declined and an individual faith on the part of the disciples began to emerge. Four
disciples, Philip, Andrew, Peter, and Judas Iscariot, are mentioned by name in this chapter, and the attitude of each toward
Jesus is at least suggested.

It was the peak of popular favor.

John alone of the Gospel writers says that the people at this
time by force sought to make Jesus their king. Assuredly His
fame must have spread through all Galilee, or the crowds never
would have followed Him. His reputation could only be en-
hanced by this miracle which He performed in response to
their importunity. The man who feeds the crowd can have
their allegiance as long as he feeds them. Even though their
loyalty was only temporary, Jesus had it at this point, and
could have asked from them anything that He desired.

It was a spectacular miracle.

The barley loaves and the fishes cannot be paralleled by the
modern concept of five loaves of dark raised bread and two
perch. The bread spoken of was more nearly comparable to
pancakes for size and shape; and the fish were not the main
part of the meal, but were probably pickled fish used as relish,
much as sardines are used now for hors d' oeuvres. This small
amount of food would scarcely make a satisfying lunch for
one child to say nothing of five thousand men, besides women
and children. As Jesus kept up an unending process of breaking the bread and fish into edible fragments, the amazement

of the audience must have grown also. The miraculous multiplication seems to have taken place in His hands, so that the distribution went on uninterruptedly until all were fed. The work is called a sign (6:14), prophetic of Jesus' sufficiency in the midst of deficiency, and of His ability to make consecrated inadequacy satisfy the need of the hungry.

It was an educational step in the faith of at least two disciples.

The barest sketch of Philip and Andrew was given, yet it revealed the temper and faith of the men.

Philip was a statistical pessimist. Challenged by Jesus, the best he could do was to produce some arithmetical calculations. The "shilling" which he mentioned was really the Roman denarius, a coin worth about seventeen cents, but with the purchasing power equal to a laboring man's daily wage (Cf. Matt. 20:2). Philip calculated that two thirds of a year's wages would not buy enough bread to provide afternoon tea for the crowd, to say nothing of a meal. He was very sure of what could not be done, but had no vision for what could be done. Hardheaded and practical, he thought in terms of cash.

Andrew was an ingenious optimist. Philip's information was given in answer to a question; Andrew's was volunteered. Philip produced figures to show what could not be done; Andrew brought food, hoping that something might be done. His faith was wavering, for he added to his offer, "but what are these among so many?" (9)—but he had faith. Though rather quiet he must have had winning ways. Any man who can persuade a small boy to relinquish his lunch possesses a forceful character.

To Philip, then, this miracle revealed the superiority of Jesus to statistical impossibilities, and to Andrew it showed that Jesus could justify any faith placed in Him.

The Walking on the Water (6:16-21)

The walking on the water should be regarded as an addition subordinate to the feeding of the five thousand in the scheme of JOHN. The writer gave less space to this event than did Matthew and Mark, but treated it with different emphasis. The story centered in Jesus' relation to the disciples rather than in their peril or in the miracle itself. It may be divided into three aspects: first, Jesus apart from the disciples; second, Jesus appearing to the disciples; and finally, Jesus received by the disciples.

While Jesus was praying in the mountain alone the disciples waited for Him on or near the shore. The boat was packed and ready for the trip to Capernaum. The "not yet" in verse 17 implied that the disciples were expecting Him to join them. Their anxiety was increasing as time passed because He had not come, and the wind was rising. The lake of Galilee was situated below sea level in a bowl in the hills, and the defiles between the hills acted as chimneys which directed the concentrated blasts of wind down upon the water. In addition, because of the relatively shallow depth of the lake, it was subject to sudden violent storms which were the terror of the fishermen who ventured upon it. The disciples, expert sailors that they were, knew the signs of the weather, and were doubtless desirous of making the crossing to Capernaum before the storm broke, or before the wind made progress impossible. When they saw that the sea was rising, and that Jesus had not come, they dared not delay any longer. They cast off and soon were out on the lake.

The failure of Jesus to meet them must have been disheartening. The difficulty of rowing would make their plight all the worse. Mark and Matthew say that it was about the fourth watch of the night when Jesus appeared. John (19) states that they had rowed over not more than thirty furlongs, or three and three quarters miles, from their point of departure in a period of nine hours, more or less. Threatened with exhaustion, they would have been at the mercy of the waves if help had not come soon. Apart from Jesus they were lost.

The appearance of Jesus must have been startling. Since they were pulling against the wind, they probably had their backs to it, and were looking back toward the shore which they had left several hours before. To see a figure approaching them, moving against the wind faster than the boat could travel, and rapidly overtaking them would be disconcerting if not unnerving. The greeting of Jesus was intended to assuage their fears and His entry into the boat insured their safe arrival.

No immediate reaction on the part of the disciples is recorded in JOHN. The miracle revealed His power over nature, and so contributed to the rounded picture of His manifested deity. The effect on the disciples doubtless contributed to their confessions recorded later in this chapter, and to the insight which the unnamed disciple possessed at the draught of fishes on the post-resurrection appearance of Jesus at Galilee.

The Discourse on the Bread of Life (6:22-71)

The discourse on the bread of life which followed as an interpretative sequel upon the feeding of the five thousand is divided into three parts corresponding to the three types of hearers in the audience. The first section, verses 22 to 40, concerns the multitude, the same promiscuous group that had witnessed the miracle. The second section, verses 41 to 59, deals with "the Jews," and is specifically said to have been spoken in the synagogue at Capernaum, presumably at a regular meeting on the Sabbath. It is quite possible that the two groups do not call for two separate occasions, but that "the Jews" represent the element that became vocal and argumentative. The address to the multitude may have been given in the open air at a public gathering, while the controversy with "the Jews" took place in the synagogue as a continuation of the same discourse. The third section, verses 60 to 71, contains an interview with the disciples and shows the effect of Jesus' words on the inner circle of His own followers.

The dealing of Jesus with the general crowd was characterized by a new harshness which was not present in most of His former discourses. There was a slight tinge of it in the interview with Nicodemus, but even there the personal appeal to the ruler whom Jesus evidently respected softened the incisiveness of His utterance. The multitude was a group of materialistic curiosity seekers who were self-satisfied in their tradition. Jesus' approach was to jar them loose from their laxity by a series of statements contradictory to their current assumptions. By the process of progressive disillusionment He sought to awaken them from a supine complacency to active faith.

This technique is dangerous in the hands of anyone but an expert. As an academic device it is all too commonly employed today by those who attempt to shatter superstition but who are not able to create positive belief. To cast a man adrift upon life after having torn away the anchor in which he trusted is little short of criminal, unless one provides him with a new and more secure anchor. Jesus could do this, for He summoned men from empty tradition to Himself.

The steps of His procedure were as follows:

Disillusionment concerning *motives*

The multitude had been so taken up with the satisfaction of their immediate physical needs that they did not perceive the real significance of the event. In the multiplication of the bread and the fishes they realized nothing more than the satiation of their bodily hunger. The sign quality of the miracle which represented Jesus as the satisfying Bread of Life never occurred to them at all.

Jesus drew the distinction between the material food which is necessary, but temporary in its value, and the spiritual bread that yields permanent satisfaction. This latter food can be given only by the Son of Man and must be obtained through Him.

The motive of the multitude in seeking Jesus was wrong because it was a desire for more bread and fish rather than for what the bread and fish symbolized. They failed to see that the ultimate end of life must be spiritual, not material possession. They did not discern that the seal of God's approval was upon Jesus, and that they could trust Him as the nourishment of their souls.

Disillusionment concerning *methods*

The mental confusion of Jesus' hearers did not clear immediately. They felt that the answer to their problem lay in some new effort that would enable them to fulfill all righteousness. "What must we do, that we may work the works of God?" (28) Paul's comment of Romans 10:3 is apropos at this point: "For being ignorant of God's righteousness, and seeking to establish their own, they did not subject themselves to the righteousness of God." Righteousness for the Jew had come to mean something accomplished by his effort rather than appropriated by faith.

In order that He might dispel the misunderstanding Jesus redefined what He meant by "the work of God." It was not some new commandment or application of an existing ordinance, but a declaration of belief. "This is the work of God, that ye believe on him whom he hath sent" (29). Acceptance of His person and claims is the method whereby the life eternal is to be found. Trust in a person rather than self-adjustment to a scheme of ordinances enables one to fulfill God's program.

Disillusionment concerning *religious antecedents*

Strangely enough the multitude, slowly reacting to Jesus' teaching, demanded a sign. It may seem inconsistent that they should ask for another when they already had received one that passed unrealized; but such is human nature. They reasoned back to the closest available analogy in the Old Testament, the manna which had been given by Moses. Their fathers had received bread from heaven. Could Jesus produce anything equally convincing? Surely if Moses could feed the people with heavenly food, Jesus must do likewise if He were to have a place of authority equal to that of Moses.

His reply was a flat contradiction of their basic assumption. "It was not Moses that gave you the bread out of heaven" (32). The manna had satisfied physical need only, and had vanished when the Israelites entered Canaan (Josh. 5:12). Christ Himself was the Bread of God, which could nourish the inner man and give life to the world. The manna of tradition was impermanent; the real manna was lasting in its effect.

Disillusionment concerning their own *understanding* and *faith*

If there is any one thing which a man ought to know with certainty beyond that possessed by another, it is his own mind. Who can know more about a man's inner thoughts and impulses than himself? Who can be a better judge of his own sincerity? In the utterance, "Lord, evermore give us this bread" (34), there was a seemingly sincere request for the living bread which Jesus could offer.

Perhaps the request can be paralleled by that of the Samaritan woman who said quite honestly, yet with inferior motives, "Sir, give me this water, that I thirst not, neither come all the way hither to draw" (4:15). Both pleas seem to have been prompted by something less than a pure faith.

Jesus reaffirmed the promise of permanent satisfaction, but denied the validity of their response by saying, "Ye have seen me, and yet believe not" (36). In the few verses that follow are found some of the most mysterious and baffling statements in the whole New Testament, paradoxically linked with one of the most encouraging truths. Jesus asserted that:

Those whom the Father gave Him shall come to Him (37a).
Those who come to Him would be certain of welcome (37b).
His reason for appearing among men was to do the Father's
will (38).

The Father's will was the preservation of those whom He
had given to the Son (39).

This preservation is the guarantee of eternal life to the
believer, sealed by the resurrection at the last day (39b).

Two elements are discernible in this declaration: the divine
element of the choice and will of the Father carried out in the
purpose and power of the Son, and the element of beholding
Him, believing on Him, and coming to Him. It is shown that
no persuasion is necessary to convince the Father that He ought
to will to save the believer, nor to persuade the Son that He
ought to carry out the Father's will. Their work is done from
all eternity, though manifest in time. There is, however, no
minimizing of the value of the individual's beholding[7] and
forming his personal estimate of the Lord Jesus for himself,
and of believing consciously and voluntarily upon Him, that
he might have eternal life. The assertion of the choice of God
as behind, before, and beyond man's own choice is not to make
the latter meaningless, a gesture of a puppet; but rather the
choice of God is all that can make it meaningful, since the
salvation of God is "not of him that willeth, nor of him that
runneth, but of God that hath mercy" (Rom. 9:16).

There is more of such teaching later in the Gospel (10:25-
29). Jesus gave it not to deter the earnest seeker, but to
awaken the self-satisfied traditionalist, who, like the Pharisee
in Jesus' parable (Luke 18:9-14), felt that he had put God
under obligation to him by his own righteousness. The appeal
to the multitude was given on the basis of the assured welcome
of all who would come for the spiritual benefits that He had to
offer.

---

7. Greek: *theoreo*

The second section of this discourse concerns the objections voiced by "the Jews." They are marked as a group separate from the multitude, though doubtless included in it during the first part of the discussion (41). Since the scene of the event was Galilee, they may be distinguished from the majority of the hearers, who were Galileans, and not so bitterly opposed to Jesus.[8]

There may also be an element of historical perspective in this attitude of the writer toward the Jews. By the time of the traditional date of JOHN, the rift between church and synagogue had become wide, and mutual antagonism was taken for granted. Perhaps between the lines of these specimens of controversy one can read the interest of the author in the conflict of his own day.

Two questions agitated the Jews: (1) the origin of Jesus; (2) the meaning of the utterance concerning the eating His flesh. They objected to His claim to be the Bread of Life because they knew His antecedents. To them He was the son of Joseph, and they were acquainted with both His father and mother. Why should a person of such ordinary origin as His make such stupendous claims as He did?

It is a curious fact that though the Fourth Gospel, of all the Gospels, presents the clearest case for the deity of Jesus as expressed by His own words, it says absolutely nothing directly about the virgin birth. Of indirect, but relevant, passages there are a few. John 1:13 implies that the new believers are born into the family of God not by human generation but by the Spirit. Is the explicit statement, apart from the meaning of the textual variant that occurs in it,[9] an echo of the firm belief

8. Contra, J. H. Bernard, *op. cit.*, I, p. 202.

9. One Latin manuscript, Codex b, the Sinaitic Syriac, the Latin text of Irenaeus, and an allusion in Tertullian read *qui non natus est,* "who was ... born." This reading makes the verb singular, with Christ as the antecedent. The reading is not generally accepted as genuine by most authorities; but its existence is witness to the fact that the text had been under discussion as early as the second century. See A. T. Robertson, *An Introduction to the Textual Criticism of the New Testament,* (New York: G. H. Doran Co., n. d.), p. 241.

that Jesus was born physically "not of bloods, nor of the will
of the flesh, nor of the will of a husband, but of God" (original
translation)? And does the comparative silence of the Gospel
concerning Joseph, though it mentions ·Maryj several times,
plus the frequent references on the lips of Jesus to God as "my
Father," indicate a latent knowledge of the great mystery? If
so, the Evangelist was silent about it. Certainly, the question
of the Jews does not preclude the virgin birth since their information about the family was casual. Their conclusions would
be based on observation of the family's life rather than on a
knowledge of its inner secrets.

The answer of Jesus to their protest implied that their query
was the result of ignorance. They had not been drawn by the
Father, nor had they learned from the Father, hence they did
not come to Him. Jesus was distinct from all others in that He
had seen the Father; He was the great objective of all spiritual
search and the arbiter of spiritual destiny, the sustainer of
spiritual life. He climaxed His utterance by stating that the
bread of life was His flesh, which He would give for the life of
the world. He regarded Himself as being supernatural in
origin and calling, and superior to the Mosaic revelation as
bread was superior to manna.

The second question of the Jews evoked by this climactic
assertion was: "How can this man give us his flesh to eat?"
(52) Without explaining to them the figurative nature of this
statement, Jesus expanded its literal expression. His device
may have been similar to that used by Matthew concerning the
parables: "Therefore speak I to them in parables; because seeing they see not, and hearing they hear not, neither do they
understand" (Matt. 13:13). If they were unready to hear, He
was not eager to press upon them truth which they would only
reject or pervert. He allowed the mystery to remain unsolved
for them. If they were ready to hear, the mysterious statement
would provoke their interest even further.

Some commentators[10] have seen in this language the Johannine expression of the last supper which is not described in this
narrative as it is in the Synoptics. The historical verity, said
they, has been eclipsed by the haze of sacramental mysticism.
It would be wiser to affirm that the spiritual verity of Jesus'
words, hidden in the arresting metaphor that He used, was
misinterpreted by His opponents. His words seemed to them
an absurd literalism because they viewed them through the
eyes of ignorance and rebellion. There may be a connection
between Jesus' allusion to eating His flesh and drinking His
blood and the last supper at which He said, "This is my body,"
and "This is my blood." If there is a connection, it is

> ..the unchanging truth so fully set forth in this discourse,
> —the believer's union with his Lord, his complete depend-
> ence upon Him for life, his continued appropriation by faith
> of His very self, his feeding on Him, living on Him, his expe-
> rience that Jesus in giving Himself satisfies every want of
> the soul.[11]

The metaphor of eating and drinking is the best possible
figure that can be employed to express the assimilation of one
body by another, the method whereby life is transferred from
the eaten to the eater. The literal eating of Jesus' flesh and the
drinking of His blood were not demanded. Jesus carefully
explained that the process was analogous to His living by the
Father, and certainly eating and drinking could not be literally
applied there. Rather His life and that of the Father were so
intertwined that He was utterly dependent on the Father for
all that He said and did (4:34, 5:19). Mutual abiding is predicated of Christ and the believer (6:56) just as elsewhere it is
predicated of the Father and Christ (14:10, 11). Although

---

10. See K. Lake and S. Lake, *An Introduction to the New Testament,*
(New York and London: Harper and Brothers Publishers, 1937), pp. 61,
62.

11. W. Milligan and W. F. Moulton, *The Gospel of John and the Acts,*
Vol. II in *A Popular Commentary on the New Testament.* Edited by Philip
Schaff, (New York: Charles Scribner's Sons, 1880), p. 86.

the figure was in itself repulsive, it expressed the meaning of
the complete assimilation of Christ into all the life of the believer, just as the life of the believer is assimilated into that of
Christ.

The last section of the discourse concerns the response of
Jesus' disciples. The word "disciples" as used in JOHN included more than the Twelve, as the context shows (60, 66,
67). There were an appreciable number of the professed believers who found this utterance difficult to understand. Their
progressive alienation was revealed in the words used to describe their action[12] (61, 66): "they *murmured*," "they *went
back, and walked no more with him.*" It might be expected
that His enemies would be mystified by His veiled statements,
but it might also be expected that His disciples at least would
be sufficiently stimulated by loyalty and curiosity to inquire
further what He meant before abandoning Him altogether.
John made clear that the defection was no surprise to Jesus.
The unbelief of the disciples had been evident to Him from
the very first, and His difficult utterances had been spoken for
the avowed purpose of disclosing their true position. Their
inability to persist in faith apart from the "gift" of the Father
(65) was His explanation of unbelief. Unbelief is natural to
the sinning heart; saving faith is the gift of God.

Jesus' realization of the reason for their defection was not
impersonal cognition of a fact. It was accompanied by a genuine concern for them. His words to the Twelve who constituted the inner circle of disciples, one of whom was to betray
Him, revealed how deeply He felt the faithlessness of those
who had left Him. No extant translation can do justice to
the poignant, heart-searching question which He addressed to
them: "*You* do not want to withdraw too, do you?" The
negative (*mé*) suggested that the question should be answered,

---

12. Italics ours.

"No." He hoped that they would remain with Him, and let His emotional feeling appear in the sentence as John quoted it.

The reply of Peter was magnificent in its sturdy faith. "Lord, to what person shall we go? You have the words of eternal life, and we have a settled conviction and a final realization that you are the Holy One of God."[13] His reply showed (1) the exclusiveness of faith, for there was none other that could command their respect; (2) the fixity of faith, for the word "believe" is in the perfect tense, which indicated an existing state resulting from and continuing a completed act; and (3) the finality of faith, because they finally realized in experience that He was "the Holy One of God." The faith preceded the realization, an order which was quite in keeping with the teaching of the Gospel, and which appeared later in Jesus' promise to Martha in 11:40.

This affirmation of Peter marked a new advance in the faith of the disciples as a group. It was the expression of a settled conclusion rather than of a single decision; a state of mind rather than an initial act of will. As the spokesman of the Twelve, Peter committed them to a definite stand on the person of Jesus. The phrase, "the Holy One of God," is used nowhere else in JOHN, and is applied to Christ only once in the Synoptics (Mark 1:24, Luke 4:34), and then by a demoniac. The apostle applied to Him in love the title that the demons applied to Him in fear. Peter's confession was a courageous act, for it committed him and the disciples to One whose popularity was waning and whose words they understood only with difficulty. It revealed the devoted heart of Peter as nothing else in the narrative did.

The rejoinder of Jesus concerning the traitor may be construed as a warning to the disciples. Apparently it was un-

13. Original translation of verses 68, 69.

heeded, for Judas did not change his ways, and the others were unconscious of his real nature, as the scene at the supper in chapter 13 showed. The language, "one of you is a devil," was drastic, for the word that He used of Judas is elsewhere applied to Satan. This picture of the last stage of unbelief added betrayal to desertion.

THE PERIOD OF CONFLICT

THE PERIOD OF CONFLICT

A. The Setting
B. The Unbelief of the Brethren
C. The Bewilderment of the People
D. The Public Appearance
E. The Popular Response
F. The Climactic Appeal of Jesus

. . . .

The Woman Taken in Adultery

. . . .

G. The Address to the Pharisees
H. The Discourse to the Believing Jews
I. The Healing of the Man Born Blind
J. The Discourse on the Good Shepherd
K. The Argument in Solomon's Porch
L. The Raising of Lazarus

CHAPTER VI

The Period of Conflict

7:1 to 11:53

MEASURED by the lines of text which it occupies, the Period of Conflict is the longest single section in the Fourth Gospel. It describes the parallel development of belief and unbelief among the hearers of Jesus, and the resultant clash of these two opposing forces. The bewilderment of some, the outspoken opposition of others, and the slow but steady development of a triumphant faith on the part of Jesus' disciples are all recorded. The difference between this period and the one preceding is that the Period of Controversy narrates mostly argument arising from unsettled attitudes, while the Period of Conflict represents fixed attitudes at war with one another.

The opening sentence of chapter 7 reflected settled hostility. Jesus, it said, continued to walk[1] in Galilee because the Jews [presumably Judeans] were seeking to kill Him. It was no longer a debate among them as to what should be done about Jesus, for they concluded that He must be destroyed. From this point on to the crisis at the close of chapter 11, Jesus was living on borrowed time as far as His enemies were concerned. To them it was a matter of catching Him in some unguarded moment; to Him it was the destiny appointed by the Father.

The chronological grouping of events in the period began with the Feast of Tabernacles, which was celebrated annually in the fall as a harvest festival, commemorative of the end of

---

1. Greek Imperfect: *periepatei*

the wandering in the wilderness. To this day it is observed by
the orthodox Jew[2] as a period of thanksgiving. It was one of
the principal Jewish feasts, and was celebrated frequently by a
pilgrimage to Jerusalem. The events within the period ended
with the last Passover of Jesus' life, which would fall in the
following spring. The Period of Conflict, then, covered the
last six months before the crucifixion.

The Unbelief of the Brethren (7:3-9)

The categorical statement that Jesus' brethren did not believe on Him (5) was amply substantiated by their attitude
expressed in this passage. Verse 3, "Depart hence, and go into
Judaea, that thy disciples also may behold thy works which thou
doest," was a sarcastic fling at His modesty. Perhaps the
Judeans would be gullible enough to accept Him even if the
Galileans, and in particular His own family, would not! The
brethren felt that He should make an open bid for the kingdom. If He had any miracles on which He could trade, why
not display them? Their level of thought was, "It pays to advertise."

The reply of Jesus showed that He regarded His career not
as an opportunity for personal aggrandizement, but as a carefully planned mission. *Time* (*kairos*) in 7:6 referred to a
suitable hour for public manifestation rather than the date of
His death. Verse 30 of the same chapter uses the word *hour*
(*hora*) and connects it with His appointed destiny rather than
with the psychological moment for action. If these two terms
had different meanings, then any idea of deception is removed
from the text. As it stands, Jesus told the brethren that He
was not going up to the feast (8), and then promptly went.
No duplicity was involved. He urged His brethren to go since
it made no particular difference when they arrived; but in His

2. See William Rosenau, *Jewish Ceremonial Institutions and Customs,*
(New York: Bloch Publishing Company, 1929), pp. 93-95, 122-124. For
Scripture references, see Lev. 23:33-44, Deut. 16:13-17, Num. 29:12-38.

case, He could appear only at the time appointed by the Father.

In addition to stating that His mission in life was different from that of humanity at large, Jesus said that the relation between Himself and the world was different from that subsisting between His brethren and the world. They were a part of it, and the world loves its own (15:19). He was not of the world and bore testimony against it, therefore it hated Him. There is in this statement a latent claim of differentiation in nature between Him and His brethren. They were content with worldly environment and opportunism; He was content only with the Father's will.

The Bewilderment of the People (7:10-13)

Jesus' presence at the various public feasts seemed to have been expected. On this occasion doubt concerning His attendance was expressed because of the avowed hostility of the leaders.

Three attitudes on the part of the populace were described.

First, the Jews sought for Him, presumably to kill Him. A comparison of verses 1 and 11 shows that such is the meaning of "seek" (*zetein*), which is employed in this sense seventeen times out of a total of thirty-four times in JOHN.[3] It was a continued attempt,[4] which showed that their attitude dominated the atmosphere of the feast (13).

In the second place, some defended Him by declaring that He was a good man. They regarded His character as being above reproach, and His works as being constructive (12).

Finally, others considered Him as an impostor, and accused Him of deceiving the people (12).

The populace of Jerusalem was thus evidently divided in mind, and uncertain of the estimate that should be placed on the words and character of the Galilean teacher. He was the

---

3. See 5:16 (in Received Text, but not in ARV), 18; 7:1, 11, 19, 20, 25, 30; 8:21, 37, 40; 10:39; 11:8, 56; 18:4, 7, 8.

4. Greek imperfect; *ezetoun*.

favorite topic of conversation during the first part of the feast, and there was wild speculation as to whether He would visit Jerusalem.

The Public Appearance (7:14-19, 21-24, 33, 34)

In the midst of the feast, Jesus came to Jerusalem and proceeded to teach. His teaching took the form of a paradox, asserting both authority (14) and subordination (16), offering a pragmatic test (17-19), and issuing in an argument (21-24).

As to authority, He took a place in the temple, and averred His right to be heard like any rabbi. There is not the slightest indication that He was embarrassed by the criticism that had been rampant, nor that He felt inferior in any way to the other teachers in Jerusalem. His effectiveness was so great that His enemies were compelled to admit that He was equal with those educated in the rabbinical schools. In His own statement, He disclaimed originality, and affirmed His dependence upon the Father.

As to this subordination, He disavowed any independent power and ascribed His teaching to God. He emphasized the fact that God had sent Him.[5] He was always conscious that He had come on a divine mission to bring a divine message. His authority was not the result of His own greatness, but of the Father's direction.

Such a claim as this naturally demanded much of His hearers. In order that they might have some method of verifying it, He offered them a simple pragmatic test: "If any man will to do his will, he shall know concerning the teaching, whether it is from God or whether I speak on my own responsibility."[6] This was the mode of testing the validity of knowledge. Resolution to do the will of God would bring with it

---

5. Out of 32 uses of the verb *pempo* (send) in the Fourth Gospel, 25 apply to Christ, as used here.

6. John 7:17—original translation.

certainty of being right. Usually the process is reversed in human thinking. Man seeks to know first, and to act afterward. The divine pragmatism says, "Do, and know." Something akin to this principle of Jesus appears in 11:40: "Didn't I say to you that if you would believe, you would see the glory of God?"[7] The concluding phrase of 7:18 emphasizes the sincerity of the man who seeks not his own reputation, but also that of the one who sent him. Falsehood and unrighteousness cannot be found in Him. This selflessness leads straight to the knowledge of God. Perhaps this dictum could be called a parallel of the beatitude: "Blessed are the pure in heart: for they shall see God" (Matt. 5:8).

It was only natural that such affirmations as Jesus made and such a pointed test as He gave should be followed by discussion pro and con. The content of the ensuing argument with the Jews was evidently connected in thought with the episode of the man at the pool in 5:1 to 16; in fact, the entire chapter seems to be related to it. Though a considerable time had elapsed since the opening of the controversy, its occasion had not been forgotten. Jesus reasoned that the Jews' persecution of Him was ill-founded. Since Moses allowed circumcision on the Sabbath, why should not the healing of a man on the Sabbath be permissible?

The Popular Response (7:20, 25-32, 35, 36)

Great confusion resulted from Jesus' words to the crowd. Some directly accused Him of insanity because He said that men were seeking to kill Him, which suggested that only Jewish officials were seriously hostile to Him (20). Others kept seeking to arrest Him (30, 32) because His pronouncements vexed them, but they did not dare to do so publicly for He was in popular favor. Still another group believed on Him since they felt that the Messiah could do no greater deeds than

---

7. Original translation.

Jesus did. Any man capable of performing miracles like His must be the Messiah. The mystery of His person was only vaguely grasped, for His declaration concerning His departure to the Father was not understood at all.

In contrast to the popular confusion about Him, John presented Jesus as being very sure of Himself. He claimed origin in God. He was sent to men from God, and He planned to return to God. In the midst of hesitancy He had poise and assurance.

The Climactic Appeal of Jesus (7:37-52)

The last day of the feast was the greatest of all. According to Jewish tradition, the eighth day was observed as a holy convocation, "which marked the conclusion, not only of the Feast of Tabernacles, but of the whole cycle of the festal year."[8] On each day the ritual included a libation of water which was taken in a golden vessel from the pool of Siloam, and which was offered by the priests as they sang: "With joy shall ye draw water out of the wells of salvation" (Isa. 12:3).[9] The ceremony may have been a memorial of God's provision of water for the thirsty Israelites in the desert, or it may have symbolized the desire for abundance of rain to bring the next harvest. There is some uncertainty as to whether it were offered on the last day of the feast; but if it were not, even more significance is given to the climactic appeal of Jesus: "If any man thirst, let him come unto me and drink" (37). In place of the physical water He proffered the spiritual; instead of a ritual He offered a reality.

John stated that this appeal of Jesus had a background in Scripture. The word "Scripture" (*graphe*) invariably referred to the Old Testament when it was used elsewhere in the Gospel, and usually to some definite passage. Nevertheless these iden-

---

8. E. Elmer Harding, "Feasts and Fasts" in *A Dictionary of the Bible,* ed. James Hastings, (New York: Charles Scribner's Sons, 1902), I, p. 861.
9. J. H. Bernard, *op. cit.,* I, p. 281.

tical words, "from within him shall flow rivers of living water" (38), cannot be located anywhere. Many passages such as Zechariah 14:8, Joel 3:18 (4:18 in the Hebrew text), Ezekiel 47:1 ff., and Psalm 46:4, 5, contain references to refreshing streams, or to living water; but no one is the exact counterpart of Jesus' words. It may be that Jesus was referring to the concept of living water in the Scripture rather than to any one specific portion.[10]

The figure of the living water was applied by John to the Holy Spirit. This explanation should be compared with Jesus' words to Nicodemus (3:5-7) and to the woman at the well (4:10-15, 23). In both of these instances, particularly the second, the spontaneous presence of the Spirit was declared to be the directive of human spiritual life and worship. Jesus' invitation to drink made an appeal to the nation in terms of its inherited ritualistic symbolism.

Following the interpretation of the figure, the first condition of the Spirit's indwelling is belief. Belief, in turn, is defined as one's coming to Jesus. "Let him come unto me and drink" and "he that believeth" are practically synonymous terms. The simplicity and definiteness of believing are stated plainly. The second condition of the coming of the Spirit is objective rather than subjective. Jesus must be "glorified" before He can come. "The Spirit was not yet given;[11] because Jesus was not yet glorified" (39). This term appears twenty-three times in JOHN, and at least four times is used to speak of Jesus' death. The implication is clear that only after Jesus' death could the Spirit begin the fullest work. The perfection of Jesus' ministry through the Spirit lay beyond the cross.

The appeal of Jesus for belief brought different response from as many different groups. There was superficial applause

---

10. Westcott in commenting on this passage says: "The reference is not to any one isolated passage, but to the general tenor of such passages . . . taken in connection with the original image." See B. F. Westcott, *op. cit.*, I, p. 278 f.

11. "Given" does not occur in the underlying Greek text.

(40) as well as division (41-44), open hostility (45-49), and hesitant faith (50-52).

Some regarded Him as "the prophet" (40), probably referring to Moses' prediction in Deuteronomy 18:15f., "a prophet . . . like unto me." Others kept saying with equal insistence that He was truly the "Messiah" (41). Neither of these groups had carefully studied Him; their pronouncements were really only opinions.

Still other critics were confused because He had come from Galilee. Prophecy had declared that the Messiah should spring from the lineage of David and from his town of Bethlehem. The ensuing argument over His origin created a division in the populace: ignorant adulation on one side, and ignorant criticism on the other.

The statement that "some of them would have taken him" (44) undoubtedly applied to the hierarchy mentioned in 7:45, since verses 30 and 32 indicated that such attempts had been made before, but to no avail. The extreme bigotry of the priestly class was made unmistakably plain by the Pharisees' scornful question: "Hath any of the rulers believed on him, or of the Pharisees?" (48) They failed to capture Him because His teaching had overawed and captivated the minds of those sent to arrest Him. Underlying the report of these officers was a subtle tribute to Jesus, "Never *man*[12] so spake." His words had even for them the ring of divinity.

The reappearance of Nicodemus is difficult to explain unless he afterward became a believer, and reported this story himself. The discussion among the Pharisees must have taken place in private, especially since a scheme to arrest or kill Jesus was being considered. It is hardly conceivable that the Pharisees would have planned the matter openly when Jesus had a large number of sympathizers. Only one on the inside would report this, and he was the only insider who would do it.

---

12. Greek *anthropos*, meaning man as a kind of being, the *genus homo*. Perhaps their word could be paraphrased: *"Man* never spake like Him; only God could speak these words."

The weight of Nicodemus' defense was placed upon an impersonal technicality, not upon a warm personal faith. Before casting aspersions upon him because he did not instantly and warmly espouse Jesus' cause, one should remember that he probably stood alone among a group of unscrupulous men who would turn on him at the slightest provocation. He made a plea for fair play, perhaps as a means of trying their temper. The abrupt dogmatism of their reply, "Search, and see that out of Galilee ariseth no prophet," (52) stifled any hope he might have had of reasoning with them and so of presenting the claims of Jesus. Their stubborn unbelief made all the more evident the sincerity of his protest, futile though it was. His belief was feeble, but genuine. In spite of the depressing rebuff that he received to his humane suggestion of fair play, he remained a loyal though rather passive supporter of Jesus.

The Woman Taken in Adultery (7:53-8:11)

This paragraph of text is not included in the earliest and best manuscripts and versions. Many manuscripts omit it entirely; others include it, but are so marked as to indicate that it was considered of doubtful authenticity; eleven relegate it to the end of the Gospel; and one group of manuscripts places it after Luke 21:38, and not in JOHN at all. Several of the old Latin versions omit it, as do three of the Old Syriac, the Coptic, Gothic, and the oldest codex of the Armenian versions. Furthermore, its text contains a disproportionately large number of variants, which is generally a sure sign that it has received less than average care in transmission. It is not quoted by the earlier fathers, whether Latin or Greek. On the other hand, a few of the later uncial manuscripts and a large number of the cursives do contain it, and it is especially mentioned by church fathers from the time of Jerome and Augustine in the fifth century.

So conservative a textual scholar as Scrivener says that "on all intelligent principles of mere criticism the passage must needs be abandoned: and such is the conclusion arrived at by all the critical editors."[13] A. T. Robertson concurs by saying: "It is clear that it is not a genuine part of the Gospel of John."[14] The new Revised Standard Version publishes it in small type to distinguish it from the main body of Johannine text.

To say that the passage is not an integral part of JOHN does not dismiss it, however. It is still necessary to account for its presence. Even those who exclude it from the body of JOHN on textual grounds admit that its tenor is wholly in keeping with the character and ministry of Jesus, and that it doubtless constitutes a genuine account of an episode of His career, though it may be misplaced. Hammond adds:

> The style and contents, indeed, in both of which it is utterly different from any of the narratives of the apocryphal gospels, convey an irresistible impression of genuineness; and it is probable that we have a piece of apostolic narrative, upon which the consent of the universal Church has set the seal of canonicity.[15]

Because of its ancient character and undoubtedly historic truthfulness, it is included in this analysis.

Chronologically, the setting of this event fits into the latter part of Jesus' life. It dovetails well with Luke 21:38, with which the Ferrar Group of manuscripts connects it; for the Lukan passage says that Jesus taught early in the day in the temple during Passion Week, and lodged (or camped in the open air) in the Mount of Olives at night. The language implies that it came after some recorded assembly, "and they went every man unto his own house"; and also that it belonged to a series of discourses given in the temple, since 8:2 contains the word "again."

---

13. F. H. A. Scrivener, *A Plain Introduction to the Criticism of the New Testament,* (Fourth edition, edited by Edward Miller. London: George Bell & Sons, 1894). Vol. II, p. 364.
14. A. T. Robertson, *op. cit.,* p. 210.
15. C. E. Hammond, *Outlines of Textual Criticism applied to the New Testament,* (Fifth edition, revised, Oxford: Clarendon Press, 1890), p. 108.

The event itself was a shock to Jesus. He was teaching in the temple court, and the people were coming to Him in a constant procession[16] to hear His words and perhaps to ask Him questions. The session was rudely interrupted by a dignified but overbearing group of men who pushed their way through the circle, leading with them a woman, bedraggled but silent and defiant. Placing her squarely in the middle of the crowd, they said dramatically:

> Teacher, this woman hath been taken in adultery, in the very act. Now in the law Moses commanded us to stone such: what then sayest thou of her?

This question bore every indication of being the outcome of a deliberate plot. The entire action was menacing and the significance was unmistakable. The Pharisees had what they considered to be a closed case. The woman had been caught redhanded and her guilt was above question. Since there was a definite law in the Pentateuch that an adulteress should be put to death by stoning,[17] the woman's fate could not be considered to be a matter of opinion. When Jesus' accusers compelled Him to render a verdict in public, they attempted to force Him into one of two positions. If He consented to the law, the multitude would feel that He no longer sympathized with the publicans and sinners. If He took issue with the scribes and Pharisees, they would assail Him as a lawbreaker and a defamer of the Mosaic covenant. The innuendo of their question was plain: "Moses commanded . . . what then sayest *thou?*" (5) Would He dare to exalt His opinion against the specific statement of the law? By what loophole could He avoid a dilemma which the case presented as they had managed it? Verse 6 states that "this they said, . . . that they might have whereof to accuse him." The tense of the verb "said"[18] means that they prodded Him repeatedly to make Him commit Himself.

---

16. Greek imperfect: *ercheto.*
17. Lev. 20:10, Deut. 22:22 f.
18. Greek imperfect: *elegon.*

The ensuing action constituted a triangle, one side of which was represented by the scribes and Pharisees, one side by Jesus, and one side by the woman. The scribes and Pharisees were actuated by malice, and not by a disinterested passion for righteousness. Their main desire was to trap Jesus, not to purge Jerusalem of its moral evils. Had they desired sincerely to abolish the immoralities of the city, they would have begun with themselves.

Their whole attitude toward both the woman and Jesus was one of cruelty. She, disheveled and sullen, was catapulted into the center of a public assembly, and her sin was shouted aloud for all to hear. There was not one syllable spoken concerning salvaging her, guilty as she was. She was merely the bait for the trap by which they hoped to take Jesus. The utter heartlessness of her captors was as immoral as was the promiscuity of the woman.

The low estimate of womanhood held by the scribes and Pharisees may be inferred from the story. If she were really caught in the very act, why did they not bring the man involved that he might share the guilt and the condemnation? Certainly he would be equally deserving of it. There were two alternatives : either the guilty man was released or had escaped, or else he was present and was one who took part in the accusation of the woman while posing as being righteously indignant over the breaking of the law. It is not incredible that the entire situation was designed in advance. How did the Pharisees know where to capture the guilty woman? Was she betrayed for the express purpose of obtaining a cause against Jesus? The language which the men used of her—"such [as these]" in verse 5—was wholly in keeping with the contempt which Jesus' persecutors evinced toward Him and toward her.

The attitude of Jesus was revealed clearly by His action. He stooped and wrote on the ground, the only occasion on record that Jesus wrote. Perhaps He was embarrassed and wished to hide the shame and anger that flushed His face as He confronted the treachery and brutality of His enemies and the misery of the woman. On the other hand, the writing may have been more than a gesture. One or two of the manuscripts[19] say that He wrote in the dust "the sins of each one of them," referring to the men. The evidence for this reading is scant, and the statement is probably an interpretation of Jesus' action added by a later hand rather than a part of the original text. Nevertheless, it is a plausible explanation of what followed.

The pronouncement of Jesus, "He that is without sin among you, let him first cast a stone at her," was a searching judgment of the scribes and Pharisees. According to the Mosaic law which they had quoted, the witnesses of a crime, who brought it to the tribunal, must be the first to cast the stones.[20] By the challenge that Jesus flung out, the accusers themselves were put in the jaws of a dilemma. If they were sinless, how had they qualified as witnesses? And if they were not sinless, how could they consistently condemn the woman? As they filed out shamefacedly one by one, they tacitly confessed their own guilt, and proved that they were in no position to act as judges of others. It was a striking demonstration of Jesus' own words: "Judge not, that ye be not judged. For with what judgment ye judge, ye shall be judged: and with what measure ye mete, it shall be measured unto you" (Matt. 7:1, 2).

Little is said of the part played by the woman in this affair, or of her reaction after it was finished. She made no attempt to escape even when her chagrined captors left. Not until they had all gone did Jesus straighten Himself and speak to the woman. The interview may not have been private, but it was not encumbered by the presence of tormenting enemies. In it Jesus' method of judging sin can be contrasted with that of His foes. They brought the woman in as a captive; He questioned

---

19. J. H. Bernard, *op. cit.*, II, p. 719—An Armenian MS. of the Gospels of AD 989, Codex U, and Jerome in *Adv. Pelagium* ii. 17 contain this addition.

20. Deut. 17:2-7

her as a free person. They regarded her as an accessory to
their convenience; He respected her as a human being. They
saw only the blackness of her past—"the very act"; He thought
in terms of her future—"sin no more." They were eager to
stone her; He was ready to save her. Yet His unwillingness to
condemn her was not laxity on His part. His very words of
forgiveness indicated that He considered her a sinner. A comparison with His pronouncement on adultery in the Sermon on
the Mount will show that in His principles He went beyond
even the letter of the law (Matt. 5:27-32).

The woman's reply, though brief, was respectful and calm.
Perhaps she sensed that in Jesus she had met a man utterly
different from any other that her sordid life had known. His
delicacy, vicarious shame, and obvious compassion separated
Him from the scribes and Pharisees, and from her former
partners in sin. She offered no excuse for her conduct, for
doubtless there was none.

Jesus dismissed her with the injunction to cease sinning,
and to enter upon a life of righteousness. The case was dismissed for lack of executioners. The Pharisees had no right to
condemn because they were sinners; the Sinless forgave because He took men's sins upon Himself. As Paul said, "There
is therefore now no condemnation to them that are in Christ
Jesus" (Rom. 8:1).

The part of the Period of Conflict comprising chapters 8:12
to 10:42 consists of a series of five argumentative discourses,
interrupted only by the story of the man born blind (9:1-41).
This miracle scarcely can be called an interruption, since it
serves to demonstrate the claims and power of Jesus, and to
illustrate graphically the intensity and the unreasoning character of the opposition to Him.

The chronological relation of some of these six divisions is
indeterminate. It may be that 8:12 connects directly with 7:52,
making 7:1 to 8:59 into a unit. The location of the temple,
mentioned in 7:14, 8:20, and 8:59, at the beginning and at the

end of the account, and the process of teaching provide continuity of place and action. The healing of the blind man probably occurred on the same visit to Jerusalem, and the discourse concerning the good shepherd terminates in 10:19-21 with an argument that relates specifically to the end of chapter 9. A marked chronological break appears with 10:22, which is dated at the Feast of Dedication. The writer's interest, however, is not in discussing chronological minutiae, but in showing the trend of action in the last fall and winter of Jesus' life.

There is a curious uniformity of structure in each of the paragraph divisions composing the general section from 8:12 to 10:42. Each begins with a challenging declaration by Jesus, each records an argument, and each ends with a definite reaction on the part of a person or group. In the reactions, there was an alternation of belief and unbelief, as follows:

"No man took him"—but there was suppressed hostility.	8:20
"Many believed on him."	8:30
"They took up stones therefore to cast at him."	8:59
"And he said, Lord, I believe. And he worshipped him."	9:38
"They understood not what things they were which he spake unto them."	10:6
"There arose a division again among the Jews because of these words."	10:19
"They sought again to take him: and he went forth out of their hand."	10:39
"And many believed on him there."	10:42

The uncertainty of the Period of Controversy had become fixed in two opposing groups of people in the Period of Conflict.

The Address to the Pharisees (8:12-30)

This paragraph, and the following one which contains the address to the Jews who had believed on Him, were two parts of one discourse which was delivered in the temple (20, 59). The use of the first personal pronoun in this section is particularly noteworthy. It recurs no less than twenty-three times. Jesus was enforcing His claims, and was contrasting Himself with the claims and attitudes of His enemies.

The address to the Pharisees grew out of His assertion: "I am the light of the world." Despite the fact that this is not discussed in detail here, it affords the underlying thought of this part of the Period of Conflict, for it makes concrete the statement of the Prologue that "in him was life; and the life was the light of men. And the light shineth in the darkness; and the darkness overcame it not." [21] The conflict described in the ensuing argument is essentially the conflict of the light of revelation and the darkness of prejudice produced by ignorance and sin. "Men loved the darkness rather than the light; for their works were evil" (3:19). The imagery may refer to the pillar of cloud and fire which guided the Israelites in their march through the wilderness, and which illuminated their way from Egypt to Canaan.[22] Those who followed it moved toward the promised land, those who did not perished in the wilderness.

The Pharisees' consequent challenge of Jesus was made on legal grounds, because no man on trial in a Jewish court was allowed to testify in his own behalf. In this contention they were carrying out a principle which Jesus Himself had enunciated on a previous occasion: "If I bear witness of myself, my witness is not true" (5:31). Jesus' reversal of His position in 8:14, "Even if I bear witness of myself, my witness is true," meant that He had shifted His argument from the basis of abstract legality to the principle of His personal competence. He, as the Son of the Father, possessed perfect self-consciousness, and was better able to bear witness concerning Himself than was anyone else. His answer to the Pharisees'

---

21. John 1:4, 5. See discussion under Prologue, pp. 66, 67.
22. See Ex. 40:34-38, Num. 14:14. Suggested by W. G. Scroggie, *St. John* in *The Study Hour Series*, (New York and London: Harper and Brothers Publishers, 1931), p. 60. No explicit reference to the Old Testament exists here, however.

incredulity was latent in His original declaration that He was the light of the world, because light needs no witness; it demonstrates its reality by its own radiance.

If, however, the dispute over the validity of His witness were not a matter of a legal technicality but of private judgment, then again He was better qualified to speak on His own behalf than were His opponents. They reasoned from their own knowledge, as all men must do. He spoke from His divine consciousness, as only He could speak. The contrast of the two viewpoints is presented clearly in the following antitheses:

Jesus			Pharisees	
I know	14		Ye know not	14
I judge no man	15		Ye judge after the flesh	15
I am from above	23		Ye are from beneath	23
I am not of this world	23		Ye are of this world	23

These contrasts between Jesus and His enemies were not intended as vilification, but as a sober judgment on the inability of the latter to discern His real identity. New categories of spiritual thinking are necessary if one is to evaluate the person of Jesus accurately.

By these differences Jesus placed Himself far above men, for the following reasons:

He had perfect self-consciousness;
His estimate of man was based on immediate intuitive knowledge, not on observation of characteristics;
His origin was heavenly, and He did not belong to the present earthly life.

Jesus' knowledge of Himself was strong at the precise point where man's is weak. Humanity knows nothing of its origin and spiritual destiny beyond what has been revealed. Jesus possessed intuitive knowledge of these things, and so was qualified to speak with finality concerning Himself. The twofold witness of the Father and of Himself should be sufficient to cover the legal requirement for the validity of witness.

In contrast to the certainty of His own knowledge, Jesus declared to the Pharisees that their unbelief was the result of ignorance. "Ye know neither me, nor my Father: if ye knew me, ye would know my Father also" (19). To this constitutional lack of spiritual perception could be attributed the Pharisees' cold hostility to Jesus.

The second paragraph of this address to the Pharisees (21-30) was a warning concerning the consequences of their attitude. "Except ye believe that I am he, ye shall die in your sins" (24). There is a curious similarity between this passage and the discourse with Nicodemus. Both interpret belief and unbelief as light and darkness respectively, and both present the cross, or the "lifting up" of the Son of Man as the point of separation between the two.[23] "When ye have lifted up the Son of man, then shall ye know that I am he . . ." (28) is His prediction that the cross will reveal His real identity. The unusual character of His sufferings and death as recorded in John brought the crowning testimony to His claims that was vouchsafed to the world.

The result of this discourse was that "many believed on him" (30). The sincerity and depth of this faith may be questioned. Nevertheless, the sincere self-assertion of Jesus caused many to accept His words as truth and to receive His message.

The Discourse to the Believing Jews (8:31-59)

There is little change in time between this address and the one immediately preceding it. Although given to "those Jews that had believed him" (31), there seems to have been no more definite response to Him nor any less severe strictures on His part than when He was dealing with the Pharisees. Probably the belief of the Jews was shallow, and Jesus knew it. He was attempting to deepen it, but His instruction encountered resistance.

---

23. Cf. John 3:18-21, 14, 15.

Jesus' initial sentence contained three concepts of major importance in all human thinking: knowledge, truth, and freedom. "Ye shall know the truth, and the truth shall make you free" (32). The word *know* (*ginosko*) occurs fifty-six times in the Fourth Gospel, and usually implies the knowledge gained from experience. *Truth* is formulated revealed reality, which is centered in the person of Christ Himself. *Free* is a Pauline word, most widely occurring in the Pauline Epistles and used in JOHN only in verses 33 and 36. It means absence of constraint and restriction, opportunity to exercise the right of acting apart from external interference. These concepts imply a progress from ignorance to knowledge, from error or misinformation or uncertainty to truth, and from slavery to liberty.

Furthermore, the statement is the conclusion of a condition: "If ye take up your abode in my word,[24] ye are really my disciples, and . . ." (31). Knowledge of the truth, acquired through experience, does not bring the liberty of which Jesus spoke. Knowledge itself is conditioned upon abiding in His word, which makes spiritual revelation prior in importance to experiential knowledge. "I believe in order that I may understand" marks the beginning of the Christian's intellectual life.

The resentment aroused by this bit of teaching showed how superficial was the belief of Jesus' Jewish hearers. Had they been believers in the fullest sense, they never would have taken offense as they did. True humility which accompanies real faith would have accepted Jesus' implications and would have gone on with Him to new spiritual progress; but the pride which this word brought to the surface revealed the latent sin in their hearts. Three points of divergence marked the contrast between Jesus' estimate of them, and their estimate of themselves.

---

24. Original translation. *Meinete* is an aorist, and is probably ingressive in force. Certainly the tense is not linear, although the word "abide" has a durative meaning.

The first difference was their concept of freedom. "We are Abraham's seed, and have never yet been in bondage to any man" (33). The Jews boasted that they were the greatest race God had made, first in His affection, and the peculiar recipients of His grace. When they declared that they had not been in bondage to any man, they stretched the truth. They forgot conveniently enough the bondage in Egypt, the oppressors in the period of the Judges, the Babylonian captivity, and the Roman yoke. Pride is usually blind to truth.

The bondage of which Jesus spoke was of a deeper and deadlier sort than political or economic slavery. "Every one that committeth sin is the bondservant of sin" (34). This was a declaration of the profound truth that slavery is not inflicted from without but from within. It is also progressive and inexorable. One sin becomes inevitably the cause of others. Sin consists not of a succession of individual offenses, each of which may be pardoned separately and no one of which has a relation to its predecessors or successors. It is more like a disease. Each fresh outbreak is symptomatic of the virus that is operating within the body, and each attack weakens the body so that subsequent seizures become more intense and more frequent. The decline of resistance accelerates the progress of the disease until finally death ensues if the malady is not arrested. As the sick man is the slave of his disease, so the sinner is the slave of sin; and unless intervention breaks the power of sin, the sinner is doomed.

A note of hope was given by Jesus in His contrast of the position of the slave with that of the Son. The slave does not remain in the house permanently; he is there only by sufferance. The Son remains because He is the heir (35). Jesus claimed authority to free men from sin, and insisted that their pride in Abraham's heritage should bend to accepting His aid, without which they must be left in spiritual slavery.

The second point of divergence was the false assumption that physical descent was equivalent to identity of spiritual character. Jesus acknowledged the Jews' ancestry (37), but imputed to them a spiritual heritage which was anything but Abrahamic. Their murderous hate toward Him stood in sharp relief to Abraham's life and faith, and pointed rather toward kinship with Satan, who had been a murderer and a liar from the beginning (44). On the one hand, they claimed God as their Father (41), but they harbored murder in their hearts (40). They despised the truth (40), they did not love God's messenger (42), they did not believe His word (46), they dishonored the Son (49), and they knew not God (55). Their action belied their claims.

The third point of divergence was the lack of accord with Abraham's prophetic outlook. The expectation of the Seed for which Abraham had been called out of Ur of the Chaldees, separated from heathenism, and launched on the career of being a father of many nations, dominated all his life. The writer of Hebrews suggests that he anticipated the resurrection in the restoration of Isaac, and that he "looked for the city which hath the foundations, whose builder and maker is God" (Heb. 11:17-19, 10). Jesus referred to this when He said, "Abraham rejoiced to see my day" (56). The hearers, although maintaining their kinship with Abraham in spirit as well as in blood, did not share their forefather's spiritual passion.

The reply of Jesus is strange. Literally it reads: "Before Abraham came into being, I am" (58). The same contrast of verbs is used that appears in 1:1 and 1:14. "Came into being" involves a crisis in time, a definite act. "Am," like the other form of the same verb in 1:1, means timeless being. There never was a time when the Son was not. He could always assert, "*I am.*" Three times in this context *I am* is used in the absolute sense: in verse 24, "Except ye believe that I am *he*, ye shall die in your sins"; in verse 28, "When ye have lifted up the Son of man, then shall ye know that I am *he*"; and in verse 58, "Before Abraham was born, I am." In no one of these passages does the third personal pronoun *he* follow the *I am* in the Greek text. The italicized form shows that it has been inserted by the translators to complete the meaning in English. In actuality the phrase *I am* is an assertion of absolute, timeless existence, not merely of a personal identity as the English equivalent would suggest.

A comparison of the use of the phrase, "*I am*," with self-revelation of Jehovah in the Old Testament shows that much the same terminology was employed. God, in commissioning Moses (Ex. 3:14), said: "Thus shalt thou say unto the children of Israel, I AM hath sent me unto you." When the Jews heard Jesus say, "Before Abraham was born, I am," they took the statement to mean not priority to Abraham, but an assertion of deity. To them it was blasphemy, and they picked up stones to cast at Him (59).

The temper of the whole argument with the Pharisees and the believing Jews is revealed by their progressive attitudes of hostility. First there was contradiction. When Jesus opened His discourse by saying, "I am the light of the world," the Pharisees said that His witness was not true.

They continued with insinuation when they said, "Where is thy Father?" (19) To question the identity of a man's father is one of the worst insults that can be offered to an Oriental, since it raises an issue concerning his paternity. The same idea is conveyed in the ill-concealed sneer of verse 41: "We were not born of fornication; we have one Father, even God." One cannot be sure whether these words were spoken as deliberate insults, or whether they were accidental; but they carry all the earmarks of subtle thrusts at the mystery of Jesus' birth.

Jesus' suggestion that they needed freedom met flat denial. "We are Abraham's seed, and have never yet been in bondage to any man" (33). Like men of the legal profession today, they felt that if a charge cannot be refuted, it can be denied;

and if the denial is sufficiently vehement and repeated often enough, it would be accepted as truth.

The Jews' next question was a deliberate insult. "Say we not well that thou art a Samaritan, and hast a demon?" (48) The Samaritans contended that they as well as the Jews were Abraham's seed. The Jews disavowed the claim of the Samaritans and classed Jesus with them because He denied the exclusiveness of the Jewish assertion.[25] The accusation that He had a demon appears also in 7:20 and 10:20. It was a cheap method of explaining away His strange sayings, and was tantamount to calling Him crazy.

The height of sarcasm was reached when the Jews said, "Surely you are not greater than our father Abraham . . .?" (53, original translation). "Who do you think you are anyway?" is the modern version of it. The sober and measured reply of Jesus showed that He was unaffected by these cynical comments. The scorn of the crowd did not change His relation to the Father; and in the full consciousness of that relationship He moved on calmly to His concluding teaching.

The final attitude of Jesus' enemies was violence. "They took up stones therefore to cast at him" (59). Violence is the last resort of defeated men, who, when reason fails, try stones. These six methods of attack show the degeneration of a shallow belief into an active and vicious unbelief, which ended in compelling Jesus to withdraw from the very temple which was His Father's house.

The Healing of the Man Born Blind (9:1-41)

The healing of the blind man is an illustration of the progress of the conflict between Jesus and His opponents, and is an outstanding example of the development of belief and unbelief. The belief is exemplified in the man; the unbelief, in the reaction of the Pharisees who examined him and finally excommunicated him.

---

25. J. H. Bernard, *op. cit.*, II, p. 316.

The chronological placement of the healing is uncertain. The episode seems to be more closely related to the context of chapter 10 than to that of chapter 8, for the dispute of the crowd reported in 10:19-21 is a direct allusion to the miracle of healing. If 10:22 sets the time for the entire discussion, the miracle took place after the middle of December about the time of the Feast of Dedication or the Feast of Lights.[26]

The episode was (1) a sign demonstrating Jesus' power, (2) an interview which afforded another instance of His dealing with men, and (3) a crisis which brought fresh response, positive and negative, to His ministry. The healing itself may be analyzed into four parts which represent a topical rather than a strictly sequential arrangement.

The Case

The action was opened by the contact which Jesus made with a beggar who was sitting by the roadside in Jerusalem. Such an occurrence was not in itself remarkable, for beggars were as common in the Orient then as they are now. The interest arose from the various viewpoints revealed in the people who observed him.

To the disciples he was a subject for theological analysis. They asked, "Rabbi, who sinned, this man, or his parents, that he should be born blind?" (2) The question recognized his miserable plight, and showed that the disciples were reflecting upon its meaning: Why should the man be *born* blind? Could his condition be accounted for by some sin on the part of his parents? The law affirmed that Jehovah would visit the sins

---

26. See B. F. Westcott, *op. cit.,* II, 30 f. "The true reading in x. 22 (*Then was the Feast of Dedication*) determines that ch. ix. and x. 1-21 is connected with the Feast of Dedication, and not, as is commonly supposed, with the Feast of Tabernacles. The latter connexion has found support from the false gloss [going through the midst of them and so passed by] added to viii. 59, which appears to have been suggested by the 'passing by' in ix. 1. As it is, ch. ix. begins abruptly like ch. vi."
The Revised Text omits the above gloss, which is not included in the best uncial MSS. representing all the leading families of texts.

of the fathers upon the children, unto the third and fourth generation of those that hated Him.[27] Or had the man himself sinned in some previous existence, so that he was suffering the consequences of that sin in his life? Some of the rabbinical teachers held to the doctrine of the preexistence and reincarnation of the human soul.[28] Perhaps the question was prompted by speculation rather than by reference to any current teaching. The disciples were bewildered by the seeming irrationality of an affliction which had befallen the man at birth, and which could not be traced to a definite retributive judgment. They were more occupied in solving the abstract problem than in ministering to the individual that had aroused it. In short, they regarded him as a sinner who was less important than their debate.

The word by which the neighbors characterized the man was "beggar" (8). He had been dependent upon their generosity for his support, and while they probably held no hard feelings toward him, they regarded him as more or less of a nuisance. He was unproductive, contributing nothing to the life of the community, and was one more mouth to feed. The neighbors were not unkindly, but indifferent.

To the Pharisees this man was only a tool. They evinced not the slightest interest in him but were eager to employ him as a witness if possible. Since the healing was performed on the Sabbath, he would be useful in incriminating Jesus whom the Pharisees sought to trap. When they found that the man was not amenable to their purposes, they contemptuously cast him off and excommunicated him.

In contrast to these three attitudes which men still take today toward those whose sufferings they are unable to explain, Jesus viewed him as "a man" (1), a personality who needed his ministrations. His explanation to the disciples is an illuminating disclosure of His entire attitude toward hu-

---

27. Ex. 20:5 and repeated in Ex. 34:6, 7.
28. See J. H. Bernard, *op. cit.,* II, p. 325 and B. F. Westcott, *op. cit.,* II, p. 31.

manity. "Neither did this man sin, nor his parents: but that the works of God should be made manifest in him" (3). He felt that the man's condition called for action rather than for discussion.

Jesus' denial of sin as the direct cause of the man's blindness raised another problem. Did His statement mean that the blindness was inflicted on the man for the express purpose of affording an opportunity for healing him? If so, did it not seemingly imply that God would cause an innocent man to suffer half a lifetime of poverty, misery, and scorn that He might later demonstrate divine power? Such a view seems repugnant if we believe in the goodness of God.

One solution that has been proposed to remove the difficulty is that of changing the punctuation.[29] If the clause beginning with "but" in verse 3 be detached from the clause which precedes it, and be attached to verse 4, it would read as follows:

> Neither did this man sin, nor his parents. But that the works of God should be made manifest in him, we must work the works of him that sent me, while it is day: the night cometh, when no man can work.

Because the earliest Greek manuscripts of the New Testament were written in uncial letters, with no separation between the letters and no punctuation, all division of text into sentences, clauses, and phrases was dependent upon the judgment of the editor. Since one editor's judgment is no more infallible than another's, the punctuation as given above provides a plausible way of removing an ethical difficulty.

On the other hand, this solution is not so simple as it seems. The elliptical construction here is not at all infrequent in Johannine writings, in fact, it is one of the characteristic turns of Johannine style. There are in JOHN thirteen parallel uses of "but" (*alla*) with either "that" (*hina*) meaning purpose or

---

29. This is the view of G. Campbell Morgan, stated in *The Gospel According to John*, (New York: Fleming H. Revell Company, n. d.) pp. 164, 165.

result, or "because" (*hoti*). In each case there is an ellipsis of the main verb before the *but that*. Among these, only the passage in 1:31, "And I knew him not; but that he should be made manifest to Israel, for this cause came I baptizing in water," has a main verb following the "but that" clause which explains its meaning.[30] The general usage in JOHN will not allow for a punctuation which ignores the ellipsis implied in "but . . . that," and which attaches the clause to the sentence following rather than to the one preceding.

Does this mean, then, that the difficulty cannot be removed?

The answer lies in the interpretation of the word "that" rather than in the punctuation of the sentence. "That" (*hina*) may indicate either purpose or result;[31] and here the latter meaning is preferable. "That the works of God should be made manifest in him" may be regarded as expressing an opportunity rather than a destiny. Without doing violence to the Johannine usage of this grammatical construction, it may be interpreted to mean that Jesus was answering in terms of fact rather than of theory, and with a view to changing rather than

---

30. In the clauses containing *all' hina* (3:17, 11:52, 12:47, 17:15) and in those containing *all' hoti* (6:26, 12:6), a contrast is indicated between the clause following *alla* and the one preceding, or its equivalent. Verse 1.8 contrasts a noun with the *hina* clause, unless the verb *marturese* can be made dependent upon an ellipsis of *elthen*, carried over from verse 7. In 13:18 and 15:25 the clause seems to be related to nothing in particular, and the ellipsis is difficult to explain. Westcott suggests (*Op. cit.* II, 32, 212) that a phrase like "this cometh to pass" should be inserted, so that the text should read: "*But* [this hath come to pass] *that* . . .". With this concurs Abbott, E. A., *Johannine Grammar*, (Cambridge, The University Press, 1906), pp. 100, 101. "Where *all' hina* is preceded by another parallel *hina* (expressed or implied) the verb in the first *hina* clause may sometimes be regarded as repeated in the second *hina* clause . . .Even where there is no preceding parallel *hina*, a preceding verb may sometimes perhaps be supplied, as, possibly, in ix. 3: 'Neither this man sinned nor his parents, but (he was born blind) in order that the works of God might be manifested in him . . .' But there (ix. 3) it is perhaps better to take *all' hina* as meaning 'but (it was ordained) in order that.'" (Anglicizing ours). As the ensuing discussion shows, Abbott goes farther in his interpretation than does the author of this book.

31. For the use of *hina* to express result, see Robertson, A. T., *A Grammar of the Greek New Testament in the Light of Historical Research* (Third Edition, New York: George H. Doran Co., 1919); pp. 997-999.

explaining the blind man's condition. Westcott sums it up concisely by saying, "His suffering is the occasion and not the appointed preparation for the miracle, though when we regard things from the divine side we are constrained to see them in their dependence on the will of God."[32]

The nature of the case was unusual, for it was the only instance recorded where Jesus performed a miracle on a person defective from birth. For that reason it was singularly difficult. Had the man's eyes been injured in some accident, slow recovery might have been unconscious, and realization of that recovery might have come at the stimulus of Jesus' touch. Had loss of sight been occasioned by hysteria, psychological factors might have effected a cure. On the contrary, the man never had possessed sight, and presumably his affliction was permanent because human skill could avail nothing.

Because of its intrinsic hopelessness the case was a favorable opportunity for divine work. Not only did it present great physical difficulties, but the questioning of the disciples had shown that it implied a metaphysical problem also. Is fate the master of man? Is there no rational accounting for circumstance? Are men victims of chance? This sign showed Jesus as the Master of human fate. Irrespective of its cause He was able to grapple with misfortune and to overcome it.

The blind man afforded an unusual study in the growth of belief. So far the Fourth Gospel has pictured it either as a quantitative historical process, expressed by the increasing number of people who professed to believe on Jesus, or as a qualitative growth of belief in an individual life over a considerable span of time. With the blind man, the growth was rapid and confined to one person. In the midst of the confusion concerning Christ which seemed to fill the minds of the people, the development of this man showed belief in clear and definite fashion.

---

32. B. F. Westcott, *op. cit.*, II, p. 32.

The Cure

The motive for the cure was compassion. Jesus had little to gain by performing the miracle, since He needed to offer no further proofs to the multitude of what He could do. He must have realized that healing this man on the Sabbath would cause an even more violent protest from the rulers than had the healing of the man at the pool earlier in His ministry. Nevertheless He did it, because of His concern for the individual.

The means of the cure has been tentatively explained as a concession to the current Jewish belief that spittle possessed magical curative powers. There may have been a better reason. Touch and hearing would be this man's two chief avenues of contact with the outside world. He had already heard the conversation between Jesus and the disciples, and would have thought it not too reassuring. The disciples were doubtless cold and unfeeling, and he would shrink from being made a subject of public dispute. The words of Jesus, "We must work the works of him that sent me, while it is day" (4), would be encouraging, but were either too good to be true, or too abstract to convey to him any direct impression of Jesus' intention. By contrast, the weight of the clay on his eyes and the terse command, "Go, wash in the pool of Siloam" (7), could not fail to have meaning for him. Even if he had not faith to believe that healing was imminent, he would at least want to wash the clay from his eyes. Perhaps the clay was used not because of any medicinal qualities, but rather to provide the man with a tangible evidence of Jesus' intent.

The cure was undeniable. Nobody who knew the man, whether disciples, neighbors, parents, ecclesiastics, or the rank and file of the multitude, challenged its reality. All acknowledged (1) that he had been born blind; (2) that the man who was professedly cured was identical with the blind beggar; and (3) that he could actually see. Neither error nor fraud could be detected.

The Confession

The confession of faith which this healing brought from the erstwhile beggar was, first of all, positive. Each time that he recounted what had happened to him he did so in simple and direct language. He had been blind; a man called Jesus anointed his eyes with clay and commanded him to wash in Siloam; he washed; he returned seeing. The statement dealt with facts, not with theories.

Furthermore, the man was not rehearsing the experience of some one else, but of himself. "Jesus . . . said unto *me* . . . *I* went . . . [*I*] washed . . . *I* received sight" (11, italics ours). The miracle was part of this man's firsthand knowledge, and his witness could not be set aside.

Both aspects of his confession, the factual and the personal, are characteristic of adequate witness to Christ. These two factors produce a faith that grows under opposition. For this reason, as the man met the incredulous queries of his friends, the timid disavowal of knowledge by his parents, and the menacing threats of the Pharisees, his testimony became progressive.

Three groups of people questioned the healed man. The neighbors, motivated by curiosity, were just eager to learn what had happened. To their insistent inquiries he replied by a simple recital of the facts. All that he knew of his healer was summed up in the phrase, "The man that is called Jesus . . ." (11).

The Pharisees, whose motive was controversy, sought to investigate the forces that produced the healing. Who was the man that had power to cure congenital blindness, and who had the temerity to perform the cure on the Sabbath? Upon being given the same facts that had been stated to the multitude, the Pharisees deduced *a priori* that Jesus must be a sinner, since He had broken the law. Others concluded *a posteriori* that He could not be a sinner since He had performed this notable miracle. When the beneficiary of the miracle was asked for his opinion, he took a new step of faith in his reply: "He is a prophet" (17).

The reaction of unbelief to this progress of belief appeared in verses 18 to 34. A heated argument ensued upon the acknowledgment that Jesus was a prophet. Stage by stage the objections of unbelief were beaten back. The man's parents, fearful as they were, recognized him as their son, and answered that he had been born blind. The miracle could not be explained as a case of mistaken identity (20, 21). In opposition to the theory of the Pharisees that Jesus was a sinner, the man reiterated the fact of his healing, and concluded by asserting that no sinner could open blind eyes. "If this man were not from God, he could do nothing" (33). Because unbelief had no argument to withstand this cogent reasoning, it resorted to excommunication. Among the Jews, two types of discipline were used: the temporary exclusion, which cut a man off from fellowship until his penitence warranted restoration; and the permanent ban, which pronounced a curse on him and separated him forever from the congregation.[33] Probably the former is meant here, since the latter would have required a formal vote of the Sanhedrin. The expression used in verse 22,[34] "put out of the synagogue," occurs only in JOHN, and is used again in 12:42 and in 16:2 in such a way as to indicate that Jewish Christians were doubtless often treated in this manner.

When Jesus heard of the unfortunate result of the controversy with the Pharisees, He was moved with pity. He sought for the man, and upon finding him, asked him a pointed personal question: "You there, do you believe on the Son of

---

33. Emil Schurer, *op. cit.,* II, ii. pp. 60, 61.
34. *aposunagogos genetai* (22) Cf. 12:42, 16:2. See J H. Bernard, *op. cit.,* II, p. 334.

God?"[35] To this direct appeal for belief the man made no immediate response, but inquired further, "Who is he, Lord, that I may believe on him?" (36) He was unwilling to commit himself without knowing why, for believing on the Son of God was an abstraction which might not have been clear to him.

Jesus answered the man's query by saying, "Thou hast both seen him, and he it is that speaketh with thee." Instantly he connected the voice with the stranger who had performed the cure. The words, "Son of God," would no longer be an abstraction, but a title of his benefactor. Immediately he responded with an act of worship (38) which is the final stage of belief.

The Consequences

This miracle illustrated clearly the consequences of belief and unbelief. Persistent faith brought healing and progressive enlightenment. As the blind man acted on the simple imperative of Jesus, he progressed from one step of faith to another, until Jesus' voluntary revelation of Himself brought the man to its highest attainment and reward.

The unbelief of the Pharisees began with misunderstanding both of the law and of the person of Jesus. The law was for them a tradition to be kept, a dead letter, not a living voice. The result of this attitude was a prejudice that blinded the Pharisees to anything but their own preconceived opinions, and so made them ignorant of the full truth. "We know not" (29) were the words they used concerning Jesus. Pride prevented their learning any more, and their bigotry caused them to drive away the very man from whom they might have taken lessons in faith (34). For this reason the miracle was made into a parable by Jesus. "For judgment came I into this world, that they that see not may see; and that they that see may become blind" (39).

---

35. Original translation which follows the reading of the ARV. Most of the critical texts, following the reading of the better manuscripts, read "Son of man."

The rhetorical question of the Pharisees, "We are not blind too, are we?" (40),[36] showed that they expected Jesus to exempt them from the condemnation of His previous utterance. His reply was devastating. If they really were blind, and admitted the fact, their confession would lead to the removal of their sin. Their inability to discern their own failure as evinced by their complacent assumption of spiritual sight aggravated the situation and made their sin all the more lasting. While the blind man gained physical and spiritual light through faith, the Pharisees lost the light they had and lapsed into complete spiritual darkness.

The Discourse on the Good Shepherd (10:1-18)

This discourse on the good shepherd is a self-sustaining unit which must have been a part of Jesus' teaching to the Jews. Bernard suggests[37] that it fits better into the sequence of thought if taken with verse twenty-nine which would connect it with Jesus' teaching in the temple at the Feast of Dedication. On the other hand, the allusion to the blind man in verse twenty-one points to a sequence of the miracle in chapter 9. The latter alternative is better, for it preserves the unity of action. The symphonic recurrence of the teaching on the sheep is characteristic of Johannine style, and does not call for arbitrary rearrangement of the text.

This section is one of the few approaches to parabolic form of discourse that appear in JOHN.[38] It can be called an allegory

---

36. Original translation.

37. J. H. Bernard, *op. cit.,* I, xxiv, xxv, II, p. 341. Bernard advocates rearrangement of the text, but his criteria are wholly subjective and lack manuscript authority.

38. The word translated "parable" in 10:6 is not *parabole* which is used in the Synoptics and Hebrews, but *paroimia* which appears four times in John and once in II Peter. It means "proverb" rather than parable and usually connotes a cryptic or enigmatic meaning. B. F. Westcott, *op. cit.,* II, p. 52, says that both Greek words are used to render the Hebrew *mashal;* but that *paroimia* "suggests the notion of a mysterious saying full of compressed thought, rather than of a simple comparison."

since the teaching is stated in bold metaphor rather than by the characteristic simile of the Synoptics:[39] "the kingdom of heaven is like . . ."

The action of the allegory is based upon the normal daily procedure of the oriental shepherd, who in the morning enters the fold where his sheep are kept, calls to them, and leads them out to pasture for the day. In case of danger he protects them with his own life against the wolves and other perils of the wilderness, and keeps them securely until he brings them back to the fold in the evening. The imagery was familiar to Jesus' hearers because shepherding was a common occupation in Palestine (Luke 2:8), and the Hebrew literature abounded in reference to it. The classic example of this figure is the twenty-third Psalm, which pictures Jehovah's personal care of His people.

The allegory in John 10 was intended to present a collective rather than an individual aspect, for each time the word "sheep" is mentioned it is in the plural. Jesus was defending His authority as the shepherd of the nation, and the "sheep" represented the chosen spiritual "remnant" who may be equated with the "remnant" or true Israel discussed in the writings of Paul (Rom. 11:1-5). The Gentiles were not excluded for they were the "other sheep" of verse 16.[40] Though directed to Jewish ears, the teaching is catholic in its scope.

In the discourse five or six classes of people were described. The shepherd was Jesus Himself, as He declared plainly (11). The "porter" or doorkeeper (3), who opened the way for Him may not be identified with any particular principle or person, but simply completed the normal picture of the sheepfold.[41] The "thieves and robbers" (1) corresponded to the pseudo-

---

39. Cf. Matt. 13:24, 31, 33, 44, 45, 47 et al.

40. See Rom. 11:11, 15:8-12.

41. B. F. Westcott, *op. cit.*, II, p. 51. "The figure is not to be explained exclusively of the Holy Spirit or of the Father, or of Moses or of John the Baptist, but of the Spirit acting through His appointed ministers in each case."

Messiahs of whom there had already been a large number.[42] The "strangers" (5) may have been the same as the thieves and robbers, or any persons who assumed leadership without pretending to be a Messiah. The sheep represented the Lord's people, who hear His voice and follow Him (27). The hireling (12) should be distinguished from the thieves and robbers, since he entered the fold as an authorized agent rather than as a marauder, and since he is condemned for cowardice and selfishness rather than for wanton attack on the sheep. By these metaphors Jesus evaluated the religious life and history of Israel.

The first place of importance in the interpretation should be given to the shepherd. No less than eighteen statements are made about him in the text.

The Shepherd:

	Verse
Enters through the door.	2
Receives the cooperation of the porter.	3
Receives the obedience of the sheep.	3
Calls his own sheep by name.	3
Leads them out.	3
Precedes them.	4

---

42. "Thieves and robbers." The first word means a sneak thief who obtains his booty by subtlety, the second is a brigand who obtains his by violence. Doubtless Jesus applied these terms to the many leaders preceding Him who had attempted to bring in the kingdom by violent means and to pose as Messiahs. There are one or two allusions to such in the New Testament. Compare Gamaliel's remark in Acts 5:36, 37, and Josephus, in his *Antiquities*, XVII, x, 4, 8 which refer to many revolts that took place before or in the time of Jesus.
"Before" (8) *pro* creates a seeming difficulty if it be interpreted chronologically, for it would make all of Jesus' predecessors to be false teachers. In order to avoid this, some grammarians have translated it "instead of," "in the room of," "in the name of." H. E. Dana and J. R. Mantey, in *A Manual Grammar of the Greek New Testament*, (New York: The Macmillan Company, 1927), p. 109, defend this translation of *pro* and allude to other examples of similar translation in Gessner Harrison's *Greek Prepositions and Cases*, p. 408. This view is not supported by J. H. Bernard, *op. cit.*, II, pp. 352, 353, nor by A. T. Robertson, in his *Historical Grammar of the Greek New Testament*, p. 622, who consider *pro* to have a temporal meaning only.

Is followed by them.	4
Is the door of the sheep.	7
Is the only *true* shepherd (inferential).	8
Is the avenue to safety and sustenance.	9
Brings life for the sheep.	10
Sacrifices his life for the sheep.	11
"Knows" the sheep.	14
Has several folds.	16
Is under necessity of bringing other sheep.	16
Sacrifices himself voluntarily.	18
Possesses power over his own life.	18
Provides security for the sheep (taken from later discourse).	28

At least four important deductions may be drawn from these statements:

Jesus is the one key to Jewish history and the only one authorized to command the allegiance of the spiritual nucleus of Judaism. To Him the gateway of prophecy, Scripture, and history had been opened; and He had entered into His commission by the legitimate channel of legal descent and of spiritual appointment.

Jesus claimed that He was destined to lead His sheep out into new pastures, which implied ability to impart a deepening spiritual revelation. Pasture, according to Psalm 23, meant sustenance and refreshment of the soul of man. "He restoreth my soul" (Ps. 23:3).

Jesus interpreted His coming death as a voluntary, vicarious offering for the sheep, and He predicted that His purpose to give them abundant life would be confirmed by His own resurrection.

Jesus declared that the Jewish "sheep" were not the only ones that He had, but that the flock would be augmented by additions from other folds. The unity of the flock is determined by a common following of the one shepherd, not by the erection of a single outward organization.

The second place of importance in the allegory belongs to the sheep. They are identified as follows:

They recognize the voice of the shepherd.	3
They follow the shepherd.	4
They refuse to follow strangers.	5, 8
Their safety and sustenance is in the shepherd.	9
They are not all of one fold.	16

Recognition of the voice of the shepherd involved familiarity with it. The summons of Jesus brought response from those who finally followed Him because in Him they recognized the accents of Jehovah who had already spoken to them in the revelation of the Old Testament. As Peter stated in 6:68, "*Thou* hast the words of eternal life." The inherent quality of Jesus' teachings identified Him as the true Shepherd of souls. This concept is supported by the Shepherd's own claim stated in verse 30, "I and the Father are one."

The symbolism of verse 9 deserves special comment. The oriental shepherd usually stood in the doorway of the sheepfold as the sheep went in or out, and passed them one by one as he counted and inspected them. He was their door to safety, to freedom, and to satisfaction of their wants. The life of the sheep was dependent upon the power and provision of the shepherd. Their recognition of him and his recognition of them established the relationship. Hearing his voice, following his leading, entering the fold through him, and the refusal to follow others was John's picture of belief.

The hireling has four characteristics:	Verse
He lacks the spontaneous responsibility of the shepherd for the sheep.	12
He is cowardly, and flees in the face of danger.	12
He has no particular concern for the sheep.	13
His sole interest is in the recompense.	13

Although no explicit comparison is stated, Jesus probably was representing the priestly party by the hirelings. The later actions of the priests and Pharisees made the metaphor apt. In the council which was held after the raising of Lazarus, they expressed their fear of Jesus' success. "If we let him thus alone, all men will believe on him: and the Romans will come and take away both our place and our nation" (11:48). They were more concerned with their place and their nation than with Jesus, who was the very reason for their national existence. Furthermore, the order of their words showed that their position meant more to them than their national life, and that they valued profit above the spiritual welfare of their charges.

The Division among the Jews (10:19-21)

The verses of 10:19-21 constitute a transitional paragraph which is closely related to the healing of the blind man in chapter 9, because those who rose in Jesus' defense appealed to the miracle as the latest proof of His integrity. The conflict in the popular mind confirms the impression given by 7:12, and by the entire context from 7:1 to 10:19, that Jesus was an enigma to the populace, and that they could not come to any conclusion about Him. Each new discourse provoked fresh discussion and heated debate.

The Argument in Solomon's Porch (10:22-42)

The argument in Solomon's porch is dated definitely at the Feast of Dedication, which is identical with the modern Jewish Feast of Lights, and which was celebrated in commemoration of the rededication of the temple after the cleansing by the Maccabean leaders. The feast took place in December, toward the end of the month, and would thus be about three months later than the Feast of Tabernacles mentioned in 7:2.

The discourse was introduced by the direct question: "If thou art the Christ [Messiah], tell us plainly" (24). The division of opinion concerning Jesus had created a tension, and the Jews requested a categorical answer. The previous teaching had been plain to those who were spiritually alert, but the half-veiled references to prophecy and the parabolic message did not satisfy the people. They wanted an open declaration.

In answer, Jesus first described the nature of true believers. They are characterized by the following:

Sensitivity	They "hear my voice"	27
Fellowship	"I know them"	27
Obedience	"They follow me"	27
Life	"I give unto them eternal life"	28
Assurance	"They shall never perish"	28
Security	"No one shall snatch them out of my hand"	28

These are the qualities that distinguish believers from unbelievers, and are both the basis and the result of belief.

By way of contrast, Jesus called His questioners unbelievers. "Ye believe not" appears three times in this context (25, 26, 38). Although He had spoken in their ears the same truths that had been presented to believers, and although He had done the same works before them that He had done before others, they still did not receive Him as the Messiah. Instead of sensitivity, they had obduracy; instead of fellowship, alienation; instead of obedience, rebellion; instead of life, death;[43] instead of assurance, danger; instead of security, perdition. By implied antitheses Jesus drew a graphic picture of the consequences of unbelief.

The final expression of hostility was not precipitated by the unfavorable contrast between believers and unbelievers, but by the claim of Jesus: "I and the Father are one." The use of the neuter gender in the numeral *one* indicated that Jesus was not representing Himself and the Father as one person, but that there was a common bond of unity in being between them. I Corinthians 3:8 employs a similar phrase: "He that planteth and he that watereth are one." This text does not assert the identity of the two individuals, nor, on the other hand, does it convey only the idea of purpose, but inward unity of function.

---

43. Cf. John 8:24.

Without a doubt the statement of Jesus recorded by John has metaphysical implications that transcend those of I Corinthians 3:8, for the remark was understood clearly as an assertion of deity.

Certain alternatives point the way to the ultimate interpretation of this text. Since Jesus claimed to be one with the Father,

> Either He was joking, and was not serious;
> Or He was lying for the sake of effect;
> Or He was insane, and not responsible for His claims;
> Or His disciples misunderstood Him;
> Or He told the truth and was deity.

Of these alternatives, the first is precluded by the occasion. The entire conversation is in a serious vein, and there is not the slightest suggestion of jocularity or of irony on Jesus' part.

The second may also be ruled out, for falsehood is out of keeping with the known character of Christ. On this particular topic, Jesus had previously stressed His truthfulness (8:45, 46, 55).

Insanity is likewise inadmissible. That charge had already been suggested by His enemies (7:20, 8:48), but was entirely incongruous with His usual poise and power. His balance of mind, finely adjusted discernment, constant emotional control, and well planned career render void the verdict of insanity.

If His followers misunderstood Him, so that the record is a warped and erroneous picture of what He really said, there is no point in discussing the person of Christ at all because there is no secure basis for any argument. Furthermore, it is unlikely that men who were reared in strict Jewish monotheism would ascribe equality with God to another man, however deeply they revered Him.

The only remaining conclusion is that Jesus spoke the truth, and that He was "one with the Father." His appeal to Scriptures is a bit of *a fortiori* argument. If the Scripture (Ps. 82: 6), "which cannot be broken," applied the term "gods" to ordinary men, should not the term "Son of God" be allowable to Him whom the Father had set apart specially and sent into the world for an unusual mission? Jesus attempted to define His unity with the Father by saying that "the Father is in me, and I in the Father" (38). This statement was later repeated in His farewell address to the Twelve (14:11). It implied a unity of fellowship between the Father and Christ which originated in unity of nature, and was analogous to the relation of "abiding" which obtains between the believer and Christ. "God is love; and he that abideth in love abideth in God, and God abideth in him" (I John 4:16). "Abiding" is the Johannine word which describes the impartation of the divine nature to the believer in regeneration and its maintenance and growth through the agency of the Spirit. The consciousness of the presence of God which accompanies this "abiding" becomes the ground of understanding the unity between Christ and the Father. The real nature of Christ is comprehensible to the believer as it is not to the unbeliever, because the former has some awareness of what divine fellowship means. Even the rudimentary step of "believing the works" (38) affords a beginning of understanding which will grow into an increasing faith.

The hostile response of Jesus' hearers compelled Him to leave Jerusalem in order to escape from their clutches, and He withdrew to Perea.

The Raising of Lazarus (11:1-53)

The account of the raising of Lazarus deserves special place in the Period of Conflict. It was the last and greatest of Jesus' public miracles as recorded by John, and brought the final demonstration of His mastery of human problems and a convincing proof of His claim to be the resurrection and the life. The progress of belief in individual consciousness and the varying ways in which belief may be manifested were illustrated in the actions and words of Mary and Martha. Finally, the effects of this miracle prompted the rulers to take summary action against Jesus, lest His popularity should become so great that their prominence and power should be eclipsed.

The event took place during the last winter of Jesus' life, following His withdrawal into Perea (10:40) and prior to the last Passover (12:1). It marked the high point of His ministry in the neighborhood of Jerusalem and made the concluding appeal to the populace on the basis of signs. The division of belief and unbelief which had already become apparent in the crowd (7:12, 40-44, 8:30, 59, 9:16, 10:19-21) became fixed after the miracle. The rulers began definite preparation to destroy Him, while the disciples became more firmly grounded in their faith.

The two verses in chapter 10 which supply the historical setting for the raising of Lazarus form a connecting link between the beginning of Jesus' ministry and its close. The allusion to John the Baptist in this passage recalls the statement in 4:1 that Jesus had left Judea the first time because of the concern the Pharisees showed over His great success. They were alarmed because He was "baptizing more disciples than John." Now upon His return to the same region, He openly discussed their hostility (Matt. 19:1ff. and Mark 10:1ff.) and accepted the belief of the people, who had received Him at least partially because of the testimony of His forerunner. "John," they said, "indeed did no sign: but all things whatsoever John spake of this man were true" (10:41). The long interim between the early contacts with John the Baptist in Perea and this later ministry had not caused the people to forget John's message nor to lessen their appreciation of Jesus. The opportunity for reflection on John's prophecies and on Jesus' deeds was a potent factor in creating belief. The raising of Lazarus was a fitting culmination to a ministry which had by its scope and effectiveness already surpassed that of John.

The careful identification of Lazarus by his connection with Mary and Martha indicated that he was not very well known to Christian tradition at the time when the account of the miracle was written. Perhaps the story of his resuscitation was told for the first time in the pages of this Gospel. On the other hand, the reference to Mary in verse 2 shows that she was well known for her anointing of the Lord's feet, for the episode had not been mentioned up to this point in the narrative. The writer would hardly expect his reader to recognize Mary by a connection which had not yet been explained in the story, if the reader were dependent solely upon this Gospel for a knowledge of her. It is fair to assume that John must have been referring to a current stock of information which his public already possessed.[44]

The emergency itself was nothing unusual in human life. Sickness and death are the common heritage of all the descendants of Adam and Eve. The importance of this crisis was due not to its singularity, but to the significance with which Jesus invested it. He gave a new interpretation of the tragedy at Bethany as He responded to the varying reactions of those who were concerned with it.

The sisters made their first appeal through the message: "Lord, behold, he whom thou lovest is sick" (3). They regarded the illness of their brother as the logical occasion for Jesus' intervention. They were sure that Jesus, of all men, would be sympathetic and helpful when His friends were in dire need.

The response of Jesus was different from their expectation. He had a supernatural outlook on the whole situation, somewhat akin to His perspective on the case of the blind man (chap. 9). To the family and friends of Lazarus, the sickness

---

44. For a discussion of the relation of Mary of Bethany to the woman whose anointing of Jesus was reported in Luke 7:36-50, see J. B. Mayor on "Mary" in Hastings' *Dictionary of the Bible*, III, pp. 279a-284a.

was a growing threat[45] that finally ended in disaster, and terminated forever the career of a beloved brother and friend. To Jesus, it was another opportunity for the manifestation of divine power, a parenthesis in the life of Lazarus that would make no ultimate difference in his welfare. "This sickness is not unto death, but for the glory of God, that the Son of God may be glorified thereby" (4).

The delay of Jesus in replying to the urgent plea of the sisters is difficult to explain on any ground other than that of His complete mastery of death. Had He been only human, He would have hurried to the bedside of Lazarus to give What He could of aid and comfort. Knowing, however, that He was the resurrection and the life, it was just as easy to raise the dead as to cure the sick, and far more necessary to His purpose which was the creation of a fixed faith in the souls of the sisters and of His own disciples. To the objection that it was unkind of Jesus to postpone aid just to carry out His own plans, there is the answer that He finally did return to Bethany in the face of bitter hostility and certain death. Because He was master of the situation, and because He was willing to jeopardize His own safety to bring consolation to the mourners, delay was not cruelty but constructive discipline.

The disciples were bewildered because Jesus was ready to return to Judea when only a short time before the Jews had attempted to stone Him (8). To their exclamation of astonishment Jesus replied that duty, not safety, was His first obligation. "Are there not twelve hours in the day? If a man walk in the day, he stumbleth not, because he seeth the light of this world" (9). He felt that as long as He walked in the clear light of the commission which the Father had assigned to Him, He would not stumble. He regarded death as only an incident in His career, and if the raising of Lazarus brought peril to Him, He would face it without shrinking.

---

45. "Was sick"—The tense is the imperfect periphrastic, which implies a protracted process or continued action.

The disciples were also puzzled by Jesus' view of death because they could not see it through His eyes. He called it "sleep" (11). The disciples misunderstood Him, and thought that He referred to the natural repose which would indicate the breaking of fever and the prospect of recovery. Jesus had to be more literal for their sakes; but His use of the term "sleep"[46] meant that He thought of death as a period of apparent unconsciousness beyond which there would be a re-awakening to life. Jesus' explanation, "I am glad for your sakes that I was not there, to the intent ye may believe" (15) expressed His desire to educate them in a faith that would transcend death. If their belief could outreach their fears, and overleap the barrier which the supposed finality of death creates, they would be prepared adequately for the shock of His coming crucifixion and for the resurrection.

The rejoinder of Thomas (16) was quite typical of the attitude of these men and of Thomas himself. Pessimism was its chief note. In spite of the hints Jesus had given concerning His duty and in spite of the victorious ring in His voice, Thomas felt sure that doom and disappointment were waiting for Him if He returned to the environs of Jerusalem. This despondency was precisely the thing that Jesus wished to cure; but more than the raising of Lazarus was necessary to do it.

Paradoxically, Thomas exhibited also a real heroism. He expected that Jerusalem would mean the death of Jesus, but he was ready to die, too, if need be. His faith was courageous but not triumphant. He was resigned to the possibility of martyrdom as a matter of duty, but he did not entertain the concept of a victory over death and all its powers. Faith had not yet passed from resolution to insight.

The conference at Bethany centered around the two sisters, Martha and Mary. Both were equally bereaved, and both addressed substantially the same reproachful words to Jesus:

---

46. The verb translated "sleep" is used 18 times in the New Testament, and in 15 of these instances it refers unmistakably to death.

"Lord, if thou hadst been here, my brother had not died" (21). The contrasts between them, however, are greater than the similarities. Martha was active. She met Jesus at the outskirts of the town (20). Mary remained in the house, lost in mournful contemplation. Martha's greeting laid emphasis on *my* brother, a hint of her aggressive and possessive personality. Mary's statement emphasized my *brother*,[47] for her tender nature was torn by the loss of the object of her love. Martha expressed a general assent to the hope of the resurrection: "I know that he shall rise again in the resurrection at the last day" (24). Mary prostrated herself before Jesus in adoration and said nothing concerning her expectations. Martha was vocal; Mary was tearful. Both had personal faith in Jesus as a man and as a friend, though it is obvious from Martha's response to Jesus' command to remove the stone that she did not anticipate any immediate restoration of her brother.

The Jews, who appeared in the background, were another group at the home of Lazarus. They had tried to console the sisters (19); they were faithful in their attendance upon the family (31), and expressed some appreciation of the attitude of Jesus (36). The best that Judaism could proffer at this time was commiseration; it had no constructive suggestions. The inability to present any positive hope to the bereaved sisters was a confession that Judaism had no clear testimony to eternal life. Only Christ "brought life and immortality to light through the gospel" (II Tim. 1:10). The limit of the Jews' faith was "Could not this man, who opened the eyes of him that was blind, have caused that this man also should not die?" (37)

With this background of confusion and incomplete faith, the action of Jesus at the tomb of Lazarus was all the more convincing. To the bewildered disciples and to the mourning

---

47. The difference appears in the word order of the Greek text, in which the last word is the most emphatic. Martha's words end with the possessive pronoun *my*, (21) Mary's words, with the noun *brother* (32).

sisters He had presented Himself as the resurrection and the life, and had challenged them to believe in Him against all appearances (25). Now He must prove His power. Could He do it?

The procedure of Jesus involved first of all His own emotional expression. Nowhere does the Gospel present sovereignty as equivalent to arrogance or to unfeeling exercise of authority. He might have been unconcerned with grief, since He knew well that it would be succeeded quickly by joy; yet He sorrowed with them. The depth of this sorrow is conveyed by a series of words in the vocabulary which contribute a new understanding of His attitude. The sisters and those with them "wept," a word which means loud crying, or wailing, an unrestrained paroxysm of grief. Jesus in less demonstrative fashion "groaned in the spirit, and was troubled" (33). Of these two terms applied to Him, the former meant literally "to snort like a horse." It connoted indignation rather than sorrow. As He looked upon the cemetery at Bethany, a silent memorial to the devastation that death had wrought on the human race, He was angered against man's great enemy. Death to Him was not an impassable barrier, but a call to battle. The second word is the same one that was used in 5:7 concerning the "troubling" of the water, and in 14:1, when He said to the disciples, "Let not your heart be troubled." He could calm their agitation because He had passed through it Himself. Nor was His emotion wholly internal, for John 11:35 says that "Jesus wept."[48] This word bespoke intensity of feeling rather than uncontrollable wailing. Jesus was not unmoved by the spectacle of death.

The second act of Jesus was a challenge to faith. Already Martha had avowed her belief in Him as the Son of God (27) and the tense of the verb that she used[49] implied a settled conviction. It was one thing to confess a theoretical belief; it was

---

48. Used only here in the New Testament.
49. First perfect active.

quite another to roll away the stone that concealed the corruption of death in expectation that the impossible would be
done. Martha protested, but Jesus insisted that she take the
initiative, and she did. Against the judgment of reason, which
told her that Lazarus' body was already a decaying corpse, she
obeyed.

The prayer of Jesus was remarkable, for He offered thanks
before seeing any results, just as He had asked Martha to act
in anticipation of what He would accomplish. He did not ask
her to place a greater faith in Him than He did in the Father.
Furthermore, His prayer was prompted more by a desire to
convince the multitude of His divine commission than by a
feeling that He must depend upon making known vocally His
requests to God. The inner fellowship of mind with the Father
would be sufficient for Him to make His wants known; but
inner fellowship would carry no conviction with a crowd.

The voice of command was the last stage of the action.
Jesus' word had calmed the sea; now it called the dead back to
life. It was a sample of the fulfillment of His own word: "The
hour cometh, and now is, when the dead shall hear the voice
of the Son of God; and they that hear shall live" (5:25).
Likewise, Paul, in teaching concerning the ultimate resurrection of the believer, speaks of "the voice of the archangel" (I
Thess. 4:16).[50] The call of Jesus was a shout of command
from the master of death.

The response was electric. "He that was dead came forth,
bound hand and foot with grave-clothes; and his face was
bound about with a napkin" (44). The Jewish system of preparing a body for burial provided for swathing it in bandage-

---

50. Literally, "in an archangel's voice." The emphasis is not on *whose*
voice, but on the *kind* of a voice. It is a descriptive, not a possessive geni-
tive.

like wrappings[51] from the armpits to the feet, leaving the shoulders bare, and with a cloth ("napkin") wrapped around the head. Such enswathement would effectively prevent any ordinary means of locomotion on the part of Lazarus. The only explanation of his appearance at the door of the tomb is that the power that galvanized him into life brought him forth to the door, so that Jesus could say, "Loose him, and let him go" (44).

The resuscitation of Lazarus could not properly be classed as a resurrection, because he resumed the same status that he had before his illness. The process of decay was reversed, and his body revitalized. So far as is known he did not possess physical immortality, though his death is not recorded.

As with the rest of the signs, both belief and unbelief followed. Many of the Jews who beheld the miracle believed; some, like the man at the pool, told the Pharisees what Jesus had done. They must have conveyed the report with no good motive, for the attitude of the Pharisees to Jesus was widely known. The words of Abraham, quoted in Jesus' story in Luke 16:31, were well illustrated: "If they hear not Moses and the prophets, neither will they be persuaded, if one rise from the dead."

Unbelief, however, cannot remain static any more than can belief. By nature it is progressive. The unbelief of the Jewish leaders had long ceased to be a polite incredulity of the claims of Jesus. His works were too numerous, too real, and too wonderful to be ignored or dismissed with contempt. Unbelief was compelled to declare its true nature which was selfishness. When Caiaphas said, "If we let him thus alone, all men will believe on him: and the Romans will come and take away both our place and our nation" (48), he conceded the cogency of Jesus' arguments and the actuality of His miracles. On the other hand, he and the hierarchy feared to risk the place of

---

51. The word occurs only here in the New Testament. It is used in a medical papyrus of the second century.

privilege and comfort which the Roman government, much as they hated it, had given them. At the council following this miracle, there was definite concerted agreement to dispose of Jesus by fair means or foul. The enmity which had made previous sporadic attempts to trap Him in speech or to capture Him now settled upon a policy of exterminating Him.

THE PERIOD OF CRISIS

THE PERIOD OF CRISIS

CHAPTER VII

The Period of Crisis

11:54 to 12:36a

A FTER the raising of Lazarus the severity of conflict had
reached a point where decisive action was inevitable.
Belief, if it were to remain belief, must become definite genuine
commitment. Unbelief, on the other hand, could no longer
tolerate Jesus' exposure and condemnation of its position. The
twelfth chapter records the consequent turning point in the
plot.

The text of 11:54 to 12:36a may be divided into four parts,
each of which deals with the relation of some particular group
to Jesus in the crucial hour.

The Retirement to Ephraim	11:54-57	Enemies
The Return to Bethany	12:1-11	Friends
The Entry into Jerusalem	12:12-19	Populace
The Visit of the Greeks	12:20-36a	Gentiles

Taken together these paragraphs describe the transition in the
career of Jesus from a public to a private ministry, for after
the entry into Jerusalem Jesus made no appeal to the crowds.
His general attitude showed that He expected a crisis. "The
hour is come" (23) is the central concept of the passage.
Hereafter the story of the Gospel moved swiftly to its conclusion.

The dating of the crisis, six days before the Passover, shows
how the suspense was maintained almost to the end of the
account. Not until the very last was the outcome certain, and
even then the climax of the book was a surprise.

The Retirement to Ephraim (11:54-57)

The brief interval between the raising of Lazarus and the return of Jesus to Jerusalem was spent in a city called Ephraim. Its exact location is unknown, but probably it was situated in the open country north or northeast of Jerusalem. Jesus had withdrawn thither in order that He might be sure of undisturbed conference with His disciples before the surrender which He knew must come. The tension of the hour must have been great; for both the populace and His enemies expected Him to come to the Passover, and both were eagerly waiting to see Him. The people were wondering whether He would dare to risk a visit to the feast, and the chief priests and the Pharisees were impatiently awaiting an opportunity to capture Him (56, 57).

The Return to Bethany (12:1-11)

The first event of the Passion Week narrated by John was the dinner given in honor of Jesus by the family of Bethany. Martha, energetic as usual, took the responsibility of serving. The double reference to Lazarus, whom Jesus had raised from the dead, conveyed the impression that his public appearance was a bit unusual. The identification of Bethany as the place "where Lazarus was," although the eleventh chapter makes clear that it was his home, and the explicit statement that "Lazarus was one of them that sat at meat with him" (2) seem a bit redundant otherwise. Perhaps the curiosity of the crowd was so distasteful to him that he avoided public appearances whenever possible.

The two chief personages in the account are Mary and Judas. The contrast between them is striking. Mary was the embodiment of self-sacrifice; Judas, of selfishness. Mary expressed her feeling in a costly gift; Judas, by cheap sarcasm. Mary took the place of a servant of Jesus; Judas constituted himself a critic. Mary possessed spiritual discernment when she anointed Jesus' body for burial (7). Evidently she had a

sympathetic insight into His mind, and felt intuitively that He
could not be with them long. Judas exhibited lack of tact that
was amazing in a man naturally as astute as he when he said,
"Why was not this ointment sold for three hundred shillings,
and given to the poor?" (5) Mary, of all of Jesus' friends,
has been remembered for her loyalty. Judas was the one disciple who has been universally execrated as a traitor.

This contrast affords a study in the development of belief
and unbelief among Jesus' own followers. Mary's natural
timidity was supplanted by the ardor of devotion which her
faith kindled. The raising of her brother Lazarus had evoked
gratitude which she could not conceal, and the presentation of
the alabaster box of ointment was a logical expression of it.
Faith blossomed into devotion.

On the other hand, Jesus' failure to claim royal titles and
prerogatives for Himself when He exercised miraculous
powers may have been the underlying cause for Judas' perfidy.
Contrary to the disciples' expectation of an outward political
coup, Jesus carefully refrained from making any pronouncements on issues of state; He talked instead to the disciples
about surrendering Himself to death. Possibly Judas felt
frustrated because the kingdom that he had anticipated was
not about to materialize. If the kingdom were not to be immediately manifested, his relation to Jesus had put him in the
anomalous position of gaining nothing and losing everything.
Not only would he fail to obtain a post in a new realm, but he
would, upon Jesus' death, be put under suspicion as a rebel. If
he should take the alternative of betraying Jesus he would
profit financially, and would square himself with the victorious
priests. The action of Judas is a perfect illustration of repu-
diation as the natural result of unbelief. Since he had refused
to yield himself to Jesus' program, he was forced to go in the
opposite direction. John presented him as restless, dissatisfied,
mercenary, and insincere.

The same process of division that was at work among Jesus' friends was taking place among the common people. Many came to the feast not as invited guests, but as spectators, because they wanted to see Lazarus, the man who had been raised from the dead. So convincing was the evidence that "because that by reason of him [Lazarus] many of the Jews went away, and believed on Jesus" (11).

The return to Bethany, then, was marked by an increase in the intensity and extent of unbelief. Under the very shadow of the cross, Jesus' friends gained in number and strength.

The Entry into Jerusalem (12:12-19)

The Johannine account of the entry into Jerusalem places greater emphasis on the action of the multitude than does the story of the Synoptics. Nothing is said of the preparation of the entry by Jesus and His disciples, nor is Jesus' personal response to the ovation recorded. John makes the event wholly an evidence of the response of the people to Jesus' claims.

Two "multitudes" are mentioned: one, the multitude of foreign pilgrims that had come to the feast and had heard that Jesus was on His way to the city; the other, the multitude of those residents who had been present at Bethany when He raised Lazarus from the dead (17). The former responded because of hearsay (18); the latter, because they themselves had witnessed the miracle.

The citation from Psalm 118:25, 26, "Hosanna: Blessed is he that cometh in the name of the Lord, even the King of Israel," was especially meaningful. Psalm 118 was one of the cycle of Psalms that was sung at the Passover season. The excerpt given is not a consecutive quotation, but a combination of parts of two verses constituting a prayer that the salvation of God might be immediately realized. "Hosanna" is not an exclamation of praise, but the Hebrew imperative which means "save now." The Passover expectation was the return of God's

Messiah to deliver His people. The crowd, by the application of this Psalm to Jesus, gave Him the place of messiahship and called upon Him to reveal His power. It was another attempt to make Him king, though perhaps more intelligent and less materialistic in its aims than the former one had been (6:15).

The act of riding upon the ass, which is given so much space in the Synoptics, is mentioned only in passing. It is, however, connected with Old Testament prophecy.[1] The ass was used by judges and kings in the Old Testament on errands of peace; the horse was used mainly as a charger in battle. By this conscious fulfillment of prophecy, Jesus offered Himself as a king of peace, not as a warrior. He asserted royal claims, but not in the military manner. The ensuing bewilderment of the disciples was caused by their inability to reconcile His willingness to be recognized as the King of Israel with His unwillingness to exert the secular authority which they thought all kings should use. Not until after the resurrection did they understand His motives.[2]

The Visit of the Greeks (12:20-36a)

A new group, the "Greeks among those that went up to worship at the feast" (20), was now introduced. They were men of Gentile birth who spoke the Greek tongue, and who probably had become Jewish proselytes, since they were pilgrims to the Passover. Like Cornelius, the Roman centurion of Acts 10 and 11, they found in Judaism something better than the futile paganism of their day. The unity of Jehovah as contrasted with the multiplicity of the heathen deities, the majesty of His righteousness as opposed to the immoralities of their gods, the direct canonical revelation of the law instead of the idle speculations of conflicting philosophies made Judaism

---

1. See Zech. 9:9.
2. Cf. John 12:16 and 2:22. Both of these passages, in conjunction with the content of chs. 20 and 21, indicate that the disciples' interpretation of Jesus' person and work as recorded in the Gospels depended upon the post-resurrection experiences which they had with Him.

attractive to thinking Gentiles. Among such were Lydia (Acts 16:14), many of the converts in Thessalonica (Acts 17:4), a part of Paul's audience in Athens (Acts 17:17) and in Corinth (Acts 18:4). There were numerous converts to Judaism in the first century, and the early Gentile church owed a large number of its adherents to those who came to Christ from paganism by this intermediate step.

The approach of the Greeks to Jesus was indirect. Perhaps they felt hesitant about speaking to the great teacher of Judaism and preferred to work through a friend. In order to gain an introduction they came to Philip with their request: "Sir, we would see Jesus" (12:21).

Just why they chose Philip as their spokesman is uncertain. His name was Greek, meaning "lover of horses," and may indicate that he had been born in a Greek-speaking community. If so, he could converse in their language and understand their ways of thinking. He seems to have been singularly approachable, a man to whom one would feel like speaking without an introduction. Evidently he treated the Greeks kindly, for he promptly carried their request to his friend Andrew, and then both carried it to Jesus.

John does not tell whether or not the Greeks ever obtained the interview that they sought. Their overture served as the introduction to a long soliloquy by Jesus, comprising verses 23 through 36a. The pronoun "them" in verse 23 might refer to the Greeks, but the closer antecedent is Philip and Andrew. Furthermore, the remainder of the passage does not mention the Greeks again. The multitude reappears in verses 29 and 34 as participating in conversation with Jesus. Except insofar as "the Greeks" were part of the "multitude," one cannot be sure that Jesus answered them at all.

The introduction of the Greeks, however, was not incidental, for the discourse of Jesus prompted by their petition was important. It was a declaration of His purpose in coming to earth and of His resolution to fulfill that purpose. It corresponded to the scene in Gethsemane as narrated by the Synoptics, for it afforded a glimpse into His inner mind at this pivotal moment of His whole career.

Jesus' announcement that "the hour" had come (12:23) struck the keynote of His thought. The consciousness of the "hour" which would mark His destiny undergirds the whole of the Johannine account thus far. The concept first appeared in 2:4, where He told His mother that His "hour" had not yet come. The time was not ripe for the assertion of His Messianic claims. In chapter 7 He delayed His going to a feast because His "hour" was not come (7:6) and the failure of His enemies to apprehend Him was attributed to the same reason (7:30). The inquiry of the Greeks, on the other hand, showed that there was a rising interest in Him among the Gentiles who were outside of the promised Messianic blessing to Israel. They were "separate from Christ, alienated from the commonwealth of Israel, and strangers from the covenants of the promise, having no hope and without God in the world" (Eph. 2:12). To be sure, by submitting to the law as proselytes they might claim its blessings, but they could do so only on Jewish, not on Gentile, ground. A new covenant between God and man was necessary if Gentile Greeks could be admitted to the divine fellowship. Jesus recognized this appeal of the Greeks as a call for just such a covenant, which could be established only through His death. Those who "once were far off are made nigh in the blood of Christ" (Eph. 2:13). The genuine interest of the Gentiles called for the establishment of a new body in which there would be neither Jew nor Gentile, bond nor free; and such could be created only by His sacrifice and suffering.

The principle involved in this new covenant was the basic reason for the cross. Jesus made known that new life can come solely by the way of death when He said, "Verily, verily, I say unto you, Except a grain of wheat fall into the earth and die, it abideth by itself alone; but if it die, it beareth much fruit" (24). This law is as universal as harvest and as inexorable as centrifugal force. Applied in the spiritual realm, Jesus impressed upon His disciples as essential to their success this fundamental truth which He must demonstrate with His own death.

The result of this realization was distress. "Now is my soul troubled; and what shall I say?" (27). Two alternatives occurred to Jesus: He could ask to be delivered from the hour of His passion, or He could go through it. The natural revulsion of the human will against the possibility of death was well illustrated by His first alternative: "Father, save me from this hour." It was His instinctive reaction to danger, but the initial impulse must not be confused with basic purpose. The second alternative expressed the real will of Jesus: "But for this cause came I unto this hour" (27b). Not caprice, but principle governed the decision of the Son of God.

This resolution was not stubborn prejudice but was a part of Jesus' personal allegiance to the Father. His attitude was the complete fulfillment of the petition which He taught His disciples: "Hallowed be thy name" (Matt. 6:9). The exaltation of the name of the Father above all considerations of personal comfort or safety was the chief concern of His life. In this He showed perfect obedience and love to God.

The attitude of obedience to the Father was a judgment of the world because the cross displayed the contrast between the obedience of Christ and the rebelliousness of man. It was a victory over the devil because the sacrifice of God triumphed over the selfishness which is the root of the devil's whole philosophy. The prince of this world has gained his place by self-seeking, through trickery, deceit, and cruelty. The Son of God draws all men to Himself by dying a humiliating death in purity and honesty and forgiveness. Ultimate victory will rest with Christ.

Twice in this passage the response of the multitude is mentioned: once when the Father spoke from heaven, and again upon Jesus' announcement of His coming death. In the former instance the people heard only imperfectly the sounds which conveyed the Father's answer to Jesus' petition. Some of them explained the voice as thunder, while others, evidently thinking that it was significant, said that an angel spoke to Him (29). None, however, seemed to have understood exactly what it meant though Jesus stated that the voice came for their sakes (30). Like the other testimony which God gave, it was available to all the public, but was received only by those whose ears were tuned to it. This manifestation was parallel to the "voice" at the conversion of Paul which the witnesses "heard" in the sense that they recognized it as a vocal sound (Acts 9:7), but "heard not" in that they did not understand what was said (Acts 22:9).

The second response of the multitude concerned Jesus' prediction of the cross. They did not understand how He could be the Messiah if He were to undergo the suffering of death. "Lifted up"[3] meant to them crucifixion; and the death of the cross made an inexplicable contrast with their concept of the Son of man. Likewise "Son of man," if the term is to be traced back to Daniel 7:13, described a Messiah coming in the clouds of heaven. Surely, they reasoned, Jesus could not be speaking of the Messiah of the Old Testament; it must be some other Son of man. Jesus did not attempt a direct answer, but issued a final appeal to faith. "Yet a little while is the light among you. Walk while ye have the light, that darkness overtake you not: and he that walketh in the darkness knoweth not whither he goeth. While ye have the light, believe on the light, that ye may become sons of light" (35, 36a). The reference to light summarized all the spiritual teaching on this subject, beginning in the Prologue, and it concluded John's use of the

---

3. *Hypsoo* is used five times in John: 3:14 twice, 8:28, 12:32, 34. The word means "to lift up" or "exalt," but in this Gospel alone as with the implication of lifting up on a cross. Morally, the cross was a degradation rather than an exaltation. Jesus must have used the word deliberately to arrest the thought of his readers. To him the cross was a triumph, not a defeat.

term as a spiritual symbol. He who came into the world as the light which enlightens every man was about to leave it through the darkness of the cross. If His hearers were to profit by His presence, they must do so while He was still with them.

All the forces of belief and unbelief which influenced Jesus converged in the brief Period of Crisis. The hatred of the Jews, the jealousy of Judas, the devotion of Mary, the expectation of the Gentile world, the purpose for which Jesus had called and trained the disciples, the conquest of Satan, and, above all, the will of the Father focussed on the choice which produced the cross and the resurrection. There was still a private ministry to be fulfilled, as 12:36b indicates; but the decisive step was taken when He said, "But for this cause came I unto this hour. Father, glorify thy name" (12:27b, 28a). From this moment on, Jesus walked with unfaltering step to the cross.

THE PERIOD OF CONFERENCE

THE PERIOD OF CONFERENCE

A. TRANSITION
  1. The Author's Parenthesis
  2. The Appeal of Jesus
  3. The Last Supper
  4. The Dismissal of the Traitor

B. CONFERENCE WITH THE DISCIPLES
  1. Conference on Preparation
  2. Conference on Relationships
  3. Conference on Revelation

C. CONFERENCE WITH THE FATHER

CHAPTER VIII

The Period of Conference

12:36b to 17:26

TRANSITION (12:36b-13:30)

A CLEAR break is made in the sequence of John's narrative with the second clause of 12:36. There is a change from public activity to private seclusion, and the purpose of the writing changes also. The two closing paragraphs of the twelfth chapter form the transition between the long public ministry of Jesus and the brief hours of private conference that preceded the passion.

The Author's Parenthesis (12:36b-43)

The paragraph comprised by 12:36b-43 is parenthetical to the story as a whole. The last words of the preceding section in verse 36a are followed in sequence by those of verse 44, for the words of 36b state that Jesus retired from the scene of action, while those of verse 44 state that He made a public appeal. Verses 44 to 50 seemingly belong with the section ending at 36a rather than in the place where they are.

There is, however, no real break in logic, if both paragraphs be taken as transitional. The former of the two is a comment of the author which was introduced to explain the meaning of the crisis in terms of belief and unbelief. The word *believe* occurs twice in opposing statements:

"..yet they believed not on him." (37)
"..of the rulers many believed on him." (42)

193

The division of the public mind which had become so apparent in the last year of Jesus' ministry was thus brought to the center of attention.

In treating the subject of unbelief, the author had three suggestions to offer. The first was that it was illogical, and contrary to normal expectation. "But though he had done so many signs before them, yet they believed not on him" (37). John wanted to impress his readers with the astounding fact that men did not believe on Jesus in spite of all that He did. The unbelief itself seemed unbelievable.

The second suggestion was that unbelief was predicted. The rhetorical question of Isaiah 53:1, "Lord, who hath believed our report? And to whom hath the arm of the Lord been revealed?" was cited (38) as a prophetic forecast of the attitude of men toward Jesus. The content of Isaiah 53 which deals with the vicarious suffering of God's servant was thus applied to Jesus and legitimately may be employed to interpret the narrative that follows. The entire passion was thus lifted out of the realm of accident, and was shown to be the consummation of the prophetic pattern for the Son of God who was also God's redemptive servant.

The third suggestion was that unbelief was a direct result of God's revelation. "For this cause they could not believe, for that Isaiah said again,

> He hath blinded their eyes, and he hardened their heart;
> Lest they should see with their eyes, and perceive with their heart,
> And should turn,
> And I should heal them.
>   (12:39, 40)

This quotation was taken from the sixth chapter of Isaiah, which contains the account of Isaiah's commission. He had been sent by God to prophesy in the declining days of the kingdom of Judah. He was forewarned that his preaching would bring no results; on the contrary, the more he preached, the less response he would get. The very message which was intended to summon men to repentance would drive them farther from God. By a striking parallelism, John cited the experience of Isaiah as an explanation of the disappointing outcome of Jesus' ministry. The same principle at work in both was the obduracy of the unregenerate heart to the message of God.

In addition to the application of this general principle to the life work of Christ, John added the startling interpretation that Isaiah said these things when he saw Christ's glory and spake of Him. A comparison with the original text shows that the "glory" was Jehovah's. Perhaps this was a hint that John identified the LOGOS, incarnate in Christ, with the Jehovah of the Old Testament.

In his discussion of belief, John remarked that many of the rulers believed on Jesus, but secretly, for fear of being expelled from the synagogue. If their belief were secret, how did the author know about it? Possibly Joseph of Arimathea and Nicodemus were among that number, and told him later. Perhaps he had access to their circles and knew their sentiments. His scorching criticism, "they loved the glory that is of men more than the glory that is of God," was his verdict on their timid faith. Only a bold confession would be sufficient in this critical hour.

The Appeal of Jesus (12:44-50)

The utterance of Jesus in this paragraph, which belonged to the close of His public ministry, was intended to convey His own evaluation of belief and unbelief.

Belief in Christ involves also confidence in God. "He that believeth on me, believeth not on me, but on him that sent me" (44). This trust is a guaranteed approach to God, because Jesus was His authoritative representative among men.

Belief in Him results in light rather than in darkness. Faith is not intellectual and spiritual complacency, resting on fixed conclusions which have long since ceased to be vital.

Facing light requires enlargement of understanding and new
ventures in experience. It is the opposite of uncertainty, aim-
lessness, and negation, for Christ said, "I am come a light
into the world, that whosoever believeth on me may not abide
in the darkness" (46). He is the only way out of the darkness of sin which enshrouds all men.

Unbelief is not a polite unwillingness to assent to some
fact, but is a flat refusal to listen to His truth and to acknowledge His claims on one's personal life. "He that rejecteth me,
and receiveth not my sayings," (48) is Jesus' definition.

Unbelief faces certain judgment by the everlasting truth
which Christ proclaimed as it was given Him by the Father.
"He that rejecteth me, and receiveth not my sayings, hath one
that judgeth him: the word that I spake, the same shall judge
him in the last day" (48). The judgment will not be a matter
of caprice or of favoritism, but of eternal justice.

God's message in Christ is thus the hope of the believer
and the condemnation of the unbeliever. "His commandment
is life eternal" (50) and "the word . . . shall judge him in the
last day" (48).

The Last Supper (13:1-20)

John's account of the last meal of Jesus with His disciples
differs in many respects from that of the Synoptics. No mention is made of the preparation by Peter and John, nor of
the procedure during the meal, nor of the discourse concerning the significance of the bread and the cup, nor of the contention for primacy that took place among the disciples at the
supper. All of those are listed by one or more of the Synoptic
writers.[1] On the other hand, the Synoptics do not relate the
story of the footwashing, nor do they repeat fully Jesus' dis-

---

1. Cf. Matt. 26:17-30, Mark 14:12-26, Luke 22:7-30.

course on the example of service. Both John and the Synoptics include Jesus' disclosure of the treachery of Judas, and his sudden departure from the group. It may never be proved to the satisfaction of all that John did or did not have in his hands a copy of one or more of the Synoptic Gospels; but it seems reasonably certain that he knew the general body of current tradition that was recorded therein, and that he purposely added to it.

On the other hand, the narrative of chapter 13 has some affinities with the Synoptic record, particularly with that of Luke. All accounts are dated in the hours just preceding the Passover; the common center of interest was the last meal with the disciples; Jesus knew in advance the identity of the traitor; the episode of footwashing is more easily understandable if it is coupled with the quarrel of the disciples over who should be the greatest; the discourse on serving as given by Luke (22:24-30) accords closely with Jesus' explanation of the footwashing as given in JOHN (13:12-20); and the disclosure of the traitor was made through the dipping of the sop. The events of the Johannine and Synoptic accounts can be harmonized satisfactorily.

There is, however, a distinctive emphasis in the Johannine story. The key statement is "Jesus knowing that his hour was come that he should depart out of this world unto the Father, having loved his own that were in the world, he loved them unto the end" (1). The stress is not on the new covenant, which is prominent in the Synoptics, but on Jesus' personal love for His disciples. The meaning can be made clear by a paraphrase of verse 1: "Jesus . . . because he loved his own that were in the world, made one final demonstration of that love." The significance is not that He loved them to the last of His life, but that He loved them to the uttermost degree of which He was capable. The historic scene that followed was a dramatic exposition of the greatness of Christ's love for the disciples. It was a preview of the meaning of the cross, in which the essential elements of the divine love for man were all represented.

First, it was a love that could not be quenched by evil. The words, " . . . the devil having already put into the heart of Judas Iscariot, Simon's son, to betray him" modify the verbs "riseth," "layeth aside," "took," "girded himself" (4). The service by which Jesus expressed His care for His disciples was offered in spite of His full knowledge of the coming betrayal by Judas (11) and of the denial by Peter (38). Notwithstanding treachery and cowardice on the part of men, and professed followers at that, the divine love was given spontaneously and freely.

Second, it was a love that was tendered by Jesus in the full consciousness of His own exalted powers. "Knowing that the Father had given all things into his hands" (3), He deliberately subjected Himself to the needs of His disciples, and sacrificed Himself for them by submitting to an authority which was beneath Him. His words to Pilate, "Thou wouldest have no power against me, except it were given thee from above" (19:11), and His calm superiority to the numerous accusations of His enemies showed that He was a voluntary, not an unwilling, victim.

Third, the love of Christ transcended the barriers of social class. The words, "Knowing . . . that he came forth from God, and goeth unto God" (3) indicate that He was fully conscious of divine origin and of divine destiny. Nevertheless He condescended to minister to those who were His natural inferiors. Divine love leaped over the boundaries of class distinctions and made the Lord of Glory the servant of men.

The act of footwashing was an amazing example of condescension. According to custom in the oriental household, a slave washed the feet of guests who had come through the dust and filth of the street. Since the last supper was held in a private home, and probably as a secret meeting, it is understandable why no slave was present to fulfill this task. Furthermore, the disciples' minds were preoccupied with dreams of elevation to office in the coming kingdom. They were jealous lest one of their fellows should claim the best place. Consequently, no one of them was likely to abase himself by volunteering to wash the feet of the others. They were ready to fight for a throne, but not for a towel!

Fourth, the love of Jesus was an active love. Twice it is stated that the supper was interrupted. Chapter 13:2 says that it was "during supper" that the action took place, and then verse 4 emphasizes the statement by adding, "riseth from supper." The disciples, as they filed into the room, had looked for someone to wash their feet, but no slave was present. Rather than humiliate themselves, they were reclining with unwashed feet. Jesus, after waiting in vain for one of them to take the place of a servant, finally assumed the responsibility Himself. The task, however disagreeable, had to be performed; and love took the initiative.

Fifth, love cleanses. The colloquy between Jesus and Peter was illustrative of a principle deeper than a mere argument over social standing. Peter's protest against Jesus' washing his feet was prompted by shame, for he deemed it unfitting that the Master should wash the feet of a disciple. Jesus' answer, "What I do thou knowest not now; but thou shalt understand hereafter" (7) and "If I wash thee not, thou hast no part with me" (8), disclose a spiritual significance which Peter did not see. Later the meaning would be intelligible in the light of the cross which provided a cleansing for all men, without which no one could have a part in the heritage of the saints. As Paul said, "God . . . saved us, through the washing of re-

generation and renewing of the Holy Spirit . . . that, being
justified by his grace, we might be made heirs according to
the hope of eternal life" (Titus 3:4-7).

Sixth, love's cleansing must be constant. The awkward
and impulsive response of Simon Peter, "Lord, not my feet
only, but also my hands and my head" (9), was characteristic of the man. He did not want to miss any blessing that
Jesus might impart to him, and he was motivated by a genuine
affection for his Master. Jesus replied, "He that is bathed
needeth not save to wash his feet, but is clean every whit." The
words *bathe* and *wash* convey two different meanings. *Bathe*
(*louo*) meant a thorough washing of the entire body; *wash*
(*nipto*) was descriptive of washing a part of the body, such
as the face or hands. The essential uncleanness of the whole
man might be removed once for all, but a constant cleansing
was also necessary to remove the incidental defilement resulting from the casual contacts of life. The washing of the feet
was typical of the daily purification of the soul from the travel
stains of pilgrimage.

Finally, the statement, "Ye are clean, but not all," showed
that Jesus intended to teach a lesson in spiritual truth as well
as to discharge the social obligation of the moment. The uncleanness of Judas, to whom Jesus alluded by His remark,
was not in his feet but in his heart. The entire episode was an
acted parable, made all the more forcible by the material necessity which had evoked it.

In contrast to the self-seeking of the disciples, Jesus took
a place of humility. He set the example of service, not of strife,
of self-abasement rather than of self-exaltation. His assumption of the towel was a representation in miniature of His
entire career, an accurate picture of Philippians 2:6-8: "Who,
existing in the form of God, counted not the being on an equality with God a thing to be grasped, but emptied himself, tak-

ing the form of a servant, being made in the likeness of men; and being found in fashion as a man, he humbled himself, becoming obedient even unto death, yea, the death of the cross."

The humiliation of Jesus was instrumental to the removal of spiritual uncleanness, and He intended that His followers should dedicate themselves to the same ministry. Their energies should be devoted to the service and cleansing of one another rather than to seeking elevation at the expense of each other. "Bondslave" and "apostle" were the terms which Jesus used to describe their work. The bondslave was the property of his owner; the apostle was at the disposal of the one who had commissioned him for his task. He who took upon Himself the form of a bondslave (Phil. 2:7) and who was the "Apostle and High Priest of our confession" (Heb. 3:1) has by His own example established forever the measure of service in these two capacities. If He is Master and Lord, as He claimed (14), the bondslave and apostle is bound to follow His precedent.

The Dismissal of the Traitor (13:21-30)

The presence of Judas among the Twelve was a hindrance to further revelation on the part of Jesus. It was no obstacle to the example of sacrifice, but as long as Judas was in the group Jesus could not speak to them as a spiritual unit. "Ye are clean, but not all" (10) showed the disunity which He recognized.

This disunity was a source of grief to Jesus. The expression "troubled in the spirit," which opens the paragraph, described the pain which Judas' defection had caused Him. On two other occasions, at the grave of Lazarus (11:33) and on the arrival of the Greeks (12:27), similar words were used; and in all three instances they apply to the struggle with death that was confronting Him. The presence of Judas caused the keenest pain, for the other two were less a matter of personal treachery than of general necessity.

The declaration of the coming betrayal served as a warning to the disciples. John did not record their nervous, self-conscious question: "Is it I?" (Mark 14:19) He did, however, mention their interest in the traitor's identity as indicated by Peter's signal and the question of the beloved disciple. The answer of Jesus through the use of the "sop" (26) was both definite and merciful. He spoke no name, and so did not call the attention of the group as a whole to the guilty man. On the other hand, those who heard His answer and who watched closely would know whom He meant. Judas, doubtless prompted by fear, withdrew suddenly. Had the others realized his purpose, they might have killed him on the spot. Furthermore, Judas knew that Jesus had discovered his falsity; and his best defense would be immediate action.

The progress of evil within Judas is traceable in the successive allusions to him in the Gospel. In 6:70,71 Jesus spoke of him as a "devil," or adversary, for that is what the name means. This is one of the few occasions where the term is used as a descriptive noun rather than as a title of Satan. In 12:4-6, he was called a "thief." In 13:2, the devil is said to have put into his heart the idea of betraying Jesus; and in 13:27 it is said that Satan entered into him. His life was the antithesis of love, and its utter selfishness ended in Satanic control and in the sin which has made his name a byword to all subsequent generations.

CONFERENCE WITH THE DISCIPLES (13:31-16:33)

The entire passage from 13:31 through the sixteenth chapter constitutes one farewell address broken only by the interruptions of the disciples who are mentioned in the thirteenth and fourteenth chapters, and by the change of place in 14:31.

The fifteenth and sixteenth chapters fall between Jesus' suggestion to quit the place of the supper (14:31) and the actual arrival of the party at the garden of Gethsemane. This intervening discourse may have been spoken in the temple, which was kept open during the night preceding the Passover for the benefit of worshippers, or while the group dallied in the upper room after Jesus declared the meeting adjourned, or it may have been given as they slowly made their way through the darkened streets of the city to the gate through which they passed over to the Mount of Olives. The exact location is less important than its unity.

The character of this discourse as a conscious effort on Jesus' part to give the disciples final instruction is marked by the sevenfold repetition of the phrase, "These things I have spoken unto you."

1. These things have I spoken unto you. 14:25
2. These things have I spoken unto you. that your joy may be made full. 15:11
3. These things have I spoken unto you, that ye should not be caused to stumble. 16:1
4. These things have I spoken unto you......that ye may remember them. 16:4
5. Because I have spoken these things unto you, sorrow hath filled your heart. 16:6
6. These things have I spoken unto you in dark sayings. 16:25
7. These things have I spoken unto you, that in me ye may have peace. 16:33

Jesus must have used this phrase to summarize the reasons for the farewell discourse. Of these occurrences, the first draws a distinction between what He had spoken, or was speaking in the flesh, and what He would continue to teach through the agency of the Holy Spirit (14:25, 26). It marked the resumption of His main line of teaching after the last interruption by Judas, not Iscariot.

Four of these instances state the purpose of the farewell discourse:

2. That they may possess joy. 15:11
3. That they might not be shocked or demoralized by the imminent disaster. 16:1
4. That they may remember His words when the crisis comes. 16:4
7. That they may enjoy peace within in spite of outward turmoil. 16:33

One of the statements may point to the result of the discourse:

5. That sorrow has filled their hearts. 16:6

The last described the method for His revelation.

6. That He had spoken to them in dark sayings. 16:25

Each of these phrases refers to the teaching which immediately precedes it, and explains the motive or method behind the spoken word. John 14:25 summarizes the colloquy of 13:31-14:25; 15:11 indicates the purpose of the allegory of the vine, and the reality behind it, namely the creation of joy. Beginning with 16:1, the division of the text follows more closely the scheme afforded by the recurrence of this phrase, and presents a review of the last revelation which Jesus was trying to impress upon the disciples.

Three general units can be distinguished in the CONFERENCE WITH THE DISCIPLES: the *Conference on Preparation* (13:31-14:31) in which Jesus attempted to prepare His followers for the shock of His sudden removal; the *Conference on Relationships* (15:1-27) in which He explained the new relations which would obtain among them after His departure; and the *Conference on Revelation* (16:1-33) in which He laid down the principles by which they might maintain their connection with Him in the future.

Conference on Preparation (13:31-14:31)

The departure of Judas was obviously a relief to Jesus. As long as he was in the company, Jesus was not free to talk on the topics that occupied His mind, for Judas had no understanding of His motives and mission. The other disciples were equally ignorant of Jesus' real purpose, as their questions later showed, but the barrier between Judas and Jesus was unbelief. While all of Jesus' followers showed some trace of love for Him and some interest in His teachings, as far as the Scriptures indicate, Judas exhibited neither.

The opening of verse 31, "When therefore he was gone out," is more than a note of time. It indicated a change of atmosphere which enabled Jesus to disclose His mind more fully to the remaining eleven. Judas had committed himself to treachery and had gone about his nefarious business. Jesus, knowing that His fate was now settled as far as outward circumstances were concerned, proceeded to prepare His disciples for the approaching catastrophe. The section, 13:31 to 14:31, contains the initial part of the farewell discourse which probably was spoken in the upper room just before they concluded the Paschal meal with the establishment of the new covenant and then went out to the last gloomy rendezvous at Gethsemane.

The structure of this section is irregular. It consists of a progressive discourse of Jesus, interrupted at intervals by the questions of certain disciples, His replies to them, then reversion to His original line of thought. If the text be arranged with the principal discourse of Jesus in one column, and the questions with their answers in another, the result will be somewhat as follows:

A CHART OF THE CONFERENCE ON PREPARATION
(John 13:31-14:31)

DISCOURSE	OUTLINE	QUESTIONS
31 When therefore he was gone out, Jesus saith, Now is the Son of man glorified, and God is glorified in him; 32 and God shall glorify him in himself, and straightway shall he glorify him. 33 Little children, yet a little while I am with you. Ye shall seek me: and as I said unto the Jews, Whither I go, ye cannot come; so now I say unto you. 34 A new commandment I give unto you, that ye love one another; even as I have loved you, that ye also love one another. 35 By this shall all men know that ye are my disciples, if ye have love one to another.	Announcement → (13:31-35) Question of Peter (13:36-38) ←	
		36 Simon Peter saith unto him, Lord, whither goest thou? Jesus answered, Whither I go, thou canst not follow me now; but thou shalt follow afterwards. 37 Peter saith unto him, Lord, why cannot I follow thee even now? I will lay down my life for thee. 38 Jesus answereth, Wilt thou lay down thy life for me? Verily, verily, I say unto thee, The cock shall not crow, till thou hast denied me thrice.
14 Let not your heart be troubled; believe in God, believe also in me. 2 In my Father's house are many mansions; if it were not so, I would have told you; for I go to prepare a place for you. 3 And if I go and prepare a place for you, I come again, and will receive you unto myself; that where I am, *there* ye may be also. 4 And whither I go, ye know the way.	The Discussion of Destiny → (14:1-4) Question of Thomas (14:5-7) ←	5 Thomas saith unto him, Lord, we know not whither thou goest; how know we the way? 6 Jesus saith unto him, I am the way, and the truth, and the life: no one cometh unto the Father, but by me. 7 If ye had known me, ye would have known my Father also: from henceforth ye know him, and have seen him.

DISCOURSE	OUTLINE	QUESTIONS
12 Verily, verily, I say unto you, He that believeth on me, the works that I do shall he do also; and greater *works* than these shall he do; because I go unto the Father. 13 And whatsoever ye shall ask in my name, that will I do, that the Father may be glorified in the Son. 14 If ye shall ask anything in my name, that will I do. 15 If ye love me, ye will keep my commandments. 16 And I will pray the Father, and he shall give you another Comforter, that he may be with you for ever, 17 *even* the Spirit of truth: whom the world cannot receive; for it beholdeth him not, neither knoweth him: ye know him; for he abideth with you, and shall be in you. 18 I will not leave you desolate: I come unto you. 19 Yet a little while, and the world beholdeth me no more; but ye behold me: because I live, ye shall live also. 20 In that day ye shall know that I am in my Father, and ye in me, and I in you. 21 He that hath my commandments, and keepeth them, he it is that loveth me: and he that loveth me shall be loved of my Father, and I will love him, and will manifest myself unto him.	Question of Philip (14:8-11) ← The Instruction Resumed → (14:12-21) Question of Judas (14:22-24) ←	8 Philip saith unto him, Lord, show us the Father, and it sufficeth us. 9 Jesus saith unto him, Have I been so long time with you, and dost thou not know me, Philip? he that hath seen me hath seen the Father: how sayest thou, Show us the Father? 10 Believest thou not that I am in the Father, and the Father in me? the words that I say unto you I speak not from myself: but the Father abiding in me doeth his works. 11 Believe me that I am in the Father, and the Father in me: or else believe me for the very works' sake. 22 Judas (not Iscariot) saith unto him, Lord, what is come to pass that thou wilt manifest thyself unto us, and not unto the world? 23 Jesus answered and said unto him, If a man love me, he will keep my word: and my Father will love him, and we will come unto him, and make our abode with him. 24 He that loveth me not keepeth not my words: and the word which ye hear is not mine, but the Father's who sent me.

DISCOURSE	OUTLINE
25 These things have I spoken unto you, while *yet* abiding with you. 26 But the Comforter, *even* the Holy Spirit, whom the Father will send in my name, he shall teach you all things, and bring to your remembrance all that I said unto you. 27 Peace I leave with you; my peace I give unto you: not as the world giveth, give I unto you. Let not your heart be troubled, neither let it be fearful. 28 Ye heard how I said to you, I go away, and I come unto you. If ye loved me, ye would have rejoiced, because I go unto the Father: for the Father is greater than I. 29 And now I have told you before it come to pass, that, when it shall come to pass, ye may believe. 30 I will no more speak much with you, for the prince of the world cometh: and he hath nothing in me; 31 but that the world may know that I love the Father, and as the Father gave me commandment, even so I do. Arise, let us go hence.	The Discourse Completed → (14:25-31)

THE FOUR QUESTIONS

PERSON	POINT OF DEPARTURE	CONTENT	ATTITUDE	ANSWER
Peter	"Whither I go, ye cannot come." 13:33	"Lord, whither goest thou?" 13:36a *Destiny*	Curiosity Eagerness Loyalty Rashness	Disillusionment Reproof Encouragement
Thomas	"Whither I go, ye know and the way ye know" 14:4 AV	"How can we know the way?" 14:5 AV *Knowledge*	Petulance Pessimism	Disclosure Self-revelation Challenge to personal contact
Philip	"If ye had known me, ye would have known my Father also; from henceforth ye know him, and have seen him." 14:7.	"Lord, show us the Father, and it sufficeth us." 14:8 *Reality*	Obtuseness Yearning	Evidence Person Words Works
Judas (not Iscariot)	". . . I will love him, and will manifest myself unto him." 14:21.	"Lord, what is come to pass that thou wilt manifest thyself unto us and not unto the world?" 14:22 *Revelation*	Confusion Amazement	Love

Since the discourse as a whole was unified by the occasion on which it was spoken, an attempt to partition it into clearly marked sections may be artificial. Such division, nevertheless, does clarify the thought which the author evidently wished to impress upon his readers when he reduced to writing the sayings of Jesus and the questions of the disciples.

The Introductory Announcement (13:31-35)

The introductory announcement of Jesus, "Now is the Son of man glorified, and God is glorified in him; and God shall glorify him in himself, and straightway shall he glorify him," set the theme for the main line of the discourse. "Glorify" was used in a specialized sense, referring to the culmination of the divine purpose in the career of Christ. The general meaning of the word is to magnify or extol, to exalt to a position of honor. John applied it here, and in a few other passages, to the death of Jesus. In 7:39 he stated that "the Spirit was not yet given; because Jesus was not yet glorified." In this verse "glorified" referred to a definite historical event because it was used for the dating of the coming of the Spirit. The same idea appeared in 12:16: "These things understood not his disciples at the first: but when Jesus was glorified, then remembered they that these things were written of him . . . " At the appearance of the Greeks, Jesus said, "The hour is come, that the Son of man should be glorified" (12:23), by which He referred to His coming passion. In the final prayer Jesus petitioned the Father, "Glorify thy Son" (17:1). By His passion, in which the death of the cross was central, the Father would be magnified among men, and Jesus would be exalted as a Savior. Paradoxically, the hour of His greatest humiliation would be the hour of His supreme glory.

The disciples, however, were totally unprepared for any such viewpoint of His death. They had been so occupied with what they thought the Messiah ought to do that they had been oblivious of what He had said He would do, although He had not failed to inform them. At the visit to Jerusalem recorded in chapter 2 He had spoken of the destruction of the temple of His body (2:20,21). In the interview with Nicodemus He had predicted being "lifted up" on the cross (3:14). He had spoken frequently of "giving himself" (6:51) and of "laying down his life" (10:11). The farewell discourse was a last attempt to prepare them for the shock which the passion would inevitably inflict upon them.

His first care, then, was to warn the disciples of His impending departure and to tell them that they could not follow Him at once. Death for Him was not a dead end street, but rather a trail which He must blaze alone as a pioneer. The Shepherd, in preparing the way for His sheep, had to explore the way before it would be fit for them to travel.

Furthermore, when He left them behind, it was necessary that they should maintain unity among themselves. The differences of temperament and the jealousies which He had already witnessed would alienate them from one another unless some powerful cohesive force were found to hold these tendencies in check. A disunited band of disciples would fall an easy prey to their enemies, and would afford a poor instrument for His subsequent plans. Therefore, He issued to them a new commandment. "Love one another; even as I have loved you" (34). This mutual love would be the permanent badge of discipleship, and the foundation of unity among them.

The Question of Peter (13:36-38)

Peter, aroused to curiosity by Jesus' prediction that He would go away, asked Him: "Lord, whither goest thou?" His query, concrete and pointed as it was, embodied the larger question of human destiny: Is there any destination after death? Jesus replied, "Whither I go, thou canst not follow me now; but thou shalt follow afterwards" (36). With characteristic impatience, Peter said, "Lord, why cannot I follow thee even now?" Jesus' "now" meant *the present period* and Peter's "now" meant *this very moment.* Peter probably was thinking of physical hindrances to following Jesus, while Jesus had in mind Peter's spiritual and moral unfitness to face the impending danger. Rashly but courageously Peter avowed his willingness to jeopardize his life for Jesus. The Master, knowing Peter better than he knew himself, questioned his

promise, and calmly predicted that before the cock crew the
following morning Peter would deny Him three times. There
was a latent irony in Jesus' prophecy. It would do Peter little
good to be given certainty about the remote future when he
could not forecast accurately his own behavior in the immediate future.

The Discussion of Destiny (14:1-4)

With 14:1 Jesus reverted to the original teaching which
He had begun before Peter interrupted Him, and at the same
time gave a fuller answer to Peter's question. The change
from a singular address "thou," in verse 38, to a plural address
"you," in 14:2, marked the transition. Jesus first had answered
Peter individually, and now was including him in the reply
which was addressed to the general group.

The counsel of 14:1 was doubtless the outcome of the attitude
of the ten as they listened to Jesus' words of warning to Peter,
and of the dismay that all of them felt when Jesus announced
that He was about to leave them. If their leader and spokesman were soon to deny Jesus, how could they trust themselves?
If Jesus were leaving them, would they not be helpless and
friendless in the midst of a hostile city? Terror must have
gripped them, and have appeared on their pale faces and in
their frightened eyes. Then Jesus gave to them another command: "Let not your heart be troubled: believe in God, believe
also in me." The first counsel was directed against disunity;
this exhortation was a cure for fear.

The second half of this command is susceptible of several
translations. As far as form is concerned, the verb *believe*
may be either indicative or imperative in either or both sentences. By the use of the double imperative, as the Revised
Version quite correctly translates it, Jesus suggested that the
proper approach to the question of human destiny is faith in
a personal God. If a personal God exists, who is the judge and
redeemer of man, there must be a destiny for man beyond the

grave. Jesus Himself had expounded the meaning of this faith in His reply to the question of the Sadducees recorded by Matthew. "But as touching the resurrection of the dead, have ye not read that which was spoken unto you by God, saying, I am the God of Abraham, and the God of Isaac, and the God of Jacob? God is not the God of the dead, but of the living" (Matt. 22:31,32). The hope of immortality is founded upon a personal relation with a living God.

Beyond this faith in God which His disciples undoubtedly possessed because of their Jewish background, He asked that they have a personal faith in Him. The words must have shocked them, since He bracketed Himself with God and asked that they believe Him equally with God. He required also by these words that they believe Him against all odds. He was doomed to death, the death that overtakes all men. Nevertheless He had the audacity to demand that they make Him an object of faith. He made Himself the key to the question of destiny, and clearly stated that their future depended on His work. He promised to prepare a place for them, and to return to claim them.

The "many mansions" did not refer to palatial residences, but rather to "abiding places." Perhaps "apartments"[2] would be a better translation. To the modern American the word "mansion" connotes a large house on a broad estate, larger and more luxurious than the ordinary middle class dwelling. In the Orient the sons and daughters of a wealthy patriarch, with their families, often lived under his roof. The one great house contained living quarters for all. By analogy, Jesus intimated that there would be room for all in the Father's house.

In discussing the important problem of human destiny, Jesus used very simple language, and spoke in clear, though

---

2. Suggested by Henry G. Liddell and Robert Scott in *A Greek-English Lexicon,* (New Edition, Edited by H. S. Jones, Oxford: Clarendon Press), II, p. 1143.

restrained fashion. Two thoughts stood out in His statement: human destiny involves both a *place* and a *person*. The place is the Father's house. However one may "spiritualize" this language, it implied definite surroundings which contribute to happiness. The person is Christ Himself, whose presence would make the place glorious. Eternal companionship with Him is the expectation of the saved.

Jesus' words made this expectation a certainty. He never would have promised to prepare a place for the disciples if He were not sure that they would reach it. In spite of Peter's denial, and of the fears and failures which He foresaw for all of them, and which they felt for themselves, He was confident of their ultimate arrival at the Father's house because He was sure of Himself. His confidence appeared in His words: "I go to prepare a place for you . . . I come again, and will receive you unto myself; that where I am, there ye may be also." Faith in Him was their key to security, no matter how well-grounded their fears for themselves might be.

The Question of Thomas (14:5-7)

The second question was put by Thomas, who contradicted flatly Jesus' last statement, "Whither I go, ye know the way," and then despairingly asked, "How know we the way?"[3] The pessimism of Thomas was thrown into sharp relief by his use of the word "know." "We know not . . . how know we . . . ?" He was in the position of the man who raised a dust and then complained that he could not see. Jesus had just explained that faith in Him was the key to destiny. Thomas' initial denial brought disheartening results because it was a false step in reasoning. Solutions to human problems are never found in skepticism, but rather in the affirmation of faith.

---

3. The alternate reading, "How can we know the way?" as given in the AV, has fair manuscript support. If accepted as correct, it makes Thomas' pessimism all the deeper, for it represents him as doubting not only knowledge, but the possibility of knowledge.

Here, as elsewhere, Jesus did not upbraid Thomas for his unbelief, but held out to him a positive declaration on which he could base his thinking. "I am the way, and the truth, and the life: no one cometh unto the Father, but by me" (14:6).

This affirmation of Jesus is one of the greatest philosophical utterances of all time. He did not say that He knew the way, the truth, and the life, nor that He taught them. He did not make Himself the exponent of a new system; He declared Himself to be the final key to all mysteries.

He was the *way*. Between the present of man's failure, and the future of God's design for him is a gulf which seems unbridgeable. Thomas recognized it, and so despaired. Jesus said, "I am the way," for in Him man is brought back to God, and through the Living Way he achieves his true destiny.

He was the *truth*. Truth is the scarcest commodity in the world. All the philosophers had sought for it; none had attained it. No one mind was great enough to grasp it; no one personality was pure enough to achieve it by conduct. Truth is neither an abstract system of integrated propositions, nor is it an impersonal ethic contained in many rules. It is both the reality and the ethic expressed in a person who is more flexible than legal rigidity and incomprehensible abstraction, and who is, notwithstanding, unchanging and consistent. Christ spoke with final authority in words adapted to human understanding.

He was the *life*. The way was a means of reaching the Father; the truth defined the righteous standards of the way; the life bespoke the dynamic which could make attainment possible. All through the Gospel of John *life* describes the principle of spiritual vitality that originates with God and that lifts men out of sin to Himself. "In him was life; and the life was the light of men" (1:4). Christianity is not a system of philosophy, nor a ritual, nor a code of laws; it is the impartation of a divine vitality. Without the way there is no going, without the truth there is no knowing, without the life there is no

living. Many others beside Christ have offered systems of
thought that purported to bridge the gap between man and
God; none other has by His own person succeeded in bridg-
ing it. "No one," He said, "cometh unto the Father, but by
me."

Jesus attributed the disciples' misunderstanding of His
words to their ignorance. "If ye had known me, ye would have
known my Father also" (7). It may be inferred from this language that the disciples had not come to an intimate knowledge
of His person, and so were incapable of apprehending His revelation of the Father. In the sense of personal acquaintance
they knew Him very well; at least, as well as anyone did. In
the sense of spiritual discernment, their knowledge of Him
was small, for they had not the faintest concept of what His
real objectives were. Since their understanding came to perfection only after the resurrection, it is fair to deduce that
true knowledge of God must include cognition of His redemptive procedure in dealing with man as well as the more obvious
demonstration of His power in the natural creation.

The Question of Philip (14:8-11)

The teaching of Jesus with reference to His relation with
the Father was too subtle for Philip. "Lord, show us the Father, and it sufficeth us" (8). Philip wanted to see the Father
as plainly as he could see Jesus. Metaphysical distinctions and
theological explanations meant comparatively little to him. He
was slow to apprehend anything of an abstract nature; he was
preeminently a "practical" man. Philip could think in terms
of statistics, when he was confronted by the problem of feeding the multitude (6:5-7); but he was totally at a loss for an
answer when Jesus stepped from the realm of the material into
the realm of the spiritual.

To say that Philip was baffled by spiritual truth is not the
same as saying that he was indifferent to it. His request revealed a consuming earnestness that was more than curiosity.

If only God could be made visible to him, if He could be brought down to the level where he could understand Him, he would be satisfied. Philip is the representative of the dull but earnest seeker, who desires to know God but who finds that no concept of Him adequately fulfills his desire. It is the New Testament echo of Job's passionate cry: "Oh that I knew where I might find him!" (Job 23:3).

The human longing for a tangible God coupled with a thoroughgoing rejection of the real God whose demands of righteousness are unwelcome, lies at the root of all idolatry. In order to satisfy his craving, man creates a God in his own image, or in the image of what he conceives God to be. The strictures of the second commandment, "Thou shalt not make unto thee a graven image, nor any likeness of anything that is in heaven above, or that is in the earth beneath, or that is in the water under the earth" (Exodus 20:4), are directed against all such ikons, images, and idols. They are at best only the imperfect portrayals of an imperfect concept, and are a perversion of the true worship which should be accorded to God alone.

The need of man still remains, and God has condescended to satisfy it. Wood and stone can never represent God, but flesh and blood may incarnate Him. The eternal Son, who is the radiance of God's glory and the impress of His essential being,[4] has expressed the person of God in human flesh. Therefore Jesus replied to Philip: "Have I been so long time with you, and dost thou not know me, Philip? he that hath seen me hath seen the Father; how sayest thou, Show us the Father?" (9) Jesus claimed such unity with the Father that His very appearance bespoke the Father's character and reality. As surely as Philip could perceive Jesus with the senses which he possessed and have the assurance of His actual physical existence, so could he be assured that the Father was real.

---

4. Paraphrased from Heb. 1:3: radiance is the Greek word *apaugasma* which means "irradiation," like the rays of the sun; impress, *charakter,* the stamp produced by a die or seal on wax.

Such an assertion demands corroboration, and Jesus gave it. He asked Philip to believe, first of all, because of His personality. "Believest thou not that I am in the Father, and the Father in me?" (10) The conscious presence of the Father which Jesus enjoyed at all times was a testimony of unity between the Father and Himself. In the deepest recesses of His soul He was as certain of the Father's nearness as He was of His own existence. Jesus' intimate relationship with the Father must have been apparent to all the disciples; and they could not deny it without denying the reality of the whole sphere of His life, to say nothing of impugning His honesty.

The subjective test of the Father's presence was supplemented by objective evidence: "The words that I say unto you I speak not from myself: but the Father abiding in me doeth his works" (10). The author of the Gospel confirmed Jesus' witness, for he said: "For he whom God hath sent speaketh the words of God" (3:34). Even Jesus' enemies had admitted that "Never man so spake" (7:46). His words carried with them an authority which could come only from a divine source. In comparison with all the utterances of the sages and saints, they were unique in their finality and power.

Lest anyone should deny the validity of His words, Jesus added also the testimony of the works. The various miracles or signs which He performed were the visible evidence of the Father's power operating in and through Him. Participation in this testimony was promised to the believer also. "Verily, verily, I say unto you, He that believeth on me, the works that I do shall he do also; and greater works than these shall he do" (12) made the disciples partners in the mission of Jesus. The "greater works" which they would do through the name of Jesus would be a witness to the immanence of the Father and to the truthfulness of the Son.

The objective of the works was the glorification of the Father in the Son. The purpose of the Son was to make the Father known to the world, and the promise contained in verses 13 and 14 was dependent upon that purpose. "If ye shall ask anything in my name, that will I do," should not be construed as a guarantee to fulfill every whim of a petitioner, but rather to complete the revelation of the Father which was begun with the incarnation. The answers to prayer in the name of Jesus are the Father's works which take place through Him.

The Instruction Resumed (14:12-21)

Verses 12 to 14, which have been treated above as completing the answer of Jesus to Philip's request, are difficult to allocate. The imperative, *believe*, in verse 11 is plural; and, by analogy with verse 1, it should be considered as the logical resumption of the address to the entire group of disciples. The continued reference to "works," however, in verse 11 unites it closely with the last of verse 10. Verse 12 continues the reference to "works"; but the main subject changes to the third person, and makes the statement a general truth rather than a personal exhortation. The full emphasis in the second person plural begins in 13. The best method of partition is to consider verse 12 as marking the division, but as transitional back to the main line of teaching after the digression occasioned by the questions of Thomas and Philip.

Having assured the disciples that He was not deserting them but rather going before to prepare a place for them, Jesus proceeded to ask for their obedience. "If ye love me, ye will keep my commandments" (15). If their distress over the prediction of His departure were genuine, it meant that they loved Him. If they really loved Him, they must show it by obedience. Love was to be the new motive for their lives; obedience to Him the new standard for their activity.

The provision for their future included also a new dynamic, the Holy Spirit. Several assertions were made concerning Him in this discourse:

He is an answer to Jesus' prayer to the Father. (16)
He is another "Comforter." (16)
He dwells permanently with the believer. (16)
He is called the Spirit of Truth. (17)
He is unknown to the "world." (17)
He will dwell *in* the believer. (17)

The term "Comforter" is misleading to modern ears. It does not mean "sympathizer" so much as "advocate," one who is called in to defend against accusation and to represent a client in court or to transact business for him. The only use of this word outside of the Fourth Gospel occurs in I John 2:1, where Christ is called an Advocate. He represents believers before the Father as the Holy Spirit represents the Father to believers. The function of the Spirit is to make the reality of God convincing to all men in the same way that Jesus did to His disciples. Had He remained upon earth, He would necessarily have been restricted by space and time as are all men. The indwelling of the Spirit in the hearts of Jesus' followers would provide a fellowship with God even closer than they had experienced in the physical presence of Jesus.

The Holy Spirit is the token of difference between the Christian and the unbeliever. "The world" cannot receive Him; He indwells the Christian. As Paul said, "If any man hath not the Spirit of Christ, he is none of his" (Rom. 8:9b). The measure of the fullness of the Spirit may vary in the individual life; but the presence of the Spirit is essential to true Christian experience. The difference between *with you* and *in you* (17) is significant, for it shows that whereas the Spirit was watching over the disciples at the time when Jesus spoke, a crisis was coming in which the Spirit would enter into the lives of the disciples and control them from within. Such an experience had not yet been theirs; it came later at Pentecost.

The promise of return in verse 18, "I will not leave you desolate: I come unto you" may be interpreted in three different ways. It may be regarded as a promise of the appear-

ances after the resurrection; or it may refer to the coming of
Jesus in the person of the Holy Spirit; or it may be prophetic
of the second coming. The last of these alternatives is least
probable, for Jesus was not discussing His return, but the
matter of further contact between Himself and His disciples.
If the promise in verse 19, "the world beholdeth me no more;
but ye behold me," be applied to His presence through the
Holy Spirit, a confusion of terms follows. The descent of the
Spirit, Jesus' incarnation, and the manifestation of the Father
are separate and are not to be identified one with the other.
A comparison of this passage with the parallel in 16:16-22,
28, 29, suggests that He was referring to His return to them
after the resurrection, when the mourning occasioned by His
death would be turned to joy because of His restoration. In
His victory over the grave there was a promise of life for
them: "Because I live, ye shall live also" (19).

Such a revelation, however, was given only to those who
were obedient. A fuller manifestation was conditional upon a
relationship of love obtaining between the disciple and the
Lord. The cross was to be the final revelation of God to the
hostile world; but the disciples could look beyond the cross.

The Question of Judas (14:22-24)

"Judas (not Iscariot) saith unto him, Lord, what is come to
pass that thou wilt manifest thyself unto us, and not unto the
world?"

Judas is doubtless identical with Judas of James mentioned
in Luke 6:16 and Acts 1:13, and with the Thaddaeus of Mark
3:18 and Matthew 10:3. He seems to have been of minor
importance, for on no other occasion is he reported as participating in any action or discussion.

The problem which he raised was that of revelation. He
could not understand how Jesus, if He reappeared to His disciples after a temporary withdrawal, could avoid showing
Himself to the world. He may also have followed the line of

reasoning adopted by Jesus' brethren: "No man doeth anything in secret, and himself seeketh to be known openly"
(7:4). If He were to manifest Himself finally as the Messiah,
why should he not declare Himself to the world in that capacity? And, if such a revelation were so restricted as not to
be perceptible by the majority of men, what assurance could
any man have of its reality? Anything that is perceivable by
all is at least acknowledged to be a fact, whether its implications
are accepted or not; but if only a minority pronounce a thing
to be true, the majority are likely to brand it as hallucination.

Jesus' answer emphasized love as the condition of revelation. The attitude of the disciple was to be the determinative
factor. "If a man love me, he will keep my word: and my
Father will love him, and we will come unto him, and make
our abode with him" (23). Direct communication with the
world was impossible because of its hatred, but He could deal
with the disciples on the basis of love. Love in turn engenders
obedience, and progressive revelation is possible only where
obedience exists. God does not give a second and greater disclosure of Himself to the man who does not respond to the
obligations amplified in the first command that he received.
Lack of love produces disobedience; and Jesus regarded disobedience as an insult to the Father.

The Discourse Completed (14:25-31)

The question of Judas created much less of an interruption
in the discourse of Jesus than did the previous questions of the
other disciples, for He was able to continue the answer to
Judas and at the same time pick up again the main thread of
His thought. The direct reply dealing with the condition of
revelation reiterated what He had said in verse 21, and resumed the discussion of the means of revelation, the active
agency of the Holy Spirit. The Spirit's advent would com-
pensate for the bodily absence of Jesus and would carry on to
complete fulfillment His promise: "I come unto you." The

post-resurrection appearances brought Him back to them in tangible form, so that they were convinced of His continued existence; but those manifestations ceased shortly. The permanent ministry of the invisible Spirit stayed to make the presence of Jesus felt and to make His counsel effective, as the book of Acts demonstrates.

Jesus outlined the functions of the Spirit in making the revelation actual. He could supply the authority of revelation because He would be an adequate and accredited representative of Jesus: "Whom the Father will send in my name" (26). He would guarantee the clarity of revelation, for He would be a capable teacher and expositor: "He shall teach you all things" (26). By the Spirit, the disciples were assured of the continuity of revelation. He could renew memory, so that the words of Jesus spoken while He was in the flesh would retain their vividness. "He shall . . . bring to your remembrance all that I said unto you" (26).

The concept of authority in revelation was conveyed by the phrase "in my name" which appears thirteen times in the Gospel of John, exclusive of a quotation from Psalm 118:25, 26. Six of these instances refer to prayer "in the name" of Jesus. Almost all mean that one person acts on the authority of another, as supported by the personality behind the name. John 5:43 illustrates the point where Jesus said: "I am come in my Father's name, and ye receive me not: if another shall come in his own name, him ye will receive." The Holy Spirit, sent in the name of Jesus, would come with His authority, and the message of the Spirit should be received as if Jesus Himself were speaking.

The instruction of the Spirit assures the clarity of revelation. Many of Jesus' teachings were obscure to His disciples because they did not have sufficient spiritual background to understand His underlying thought. He did not bequeath to

them a fixed system of propositions to be memorized in order
to insure their perception of His truth. Instead He promised
them the presence of the active living Spirit, who could speak
for Him with convicting power. The writer, John, spoke of
this when he said in his First Epistle, "Ye have an anointing
from the Holy One, and ye know all things" (I John 2:20).
The completeness of this teaching is affirmed by another passage in the same epistle: "And as for you, the anointing which
ye received of him abideth in you, and ye need not that any
one teach you; but as his anointing teacheth you concerning
all things" (I John 2:27). Such teaching is direct and appeals
to the inner consciousness of the believer rather than to his
outward ear. It creates a spiritual sensitivity that the world
does not possess.

The continuity of revelation is likewise guaranteed by the
Holy Spirit. Because the disciples were human, they were
likely to forget what Jesus said. Some of His words were
doubtless often repeated and so would have remained long in
their memories; other sayings no less important would have
been overlooked easily because they were uttered casually or
when the disciples were inattentive. Besides, if His words
were remembered in their exact form, the understanding of
them might change. Even if they were committed to writing
immediately so that their substance could not be lost, false or
inadequate interpretation could rob them of their true meaning. The voice of the Holy Spirit alone could stimulate the
disciples' minds to recall the utterances of Jesus and could
explain them correctly as needed.

Calling to remembrance, however, implies learning, for men
cannot remember what they never knew. Jesus did not intend
that the Holy Spirit should be regarded as a substitute for
learning. He expected that the disciples would pay close attention to His teachings, so that the Spirit might direct the use
of what they had acquired.

With verse 27 the discourse on revelation was completed, and Jesus returned to the original procedure of giving farewell instructions and comfort. The final gift was peace, defined in terms of Himself, "my peace" (27). Paradoxically, He bequeathed it to the disciples in the very moment when it seemed farthest from Him. Jesus had said a few days before, "Now is my soul troubled" (12:27), and He was yet to experience a fuller agony in Gethsemane, where He "began to be greatly amazed, and sore troubled" (Mark 14:33). His peace did not consist in freedom from turmoil and suffering, but in a calm undeviating devotion to the will of God. Like the compass of a ship, which steadily points north no matter how the ship may be rocked in a storm, Jesus' mind was at rest because of His trust in the Father. Precisely for this reason He bequeathed a different peace from that of the world which consists of temporary compromise or of heedless complacency. Jesus found tranquility in adherence to the will of God even on the verge of the cross.

The threefold result of Jesus' voluntary death is aptly summarized in the last few verses of the fourteenth chapter. The effect on the disciples was defined in His words: "And now I have told you before it come to pass, that, when it is come to pass, ye may believe" (29). The careful predictions of His passion seemingly had been lost on His followers, but Jesus said that in the hour of testing they would believe because His words would be fulfilled.

To Satan, "the prince of the world," mentioned by the same title in 12:31, the farewell of Jesus was defiance. Like a traveler who crosses unscathed the kingdom of his enemy, Jesus traversed the realms of death but was not taken captive. He knew that Satan had no claim on Him, and so He was able to pass through the devil's power without fearing the consequences.

To "the world" the coming death was intended to be the clearest and fullest demonstration of Jesus' love to the Father. "That the world may know that I love the Father, and as the Father gave me commandment, even so I do" (31). The world did not love the Father and had no true conception of what such a relationship meant. The death of Christ was an utter contrast to the spirit of the world which was epitomized in the jest of His enemies: "Save thyself, and come down from the cross" (Mark 15:30).

With these words of encouragement and warning, Jesus closed the first stage of the discourse. "Arise, let us go hence," was the signal for the end of the meal, and for the departure from the city.

Conference on Relationships (15:1-27)

The Relation of the Believers to Jesus (15:1-11)

The first and most important relationship which the disciples should maintain was with Jesus. In order to enforce its meaning, He used the allegory of the vine. This device was not unfamiliar to the disciples, for the culture of the vine was one of the common occupations of that day in Palestine. Vineyards were everywhere, and it may be that they passed several on the road from Jerusalem to Gethsemane. The vine was also known as an emblem of their own nation, just as the eagle is the emblem of the United States. Over the temple of Herod which was then standing was the symbolic decoration of a great golden vine. Isaiah had used the same figure to point out how Israel had disappointed God by its unproductiveness (Isa. 5:1-7). He concluded the parable by saying: "For the vineyard of Jehovah of hosts is the house of Israel, and the men of Judah his pleasant plant: and he looked for justice, but, behold, oppression; for righteousness, but, behold, a cry." Jesus made a different use of the same imagery by applying it to the relation between Himself and His disciples.

Five points of resemblance between the vine and this relationship are given:

The Right Stock	"I am the true vine" (1).
The Right Expert	"My Father is the husbandman" (1).
The Right Culture	"Every branch in me that beareth not fruit, he taketh it away: and every branch that beareth fruit, he cleanseth it, that it may bear more fruit" (2).
The Right Contact	"Abide in me, and I in you" (4).
The Right Fruitage	"The same beareth much fruit" (5).

The first essential in planting a vineyard is to have the right stock. Every nurseryman guarantees that the plants that he sells will run true to type. Since the word "true" in verse 1 means "genuine" or "real," Jesus claimed to be the one true stock. Just as there must be an original vine from which all specimens of a given variety are taken, so He alone is the source of the heavenly life of the spiritual vine.

Every vineyard must be pruned by an expert. The vinedresser had to know how and when to prune and fertilize the vine, so that it would produce the maximum crop. The spiritual vineyard is tended by God Himself, who knows best how to train and develop the personality of man.

Viticulture, however, consists mainly of pruning. In pruning a vine, two principles are generally observed: first, all dead wood must be ruthlessly removed; and second, the live wood must be cut back drastically. Dead wood harbors insects and disease and may cause the vine to rot, to say nothing of being unproductive and unsightly. Live wood must be trimmed back in order to prevent such heavy growth that the life of the vine goes into the wood rather than into fruit. The vineyards in the early spring look like a collection of barren, bleeding stumps; but in the fall they are filled with luxuriant purple grapes. As the farmer wields the pruning knife on his vines, so God cuts dead wood out from among His saints, and often cuts back the living wood so far that His method seems cruel. Nevertheless, from those who have suffered the most there often comes the greatest fruitfulness.

The process of pruning must never sever the fruitbearing branch from the main vine. Cuttings will often bear leaves independently through the vitality resident in them, but they will never bear fruit. "As the branch cannot bear fruit of itself, except it abide in the vine; so neither can ye, except ye abide in me" (4). The word "abide" which occurs ten times in this passage (1-10), means the maintenance of an unbroken connection rather than repose, and bespeaks the necessity of a constant active relationship between the believer and his Lord, if the resultant life is to be productive.

The ideal measure of productivity is stated by a threefold progression:

"Every branch that beareth fruit" (2).
"He cleanseth it, that it may bear more fruit" (2).
"The same beareth much fruit." (5).

Fruit, more fruit, much fruit is the divine order. Growth brings increase of fruitfulness, and the more mature a believer becomes, the more may be expected of him.

The nature of the fruit is not stated categorically, but the context following the allegory suggests what the fruit is. Fruitfulness is implied in a prayer life that brings answers: "If ye abide in me, and my words abide in you, ask whatever ye will, and it shall be done unto you" (7). Fruitfulness appears in obedience, which is a sure mark of the believer as disobedience is a mark of the unbeliever. Joy is mentioned here as a spiritual fruit, as well as in the familiar quotation of Galatians 5:22: "But the fruit of the Spirit is love, joy, peace, longsuffering, kindness, goodness, faithfulness, meekness, self-control; against such there is no law." John also includes love (12), as does Paul. These qualities of love toward others, joy within one's own heart, spontaneous obedience to Christ, and a prayer life that brings concrete answers are convincing proofs of the actuality of the life of God in the soul of man. "By their fruits ye shall know them" (Matt. 7:16).

The Relation of Believers to Each Other (15:12-17)

Having explained the essential relationship of believers to Himself, Jesus proceeded to show His disciples what their relationship to each other should be. The differences of temperament among them and the jealousies that had arisen over the positions which they expected to hold in the coming kingdom made their group unstable. Jesus knew that if they were to maintain an adequate testimony for Him they could do so only as a unit. Disunity would mar their work, if indeed it did not vitiate that work altogether. For this reason He gave them the eleventh commandment: "This is my commandment, that ye love one another, even as I have loved you" (12).

The comparative clause in verse 12, "even as I have loved you," gave the standard by which all real love can be measured and understood. Paul used a similar comparison to establish a standard for marital love when he said, "Husbands, love your wives, even as Christ also loved the church, and gave himself up for it" (Eph. 5:25). Christ did not ask from His disciples more than He Himself gave, and He set the norm by His own life. "Even as I have loved you" may refer either to the recognized quality of His love as it already had been manifested, or it may refer proleptically to His coming death as the supreme act of love, as in 13:1.

The first element of this lofty love was sacrifice. "Greater love hath no man than this, that a man lay down his life for his friends" (13). This marked the highest achievement of human love. Divine love went beyond this, for Jesus laid down His life for His enemies. As Romans 5:8 says, "God commendeth his own love toward us, in that, while we were yet sinners, Christ died for us." By emphasizing the word *man* in verse 13, the full meaning of the text may be brought into

plain view. Men give their lives for their friends; Jesus gave
His life for His enemies.

A second aspect of love was intimacy, illustrated by Jesus'
contrast of the words *friends* and *slaves*. The bondservant
might be loved by the master, and might be treated kindly; but
he never would be regarded as an equal nor given an insight
into the master's mind. He would be expected to obey without
knowing the reason why. Jesus, on the other hand, took His
disciples into His confidence, "for," He said, "all things that I
heard from my Father I have made known unto you" (15).
He shared with them the secrets of heaven.

A third quality of divine love was initiative. Jesus had not
waited for men to appreciate Him and to invite Him into their
lives, but He had first chosen them. "Ye did not choose me, but
I chose you, and appointed you, that ye should go and bear
fruit" (16).

The final aspect of love was productiveness. The continuation of verse 16 is: "I chose you, and appointed you, that ye
should go and bear fruit, and that your fruit should abide:
that whatsoever ye shall ask of the Father in my name, he may
give it you." Jesus' love for the disciples was to be the secret
of their effectiveness. Out of the timid band who fled from
His enemies in the garden and who cowered in the upper room
after the resurrection, Jesus made convincing witnesses. Immediate and permanent fruitage was the gift of His grace to
them.

The Relation of Believers to the World (15:18-27)

The third relation which the believer must maintain is with
the world. Jesus never intended that he should live in pious
isolation, but in active contact with the problems of men.
Nevertheless, He drew a sharp line between the believer and
the "world" which comprises the mass of men who live without God. Between the two is a hostility which is as deep and

as inevitable as their nature—a hostility which goes back to
the enmity of the carnal mind against God.

Jesus, in stating the attitude of the world, carefully forewarned the disciples of its hatred because He did not want
them disillusioned when they met it. "If the world hateth you,
ye know that it hath hated me before it hated you" (18). The
type of grammatical condition which John used implied the
actuality of the hatred; it was not hypothetical. Jesus recognized it as a chilling reality; but He comforted the disciples
by assuring them that He shared with them all the ostracism
and contempt which the world could heap on them.

The attitude of the world seemed at first to be inexplicable.
How was it possible that men as a whole could fail to appreciate the sheer goodness and inestimable worth of Jesus? Why
should the world hate men who were following Him as the
servant follows his master? Jesus gave three reasons for its
hostility: first, a difference in nature between the world and
the disciples; second, the disciples' close association with the
rejected Christ; and third, the conviction of sin which Jesus'
message brought upon the world.

Throughout all nature, whether in the animal or human
world, there is a tendency to dislike any individual that differs
from the average type. Birds will drive from the flock one of
their number that differs radically from them in plumage. Men
look with suspicion and jealousy upon one who possesses abili-
ties or features that make him stand out from the crowd. "If
ye were of the world," said Jesus, "the world would love its
own: but because ye are not of the world, but I chose you out
of the world, therefore the world hateth you" (19). The very
fact that He has chosen men out of the world places them in a
different category from others. They have a new nature, a new
aim in life, a new productiveness. The world does not understand their motives nor feel comfortable in their company.

Again, voluntary attachment to Christ brings with it the
hatred which was directed against Him. "If they persecuted
me, they will also persecute you; if they kept my word, they
will keep yours also. But all these things will they do unto you
for my name's sake, because they know not him that sent me"
(20b, 21). Jesus accepted the hatred of the world as a matter
of course; and He gave His disciples to understand that they
must do likewise as the logical consequence of following Him.

Lastly, the chief reason for the hatred of the world was
Jesus' exposure of its sin. As the clear sunlight reveals stains
and flaws which escape notice in lesser light, so His presence
revealed by contrast the darkness of the world's sin. Two
claims in this passage describe the effect of Jesus on the world:

> "If I had not come and spoken unto them, they had not had
> sin" (22).

> "If I had not done among them the works which none other
> did, they had not had sin" (24).

The words and deeds of Christ showed by contrast how evil
men can become. His presence made their sin deliberate and
inexcusable. Ignorance could no longer palliate their guilt. As
was stated in 3:19, "Men loved the darkness rather than the
light; for their works were evil."

Two antidotes to the attitude of the world are proposed in
the concluding verses (26, 27) of this part of the discourse:
the witness of the Spirit, and the witness of the believers. The
witness of the Spirit is powerful because He comes with supernatural insight and conviction to demonstrate the reality of the
unseen Father. The witness of the disciples is also potent because it presents the unanswerable argument of transformed
lives. Everyone knew what these men had been, and could see
what they became through their contact with Jesus. Jesus
expected that the Holy Spirit and the disciples through whom

He would work would maintain the words and deeds which He had begun, and through which the evil of the world would meet its living refutation.

Conference on Revelation (16:1-33)

The Revelation Explained (16:1-6)

Having made clear that the hatred of the world was inevitable to the disciples if they would follow Him, Jesus proceeded to make more vivid what that hatred would mean. Expulsion from the synagogue, as in the case of the blind man (9:22, 34), and even death would be their lot. Such treatment they were not to regard as abnormal. It would be the logical result of unbelief, which was in turn a consequence of ignorance. "And these things will they do, because they have not known the Father, nor me" (3). In this fashion Jesus sought to divest the disciples of any vain hope.

The Consequence of Revelation (16:7-15)

The reaction of the disciples to Jesus' predictions was depression (6). To dispel the gloom, He informed them that His departure was not just an inevitable calamity which must be endured, but a necessity to the progress of the work. It would be profitable[5] for Him to go, because His death would enlarge His ministry through the activity of the Holy Spirit.

The functions of the Spirit as Jesus outlined them had a twofold relation: to the world and to the believer. An analysis of the text instantly reveals the parallelism.

(See next page)

---

5. Greek: *sumpherei,* profitable, expedient. The word appears in John in three passages only: 11:50, 18:14 where allusion is made to 11:50, and 16:7. The contrast of usage is striking, for in 11:50 and 18:14 Jesus' death is "profitable" for the leaders who feel that they must remove Him to save their own place, while in 16:7 He says that His death is "profitable" for the blessing of others through the Holy Spirit.

8   And *he,* when he is come, will convict the world

	in respect *of sin,* and *of righteousness,* and *of judgment*:
9	of sin, because they believe not on me;
10	of righteousness, because I go to the Father, and ye behold me no more;
11	of judgment, because the prince of this world hath been judged.

12	*I* have yet many things but ye cannot bear	to say unto you, them now.
	when he, the	Spirit of truth, is come,
13	Howbeit/............	he shall guide you into all the truth:

for he shall not speak from himself;
   what things soever he shall hear,
but / . . . these shall he speak:

and he shall declare unto you the
   things
                              that are to come.

14   He shall glorify me:

for he shall take of mine,
and shall declare it unto you.

15   All things whatsoever *the Father* hath are mine:

therefore said I,

that he taketh of mine,
and shall declare it unto you.

Three aspects of the work of the Holy Spirit are marked by the three main verbs, "he . . . will convict" (8), "he shall guide" (13), "he shall glorify" (14). The first two are qualified by the temporal clause, "when he is come," which indicates that these relate to the work of the Spirit in time as it affects the world and the disciples. The third aspect indicates the relation of the Spirit to Christ, who is the source of the Spirit's teaching. The first epitomizes the relation of the Spirit to the world by the word "convict"; the second, the relation of the Spirit to the disciples by the word "guide"; the third, the relation of the Spirit to Christ by the word "glorify." "Convict" means to refute an adversary completely, to prove guilt so as to bring an acknowledgement of the truth of the charge. It implies a successful action against an opponent that results in establishing his guilt. "Guide" implies leadership for a person who is interested in traveling on the right path, but who needs help in finding it. "Glorify" has several meanings in JOHN, but here can be understood as "display to the best advantage," "extol." The two former words, "convict" and "guide," mark the difference between the believer and the unbeliever. The unbeliever is guilty of deliberate rebellion against God and of rejection of His claims, and needs to be brought to face God's judgment. The believer may not have progressed far along the way of truth, but is desirous of going on in the right direction, and needs the good offices of the Spirit to conduct him on his way.

The Spirit and the World (8-11)

The Spirit's work of conviction applies in three realms: sin, righteousness, judgment. The causes assigned do not seem relevant at first. Why should men be convicted of sin because of unbelief rather than because of some concrete offense, such as murder, theft, or adultery? What has Christ's return to the Father to do with personal righteousness? How can the judgment of an invisible person whose very existence is dubious to

many be regarded as a proof of judgment? The points of connection seem farfetched.

The causes, however, are not so vague as they seem. If
Jesus is the Son of God, as this Gospel declares Him to be, then
rejection of Him is the greatest and most fatal sin of all. Such
sin is the product of an ingrained distaste for righteousness.
It is the deliberate refusal of God's will. It cannot be attributed
to ignorance only, or to misfortune, or to fate, or to any one
of a thousand reasons by which men excuse their behavior;
for Christ is self-authenticating, and those who reject Him do
so because they do not want Him.

In order to define sin there must be a standard. There can
be no transgression where there is no law, no darkness where
there is no light, no sin where there is no holiness. Righteousness is not established in a code nor in a pattern of conduct,
but in law as spoken and in conduct as exemplified in Christ.
If He is to be established as righteous, however, it cannot be
by popular vote. Men are prejudiced and their assent to any
man's claim will not enact it, nor can their dissent destroy it,
but the verdict of God alone can settle finally any such claim.
The return of Jesus to the Father was the ultimate proof that
He was the perfect pattern for righteousness, accepted by the
Father. This principle was illustrated by Peter's statement in
the sermon at Pentecost when he said that Jesus of Nazareth
was "a man approved of God" (Acts 2:22); that He was
executed "by the hand of lawless men" (Acts 2:23); but God
raised Him up, so that, "Being therefore by the right hand of
God exalted, and having received of the Father the promise of
the Holy Spirit, he hath poured forth this, which ye see and
hear" (Acts 2:33). The Father placed the stamp of divine
approval upon His ministry by raising Him from death, and
established Him as the enduring embodiment of holiness.

Whenever sin and righteousness meet there must be judgment. The word "judgment" means an ethical decision: ap-
probation of such qualities or acts as may be deemed good,

and simultaneous condemnation of such qualities or acts as may be deemed evil. The vindication of Christ by the resurrection as the incarnate righteousness of God was at the same time God's rejection of the prince of this world as the personification of all that is evil. In chapter 12:31, Jesus, in speaking of His passion, said, "Now is the judgment of this world: now shall the prince of this world be cast out." The cross was the condemnation of all that the world contained—its pride, its envy, its hatred, its rebellion, its unbelief. The function of the Spirit is to apply that condemnation to the world, and to make it conscious of the reality of judgment.

To convince any unbeliever of sin, righteousness, and judgment is beyond human ability. It may be possible to fix upon him the guilt of some specific sin if there is sufficient evidence to bring him before a jury; but to make him acknowledge the deeper fact, that he is a sinner, evil at heart, and deserving of punishment because he has not believed in Christ, is quite another matter. To bring a man to some standard of ethics is not too difficult; for almost every person has ideals that coincide with the moral law at some point. To create in him the humiliating consciousness that his self-righteousness is as filthy rags in comparison with the spotless linen of the righteousness of God cannot be effected by ordinary persuasion. Many believe in a general law of retribution; but it is almost impossible to convince them that they already stand condemned. Only the power of the Holy Spirit, working from within, can bring about that profound conviction which leads to repentance. The Spirit anticipates and makes effective the ministry of the disciples in carrying the message to unbelievers.

The Spirit and the Believer (12, 13)

The Spirit's work with the believer is quite different from His work with the unbeliever. Three aspects of His functions are outlined:

He shall guide into all truth.
He shall not speak of Himself, but of what is given to Him.
He shall declare things to come.

The first promise implied that Jesus had not been able to impart to the disciples all that He knew, or all that they needed. He said that He had many things to tell them, but they were not able to bear them (12). Learning the truth of God would be a slow process, interwoven with the growth of their personal experience. Personal experience, however, would not be enough in itself. Vagaries and errors would quickly lead them astray unless the living Spirit provided them with His guidance. He was promised to them in order to meet these emergencies, so that they might be kept in the right path.

Through the Holy Spirit every Christian can be provided with individual authoritative instruction. Spiritual knowledge is not identical with dogma, though the body of Christian truth which has been transmitted through the historical church undoubtedly has for its core the final revelation of God. The creation, revelation, transmission, preservation, and application of that truth is made possible by the living personal Spirit who comes to each one of the disciples. The recurrence of the Spirit's impact upon individual lives keeps the truth from becoming dead tradition; the persistence and cumulative effect of His work historically recorded guards men from extravagances and mistakes.

How is it possible to distinguish the voice of the Holy Spirit in the noise of conflicting dogmas and creeds? The second statement of Jesus applies: "He shall not speak from himself; but what things soever he shall hear, these shall he speak" (13). The Spirit does not advertise Himself. He presents the teaching which is consistent with the previous revelation and which comes from the heart of God.

The Spirit's work includes the unfolding of the future. The last clause of 16:13 constitutes the warrant for the inspiration of the New Testament. The Spirit was empowered to add to what Jesus had said in person to His disciples, and to predict the future. The discernment which the Spirit could generate and the definite knowledge which He could impart became the basis of the gift of prophecy and the creation of the authoritative canon which composes the New Testament.

The Spirit and Christ (14, 15)

Like a spotlight which brings some object into brilliant relief against the blackness of the surrounding night, but which calls no attention to itself, the Spirit's chief mission is to make men conscious of Christ rather than of Himself. Consequently, any movement which purports to be led by the Spirit, and which focuses interest on its phenomena rather than on the person of Christ belies its own claims. Like the servant of Abraham, He promotes another's cause, not His own.

Jesus' exposition of the work of the Holy Spirit affords a practical understanding of the meaning of the Trinity. Each of the persons, Father, Son, and Holy Spirit, is separate in personality and is distinguishable from the others. In function the Father plans, the Son perfects, the Spirit executes and reveals. The Father sent the Son; the Son sent the Spirit; the Spirit represents the Son as the Son represented the Father. The three interact and also act separately; they are three individuals, but yet one God. All that the Father has belongs to the Son; and all that the Son has to teach is administered through the Spirit (15, 12, 14). Jesus offered no philosophical statement of the Trinity. His language was extremely simple, though the profundities of His words are still unplumbed.

The Revelation by the Resurrection (16:16-24)

The content of the sixteenth verse sets the keynote for the next section of the discourse. "A little while, and ye behold me no more; and again a little while, and ye shall see me." The disciples found this puzzling; for they argued its meaning among themselves, but hesitated to make inquiry concerning

it. The explanation seems to make it plain that Jesus was thinking of the resurrection when He said that He would disappear
and reappear. In verse 20, He said, "Verily, verily, I say unto
you, that ye shall weep and lament, but the world shall rejoice."
The sorrow of the disciples and the parallel joy of the world
must refer to His death, since both were expressed at that time.
The attitude of the world was not mentioned again, because the
world regarded His death as final. Jesus compared the disciples' joy to that of a woman in travail, who forgets her pain
when the child is born. Their gloom was turned into joy when
they realized that the tomb was empty and that He must have
risen. That joy, He said, would be permanent. "I will see you
again, and your heart shall rejoice, and your joy no one taketh
away from you" (22).

Closely connected with the revelation of the resurrection was
the new doctrine of prayer. Two distinct words were used
in the context which are translated by the single English word
"ask." The former of the two, *erotao,* translated "ask a question" in the American Revised Version of verses 23a and 26b,
may have meant to question or to invite. It was used generally
among equals in the sense of "demand," "invite," or by a superior to an inferior. The other word, *aiteo,* translated "ask,"
in verses 23b, 24, and 26a, means to offer a petition, to prefer
a request, and is generally used by an inferior toward a superior.[6]

Verse 23 may be understood to mean that the revelation of
the Spirit and of the resurrection would be so plain that all
questions as the disciples had just asked would be superfluous,
but the sequence of thought with what follows concerns prayer
rather than information. The passage may well denote that
in the coming day the disciples would no longer regard Jesus
as an equal, from whom they might on occasion ask a favor,
but that they would recognize Him as the beloved Son in whose
name they as suppliants would present their requests to the

---

6. See R. C. Trench, *op. cit.,* pp. 143-145.

Father (23b). He could approach the Father as they had been coming to Him, as an equal; while they could come to the Father only through the proper mediator.

The Revelation by Proclamation (16:25-33)

The recurrence of "These things have I spoken unto you" (25) marks another transition of thought. The discourses of Jesus up to this point have been couched in parables or figures. The questions of the disciples had been provoked by the obscure manner in which Jesus had disclosed His thought. At this time He turned to a statement of His mission. "I came forth from the Father and have come into the world: again I quit the world and proceed to the Father" (28).[7] Three times it is asserted that He came from the Father, and in each of these instances the text of JOHN uses a different preposition.

"I came forth from the side of the Father" (27).[7]
"I came forth out of the Father" (28).[7]
"We believe that you came forth from God" (30).[7]

It is unlikely that the prepositions (*para, ek,* and *apo*) were used interchangeably, since John differentiated the uses here and since he was not generally averse to repetition. The variation may be attributed fairly to design. The first preposition carried the idea of authority, sometimes with the connotation of commission. It was employed in the Prologue (1:6) where John the Baptist's commission was stated. The second preposition implied source, "from within." It carried the idea of nature, for He who came out from the Father revealed the Father's nature to the world. The third expression was the disciples' word, which meant separation. Jesus had been in the company of the Father and now was separated from Him. In the lowest sense it implied preexistence, which the disciples had acknowledged.

---

7. Original translation.

The declaratory revelation on the part of Jesus that He had come from God evoked a definite reaction of belief from the disciples which exceeded any previous expressions that they had made. Twice it was asserted: once by Jesus, " . . . Because ye have loved me, and have believed that I came forth from the Father" (27), and once by their own confession, "by this we believe that thou camest forth from God" (30). This affirmation transcended that given by Peter in 6:69: "We have believed and know that thou art the Holy One of God." In the former instance, Peter was ascribing to Jesus a title; on this occasion, the disciples were testifying to belief in His origin and divine nature.

The reply of Jesus was pathetic. "Do you now believe?" (31) He was still unsure of their faith as He was when, after Peter's confession, He said: "Did not I choose you the twelve, and one of you is a devil?" (6:70) At this very time His misgivings had been justified and He knew perfectly well that the allegiance of the rest would soon prove transient. "Behold, the hour cometh, yea, is come, that ye all shall be scattered, every man to his own [home], and shall leave me alone" (32). The hour of His greatest revelation would be the hour of their greatest failure (25,32).

Jesus' constancy was marked by His declaration of faith in the Father. "I am not alone, because the Father is with me" (32b). Because of His faith, the prospect of the disciples' defection did not alter His fixed purpose. He went His way unflinchingly.

The last recurrence of "These things have I spoken unto you" explained the design of the discourse as a whole: "that in me ye may have peace" (33a). "In me" recalled the word "abide" used in chapter 15. The close relationship with Christ which the disciple sustains affords him surcease from conflict, from fear, and from doubt. "In the world" is tribulation; "in Christ" is peace. Victory over the forces and circumstances

that circumscribe human life is attainable through Him, for
He has overcome the world by His cross.

CONFERENCE WITH THE FATHER (17:1-26)

The seventeenth chapter of John is the farewell prayer of
Jesus for His disciples. It is the explanation of the cryptic
phrase in Luke 22:31,32: "Simon, Simon, behold, Satan asked
to have you, that he might sift you as wheat: but I made sup-
plication for thee, that thy faith fail not." In thus addressing
Simon, He was assuring that wavering disciple of security.
In John 17, He gave the guarantee of the disciples' survival
of the trying period which was occasioned by His death.

The prayer itself was probably spoken after the little party
had left the room where the last supper was eaten, and before
they crossed the Kidron valley to the Mount of Olives. Perhaps Jesus stopped under the shadow of the wall of the city to
breathe this petition while His words of warning were still
fresh in the disciples' ears. Its content was largely intercessory,
and concerned the needs, first, of Himself (1-5), second, of the
disciples (6-19), and third, of future believers (20-26).

The first section (1-5) contains two imperatives: "glorify
thy Son" (1), and "glorify thou me" (5). For Himself Jesus
asked two things: a glorification of His position as the Son that
His authority to give eternal life might be manifest to all, and
a glorification of His person, that He might return to the
glory which He shared with the Father before the existence
of the world. The prayer claimed as His right a place of equality with the Father.

The second section (6-19) contains another pair of imperatives relating to His disciples: "keep them" (11) and "sanctify them" (17). The Lord's two chief desires for them were
protection from evil, lest they be injured by it; and perfection
in holiness, that they might be completely set apart for the divine use. The perils of the moment were great, and they needed sorely God's care over their lives.

The third section (20-26) contains two petitions: "I pray" (20) and "I desire" (24). Both related to all believers whose faith comes through the testimony of the disciples, and so embraced the entire church of God. The former petition sought for unity; the latter requested that the believers might be with Him in His glory. The present testimony and the future destiny of the believers were thus included.

These three sections are like three concentric circles, the second of which is larger than the first, and the third of which is larger than the second, and inclusive of all three. All, however, have a common center. The prayer as a whole is keyed to one central idea, *eternal life;* for it is Jesus' petition that He may be glorified in order that eternal life may be made available to men.

From another viewpoint the prayer may be interpreted by a scheme somewhat different from the foregoing divisions.

First is the statement of the occasion: "The hour is come" (1). The phrase, "the hour," has appeared sporadically in the preceding body of the Gospel. At the wedding of Cana, Jesus informed His mother that His hour had not come, but, with the advent of the Period of Crisis He said, "The hour is come, that the Son of man should be glorified" (12:23). His one desire was that the Father might be glorified in Him, and He in the Father. The greatest glory of God is the impartation of eternal life to men by bringing them to God in faith. Revealing this life was the climax of Jesus' spiritual work.

Second is the definition of His work: "That to all whom thou hast given him, he should give eternal life" (2). If the language sounds as though salvation were restricted to a predetermined few whom God has given to Christ, it should be remembered that this prayer was addressed to one member of the Godhead by another, and that in reading it men are listening to the family conversation of deity. From the human viewpoint, there can be no question that salvation in Christ is sincerely offered to all, as the "whosoever" in 3:16 indicates.

No restriction of class, race, color, social standing, nationality,
or character is imposed upon any prospective believer. Anyone
who hears may believe, and is welcomed by Christ. On the
other hand, not everybody has believed on Him or will believe.
The text states plainly that the Son gives eternal life to those
whom the Father has given to Him, with the tacit assumption
that there are some to whom the Father has not given that life.
Since there are no surprises to God, He knows from the first
the individual destiny of man, and He is able to determine who
are to be the recipients of grace. The passage parallels the
strange one in Acts: "As many as were ordained to eternal
life believed" (Acts 13:48). As far as preaching is concerned,
salvation is universal in Christ. From the divine point of view,
salvation is elective for those whom the Father has given to the
Son.

Christ's work was the impartation of life. His teachings,
His signs, His person, His death and resurrection were all a
part of His calling. The prayer which He offered is, in a
sense, a report of His fulfillment of His commission before returning to the Father.

The definition of eternal life is important because Jesus
differentiated it from the current concept of endless existence.
"And this is life eternal, that they should know thee the only
true God, and him whom thou didst send, even Jesus Christ"
(3). The word *know* (*ginosko*) suggests living contact rather than imparted information. Experience is the sum total of
man's contact with His environment, and his highest experience is naturally the product of his highest contacts. The highest contacts of the world are at best temporal, for the world
is temporal; and so they give only a temporal life. However
fully man lives in the world, he ultimately reaches the point
where nothing is new because he has reached human limits.
Only the knowledge of God can give enduring satisfaction, because God alone is eternal. Contact with God will provide the
fullest experience, and the experience of God's eternal being

will be eternal life. The present tense of the verb *know* indicates also that "eternal life lies not so much in the possession of a completed knowledge as in the striving after a growing knowledge."[8] Eternal life is growing and expanding, not static.

The objects of this knowledge are personal: "the only true [real][9] God, and Jesus Christ" whom He sent. Eternal life is the end of the philosopher's quest for ultimate reality, and of the scientist's search for truth. It is not the quest of the academician alone; it is the plain man's satisfaction because it is a personal acquaintance. "I know him whom I have believed" (II Tim. 1:12), not "what I have believed," is the final expression of triumphant Christian experience.

The prayer of Jesus defines eternal life in practical as well as in abstract terms. Functionally life is best understood by its privileges and effects. A number of them are listed as illustrating its meaning, and are embodied in the successive statements and petitions of Jesus concerning the disciples.

The first is enlightenment. Jesus had imparted to them the words of the Father which were life-giving, for on another occasion He had said, "The words that I have spoken unto you are spirit, and are life" (6:63). The response of the disciples to His instruction is' described in the verbs of verse 8: "They received . . . they knew . . . they believed." Acceptance of His testimony, experimental realization of its truth, and personal commitment to Him were the gateway to life.

The second is preservation. Two words are used in verses 11 and 12, "kept" and "guarded." The former means protection by restraint and is frequently used in JOHN of "keeping" commandments or words in the sense of obeying them. The second word appears only twice in the Fourth Gospel. It

---

8. B. F. Westcott, *op. cit.,* II, p. 242.
9. Greek: *alethinos,* which means *true* in contrast to unreal or shadowy. It establishes God's actuality or verity rather than His truthfulness or veracity.

refers to protection from external peril.[10] Taken together, the words give a picture of complete deliverance from all perils, within and without. Eternal life means a lasting security.

The third is joy. The possessive adjective *my* (13) which is employed is frequently used by John with a qualitative as well as with a possessive sense. Christ is speaking of a joy that is peculiarly His, made what it is because it is His. The same phraseology is used in 14:27 and 15:11. The joy of Christ was the gladness that came from His perfect accord with the Father and from His perfect obedience to the Father's will. The disciples might share in His joy as they realized the security which He pledged to them, and which He could make good by the power of His resurrection life (Cf. 16:22). Jesus' kind of joy was not dependent upon the accidental occurrences of life which bring elation or depression in their wake, but was drawn from the knowledge that whatever happened, the Father would undertake all responsibility for Him.

The fourth is sanctification. Sanctification means to be made holy by being set apart for a special purpose. Negatively, the word implies separation from all evil, and so is used in contrast to being involved in the world. Positively, it means dedication and is illustrated by Jesus' statement, "I sanctify myself" (19). In one sense He could not make Himself more holy than He was, but if the word *sanctify* be understood as "dedicate" the meaning at once becomes clear. Jesus set Himself aside from all defilement, repulsed all temptation in order that He might discharge completely His spiritual responsibility to the disciples. Representatively, the disciples were sanctified in Him, so that they could claim complete sanctification by faith, "For by one offering he hath perfected forever them that are sanctified" (Heb. 10:14). Jesus' will was the instrument, as the

---

10. See B. F. Westcott, *op. cit.*, II, p. 251. "The difference between the verbs themselves appears to be that *terein* [the former] expresses the careful regard and observance of that which is looked at as without (*e. g.* Matt. xxvii. 36), while *phulassein* describes the protection of something held as it were within a line of defence from external assaults."

writer of Hebrews says: "By which will we have been sanctified through the offering of the body of Jesus Christ once for
all" (Heb. 10:10). In the voluntary dedication of the Lord
Jesus Christ to the work assigned to Him by the Father, He
sanctified Himself, and accomplished the sanctification of believers also. The tense of the verb in 17:19 suggests that His
disciples were already sanctified, and that they should act on
that promise rather than on the assumption that they were
working toward sanctification.

Closely connected with the sanctification of the believer is
his commission. "As thou didst send me into the world, even
so sent I them into the world" (18). Sixteen times this word
is used of Christ as sent by the Father. It usually meant appointment to some task, plus the equipment for doing it. Eternal life is a commission to the fulfillment of God's work. As
men labor in Christ, they live in Christ, for they can know Him
only by working with Him. The eternal quality of Christ's
life was revealed by His purpose to do the Father's work. He
began His prayer by saying that He had fulfilled the work
which had been given Him to do. Eternal life for men is not
luxurious idleness, but purposeful labor in which they realize
the best destiny that the Father offers them.

Unity is another factor in eternal life. The final prayer of
Jesus for the believers as a whole was that they should be one
(22). A clear distinction should be drawn between four closely allied concepts: unanimity, uniformity, union, and unity.
Unanimity means absolute concord of opinion within a given
group of people. Uniformity is complete similarity of organization or of ritual. Union implies political affiliation without
necessarily including individual agreement. Unity requires
oneness of inner heart and essential purpose, through the possession of a common interest or a common life. No one of
these is dependent on any other. Unanimity of belief does not
necessarily mean uniformity of ritual; nor does uniformity of

ritual presuppose organic union; nor does organic union involve unity of spirit. Within the church of historic Christianity there have been wide divergences of opinion and ritual. Unity, however, prevails wherever there is a deep and genuine experience of Christ; for the fellowship of the new birth transcends all historical and denominational boundaries. Paul of Tarsus, Luther of Germany, Wesley of England, and Moody of America would find deep unity with each other, though they were widely separated by time, by space, by nationality, by educational background, and by ecclesiastical connections. Such unity was what Jesus petitioned in His prayer, for He defined it as the unity which obtained between Himself and the Father, "as thou, Father, art in me, and I in thee, that they also may be in us" (21). This relationship lay in a common nature rather than in an identity of minds or of persons. Jesus did not pray for absolute unanimity of mind, nor for uniformity of practice, nor for union of visible organization, but for the underlying unity of spiritual nature and of devotion which would enable His people to bear a convincing testimony before the world.

The last aspect of eternal life that is treated in this chapter is fellowship. The closing petition was: "Father, I desire that they also whom thou hast given me be with me where I am, that they may behold my glory, which thou hast given me" (24). The knowledge of God through Christ can be made complete as Christ's disciples enjoy everlasting companionship with Him in the place where He abides. Jesus predicted an eternal society of those whom the Father had given to Him, redeemed by His death and bound to Him indissolubly forever. In this fellowship life would find a congenial environment and would develop unhindered by evil. Such was His desire and plan for all those possessing eternal life.

With the end of the seventeenth chapter, the Period of Conference closed. In the brief hours from late afternoon until almost midnight, Jesus had made His last address to the disciples and His final report to the Father. He had brought His followers to the point of declaring belief in Him (16:30,31); and had commended them to the Father's care. The concluding stage of the conflict of belief and unbelief was about to begin, and He must go forth to face the storm.

THE PERIOD OF CONSUMMATION

THE PERIOD OF CONSUMMATION

A. The Betrayal
B. The Trial before Annas
C. The Interview with Pilate
D. The Crucifixion
E. The Burial
F. The Resurrection

   1. The Evidence of the Resurrection
   2. The Effect of the Resurrection

CHAPTER IX

The Period of Consummation

18:1 to 20:31

THE Period of Consummation which covers the close of
Jesus' life is so named because its content revealed the
consummation of the tension of belief and unbelief. Unbelief
reached its deepest infamy in the rejection and crucifixion of
Jesus. Belief reached its highest achievement in the action of
the disciples at the time of the resurrection and afterward. The
earthly work of Jesus was completed by these events. His
statement in 17:4: "I glorified thee on the earth, having accomplished the work which thou hast given me to do" compared with the utterance from the cross, "It is finished" (19:
30), shows that He regarded His death as the apex of His
career and the fulfillment of His commission. A comparison
of the accusation of the priests " . . . he made himself the Son
of God" (19:7) with Thomas' confession, "My Lord and my
God" (20:28) illustrates well the respective climaxes of unbelief and belief. In this period the plot of JOHN reached its
conclusion.

Within this section the Fourth Gospel bears the closest resemblance to the Synoptics. The similarities are more numerous than the divergences though there are several of the latter.
John added to the story the trial before Annas (18:12-24),
some detail about the hearing before Pilate, the committal of
Mary to the beloved disciple (19:25-27), the four last words
from the cross, the visit of Peter and the other disciple to the
tomb (20:3-10), the interview with Mary Magdalene (20:
11-18), the remarks of Thomas (20:24-29), the appearance

to the seven disciples at Galilee (21:1-24). The author omitted
the agony in Gethsemane, the rending of the veil, the group
of women at the tomb, the walk to Emmaus, the great commission, and the ascension. Definite reason cannot be given
for the inclusion or omission of each of these several items,
but the principle of selectivity which the author gave in his
key to the Gospel was doubtless applied. The choice may have
been governed by the desire to use fresh material, or it was
connected with the principle of relevancy to the central theme
of belief and unbelief.

There is more detailed treatment of individual personalities
in JOHN than in the Synoptics. The consummation of belief
and unbelief consequently seems to be much more a result of
spiritual development than of an historic process. John's Gospel narrates a story, and makes that narrative a personal appeal to the reader.

The Betrayal (18:1-11)

The feature of the betrayal which John made most important was the voluntary surrender of Jesus. A hint of this emphasis was foreshadowed in chapter 10: "No man taketh it
[my life] away from me, but I lay it down of myself."

The surrender was conscious. Verse 4 says that "Jesus
therefore, knowing all the things that were coming upon him,
went forth." While the statement related directly to His going
to meet the party that had come to capture Him, it was indicative of His entire attitude. He went to the garden with the
full knowledge that Judas had gone to bargain with the priests
for His betrayal and would look for Him in this familiar rendezvous.

The surrender was voluntary. Between the dismissal of Judas from the upper room and the actual arrest in the garden,
at least two hours must have elapsed. In that time Jesus could
have left Jerusalem and have been well on His way across the
river to Perea, or to some hiding place where the Jewish lead-

ers could not have found Him. Judas' betrayal would have re-
coiled on himself, since he would have failed to produce Jesus,
and undoubtedly the priests would have wreaked the vengeance
of their disappointment on him. At one stroke Jesus could
have saved Himself and could have disposed of the traitor.
Why should He have gone deliberately to the place where Judas would surely look for Him, and wait until the traitor came
to capture Him?

Furthermore, when the mob with Judas at its head finally
arrived, Jesus walked boldly out to meet it. Upon being informed that they were looking for Jesus of Nazareth, He said:
"I am he" (5,8). His courage frightened the would-be captors so that they shrank back from Him and fell on the ground
(6), and still He waited for action. His capture was not effected by their superior astuteness or power, but by His ready
consent.

The surrender was vicarious. "Jesus answered, I told you
that I am he; if therefore ye seek me, let these go their way:
that the word might be fulfilled which he spake, Of those whom
thou hast given me I lost not one" (8, 9). He gave Himself
in the place of the disciples, all of whom made good their
escape. The essence of the atonement was illustrated by this
act of Jesus, who purchased their security by His sacrifice.

The surrender was loving. Peter, in a fit of loyal zeal, drew
a sword and cut off the ear of Malchus, a servant of the high
priest. The probability is that in nervous haste he struck three
inches wide of his original aim. Certainly it was not Peter's
intention to damage only an ear. By contrast with this action,
Jesus' rebuke of Peter and the healing of the servant, which
John did not record, though Luke did (Luke 22:51), indicated
that the entire surrender was motivated by love. Love for the
Father was primary. "The cup which the Father hath given
me, shall I not drink it?" (11). In other words, if the Father
permitted suffering, He would gladly endure it. Love for the
disciples also was a compelling factor, for He sought to spare

them arrest and trial. Love for His enemies appeared in the healing of Malchus, and in the absence of any tirade against Judas.

The contrast of Peter and Judas in this paragraph heightens the difference in the characters of the two men. Judas arrived with armed men to capture Jesus; Peter drew arms to defend Him. Judas apprehended Him by stealth; Peter defended Him openly. Judas betrayed Him in cold blood; Peter attacked Jesus' enemies. In this account Jesus treated Judas with silence; He rebuked Peter sternly. Judas' crime was deliberate throughout; Peter's blunder in drawing the sword was prompted by a loyal though mistaken impulsiveness. The chilly indifference of unbelief and the erratic action of a belief which had not yet reached stability were alike destructive.

Thus the attitude of the disciples was revealed. They were frightened, rash, unstable; nevertheless, they were loyal at heart. Their desertion was not stated, but the group disappeared from the narrative to reappear only after the resurrection. Their fright accounted for their dispersion, and even at their reunion they had shut the doors "for fear of the Jews" (20:19). The essential belief of these men was evinced in the fact that they gathered together at all. Belief was not complete, but it was real.

The Trial before Annas (18:12-27)

The trial before Annas took place at his private lodgings, in which Caiaphas may or may not have participated. Annas, the father-in-law of Caiaphas, had been high priest between the years 7 and 14, and following him at intervals, five of his sons and his son-in-law held the office. He wielded a powerful influence, and was regarded as high priest emeritus. In this case he was consulted that he might render a preliminary opinion to establish the nature of the accusations which should be ratified by the Sanhedrin in a formal meeting on the following morning.

The point of transition from the house of Annas to the presence of Caiaphas has been disputed by various scholars. If the term "high priest" in verse 15 referred to Caiaphas, to whom the title was applied in verse 13, then the account from verse 14 on to the end related to the trial before Caiaphas; and no detail of the hearing before Annas was given at all. Verse 24, which states that "Annas therefore sent him bound unto Caiaphas the high priest," would then have to be translated "Annas had sent him bound . . . ." Such a rendering does violence to the tense of the verb. If this episode in its entirety be considered as taking place before Annas, verse 24 marks the transition, but leaves unexplained the fact that Matthew connected the denial of Peter with the appearance before Caiaphas.[1] Reconciliation has been attempted by suggesting that the hearings took place in different rooms of the same building.[2] The two were closely connected, and were essentially part of the same procedure.

The incident as John gave it presented two main features: the questioning before the high priest and the denial of Peter. The examination was not reproduced in full detail, because the author wished to lay his main emphasis on the alternate views of Jesus which the questioning evoked. The inquiry itself began as a routine matter, for any suspected agitator would be asked who his followers were and what doctrine he taught. Jesus promptly referred the high priest to public witness. "I have spoken openly to the world . . . and in secret spake I nothing . . . ask them that have heard me . . ." (20, 21). Why should He testify against Himself in a prejudged case when His judges could ask those who had heard Him, if they

---

1. See Matt. 26:57. Perhaps the Synoptic accounts telescoped the entire event into one hearing before the priests, while John preserved the trial before Annas as a separate event.

2. For an excellent detailed discussion of this, see H. W. Watkins, *The Gospel According to St. John,* in *The Handy Commentary,* (C. J. Ellicott, Ed., London, Cassell and Company, Ltd., n. d.) pp. 371-374. Westcott, *op. cit.,* II, pp. 275, 276, thinks that verses 19-24 relate to the hearing before Caiaphas.

really wanted the truth? When the temple officer struck Him
for so abruptly replying to the priests, He set the alternative:
"If I have spoken evil, bear witness of the evil: but if well,
why smitest thou me?" (23). If He had done wrong, it
should be proved legally: if not, He did not deserve to suffer.
The few words of this hearing showed that the trial would be
unfair because unbelief had already condemned Jesus, and was
merely seeking testimony to justify its attitude.

The denial of Peter (15-18, 25-27) was a contrasting sequel
to the representation of his character which was begun in the
thirteenth chapter. His loud protestations of unswerving loyalty to Jesus, and his bold but rash act of attempting to defend
Him with the sword were wholly undone by his sudden denial.
The record was necessary to explain the words of Jesus in
13:38: "Wilt thou lay down thy life for me? Verily, verily,
I say unto thee, The cock shall not crow, till thou hast denied
me thrice." The sudden collapse of Peter's inflated purpose
revealed the inherent weakness of the flesh apart from supernatural grace.

The Interview with Pilate (18:28-19:16)

The trial before Pilate is given more space in JOHN than
in any one of the Synoptics, in spite of certain omissions from
John's narrative. He does not mention the initial accusation
presented to Pilate (Luke 23:2), nor the repeated accusations by the priests (Matt. 27:12; Mark 15:3), nor the hearing before Herod (Luke 23:4-12), nor the priests' agitation
for Barabbas (Matt. 27:20, Mark 15:11). The first charge
was assumed rather than expressed, and the committal to Herod was probably omitted by the author because it had no bearing on the character of Pilate. John's portrayal of this incident
was designed to bring the personalities of Pilate and Jesus into
sharp relief. As he narrated it, the judicial aspect of the occasion became less prominent, and the character of Pilate became

more important. It was a trial of Pilate before Christ instead of Christ before Pilate.

The first impression given of Pilate was his reluctance to take part in the action. The fact that he was available for conference at an unseasonably early hour probably meant that he had been forewarned. On the preceding night the Sanhedrin may have informed him that they were about to apprehend a dangerous prisoner whom they would bring to him for the final sentence. Action in criminal cases was subject to Pilate as the ruling Roman governor, since Rome had divested the Jewish Sanhedrin of the authority to inflict capital punishment. He was in no very genial mood when the priestly group, leading Jesus bound, appeared in his courtyard.

The question of Pilate, "What accusation bring ye against this man?" (29) was a part of the usual legal routine. Formal complaint had to be lodged before he could proceed with the case. The sullen, half-insolent reply, "If this man were not an evil-doer, we should not have delivered him up unto thee," showed that the priests had not brought the prisoner for examination, but to have their sentence confirmed. The answer carried a veiled contempt, as if they were telling the governor that their judgment was sufficient, and that his business was to carry out their behest. Pilate replied by a command which was virtually a taunt: "Take him yourselves, and judge him according to your law" (31). He sarcastically told them that they should finish what they had started. Why should they expect Rome to be the executioner for their law? And if they were unable to do it, so much the worse for them!

The author intimated that the situation brought about a closer fulfillment of Jesus' words. Had the Sanhedrin possessed the right to execute Jesus, they undoubtedly would have stoned Him to death, for stoning was prescribed by the law (Lev. 20:27). Crucifixion was the Roman method which Jesus had foretold (3:14, 12:32, 33). The administering of the penalty by Rome made His death an imperial, not a provincial, affair.

Pilate's unwillingness to act on Jesus' case was manifested throughout the interview. He pronounced the prisoner innocent of any crime (38) ; he sought to release Him in accordance with the annual custom of pardoning a prisoner at the Passover (39) ; he tried to placate the priests with a halfway punishment and a sentimental presentation (19:5) ; he pleaded with the crowd (12) ; and he employed sarcasm, "Shall I crucify your King?" (15). All of these devices availed nothing; the priesthood was resolute in will, and forced Pilate's hand.

Another feature of Pilate's attitude was uneasiness. He made at least four trips between the outer court where he met the Jews (18:28) and the inner chamber or hall where he took Jesus for questioning.

> Pilate went out to meet the delegation and the prisoner. 18:29
> Pilate went in and called Jesus for consultation. 18:33
> Pilate went out again to report his verdict. 18:38
> Pilate went in again to order the scourging. 19:1 (inference)
> Pilate went out again to present Jesus. 19:4
> Pilate went back again to question Jesus further. 19:9
> Pilate brought Jesus out again for the final verdict. 19:13

Apart from any comment by the author, the very physical motion betrayed his inner conflict and his vacillation. He was certain only of the fact that Jesus was innocent. Pilate's behavior on this occasion was quite different from the character of blunt and obstinate decisiveness which history has assigned to him.

A third aspect of the attitude of Pilate was his readiness to hear Jesus. The opening interrogation, "Art thou the King of the Jews?" (18:33) was evoked by the charges which the chief priests had transmitted to him. From their standpoint it was the most damaging accusation possible, because it would be regarded by the Roman governor as tantamount to treason. To Pilate's mind, it was half a joke. His question could well be translated, "So YOU are the King of the Jews, are you?" His amusement was ill-concealed, and perhaps he did not know whether to be severe or facetious. The bedraggled figure before him did not look like most of the defiant rebels whom he had arrested as claimants to the Jewish throne. Possibly he thought that the priests were trying to play a practical joke on him. The emphatic use of the second personal pronoun in Pilate's question showed that he did not expect to receive the kind of person that stood before him.

The dignified reply of Jesus, "Sayest thou this of thyself, or did others tell it thee concerning me?" (34), took Pilate by surprise. The defendant vouchsafed no violent protestations of innocence, nor was He sullenly defiant. He treated Pilate as an equal, not as a superior; and questioned him in turn. Jesus politely but firmly asked him whether he were acting on his own initiative, or whether the charge were second-hand. He challenged directly both his motives and his justice.

Pilate exploded with indignation. "Am I a Jew? Thine own nation and the chief priests delivered thee unto me: what hast thou done?" (35). His contempt for the Jews and his impatience with Jesus' impugning his motives came to the surface immediately. This annoying but mystifying prisoner must be put in his place.

Jesus, however, serenely proceeded to explain that His kingdom was not of this world. Were it so, His servants would have taken the world's method of establishing it by fighting.

Pilate's anger subsided into baffled curiosity: "Art thou a king then?" (37). Although well acquainted with royalty, he could not classify Jesus with any king that he knew; nevertheless he was not ready to deny the claim because of the strange assurance that Jesus possessed.

Jesus, realizing Pilate's growing interest, gave him a little bait to draw him on. "Thou sayest that I am a king. To this end have I been born, and to this end I am come 'into the world, that I should bear witness unto the truth. Every one that is of the truth heareth my voice" (37). This was a subtle appeal, for a judge was supposed to adhere to the truth. Logically, then, if Pilate were devoted to truth, he would hear it in Jesus' voice; if not, he would brand himself as not belonging to the truth.

Pilate's reply, "What is truth?" has been variously interpreted as a cynical disavowal of the possibility of knowing any truth, as a contemptuous jest at anything so impractical as abstract truth, or as a wistful desire to know what nobody thus far had been able to tell him. In any case, he probably was not jesting, for the occasion was too serious. He was convinced of Jesus' innocence of the charge against Him, and he sought to release Him. His attitude had swung from scornful surprise to that of respectful though puzzled regard. With a few words, Jesus had confronted him with the real issue at stake: his attitude toward truth. Had he realized it, the answer to his question, whether prompted by cynicism, scorn, or sincere desire, was within arm's reach of him, for Jesus was the Way, the *Truth,* and the Life (14:6). Pilate was facing the opportunity of a lifetime.

The suspense of this moment must have been tremendous both for Pilate and for Jesus. It was portentous for Pilate because he was torn between the alternatives of saving an obviously innocent man and the possibility of losing his own position. The real temper of Pilate was revealed in his attempt to solve the dilemma by a futile compromise, and his ensuing action became a moral retreat which turned into a rout.

It was a critical moment for Jesus because the soul of Pilate hung in the balance. Jesus suffered no illusions concerning the outcome as far as He was affected. He had already predicted His death and He expected it. Nor could He have been ignorant of the ultimate verdict and of its effect on His judge. Nevertheless, His appeal was made in all sincerity. Pilate's negative decision would make even more poignant the suffering which rejection by His own people and political selfishness had occasioned.

Pilate's moral rout was revealed in the rapid deterioration of his attitude. Confronted by the necessity of choice, he had become progressively interested in Jesus and increasingly serious. From the time of compromise until he surrendered to the will of the malicious priesthood there was a steady decline. The first step down was fear. When the Jews added the religious charge to the civil and said, "We have a law, and by that law he ought to die, because he made himself the Son of God" (19:7), Pilate was afraid. "Son of God" did not connote blasphemy to him, as it did to Jewish ears, but brought to his mind the legendary tales of the offspring of the gods who visited men occasionally and who performed remarkable deeds. Was not Aeneas, the subject of Virgil's great epic, the son of Venus, and sponsored by his divine mother? Perhaps, he thought, this mysterious stranger *was* half divine! He ought at least to make sure. Again he questioned Jesus, "Whence art thou?" But Pilate had rejected Jesus' first overtures. He was not interested in truth for its own sake, but only as an expedient to save himself. Consequently, Jesus had nothing to say to him, and He remained silent. There can be neither assurance nor comfort for the man who wilfully compromises with truth.

Pilate's initial fears became frantic terror, which expressed itself in braggadocio. "Speakest thou not unto ME?[3] knowest

---

3. Capitals ours to convey emphasis of Greek *emoi*, the emphatic form of the personal pronoun.

thou not that I have power to release thee, and have power to crucify thee?" (10). The irony of his statement is plain. If he had the authority to release Jesus, whom he had already pronounced innocent, why did he not exercise it? Theoretically he had the power; practically he was bound by his own sins and by the political commitments he had made.

Jesus' words show that He was absolutely in possession of Himself and superior to Pilate. His utterance contained pity and reproof, much as one would speak to a naughty child to undo his self-deception and to discipline him. In all of Pilate's cowardice and carelessness Jesus showed a real concern for him. Perhaps he was not far from the kingdom of God.

The last attitude of Pilate was bitterness. The question, "Shall I crucify your King?" embodied in one stinging piece of sarcasm all of Pilate's hatred toward the Jews who had goaded him into what he knew was a wrong moral decision. The old Pilate, haughty, cruel, and cynical, reappeared. In the final inscription over the cross, his cold arrogance became fixed: "What I have written I have written" (22).

A study of the attitudes of Pilate thus reveals that he passed from perfunctory official indifference through curiosity to intense personal concern, and then, because he did not dare to act on what he knew was right, he gave way to hesitation, fear, arrogance, and bitterness. He was aroused by Jesus' presence and bearing, but he was reluctant to conform to the truth as the occasion presented it, and so he lost Jesus altogether. The story of Pilate is the tragedy of unbelief.

The Crucifixion (19:17-37)

No one of the Gospels deals at length with the crucifixion of Christ, and no two of them coincide exactly in the narration of detail. The greatest number of variants from the common tradition occur in JOHN; but the distinctive element in this

Gospel is not an accident. The aspects which the Fourth Gospel contain were selected carefully for the purpose of concluding the main theme: belief versus unbelief. John 19:35 says explicitly that the record of an eyewitness is stated and corroborated "that ye also may believe." The problem in analyzing this section is to establish the relation between the facts emphasized and the potential belief of the reader.

The narrative of the crucifixion may be divided naturally into six paragraphs, each of which contains a unit of action taken from the scene as a whole.

The act of crucifixion	17,18
The placing of the title on the cross	19-22
The division of the garments	23-25a
The provision for Jesus' mother	25b-27
The final cry from the cross	28-30
The piercing with the spear	31-37

The crucifixion was mentioned in the fewest possible words. John, who alone of all the disciples witnessed it, said the least about it. The paragraph merely states the act, the place, and the fact that two others shared the same fate as Jesus. The reticence of the writer indicates that he did not lay great value upon stressing the physical suffering. Besides, in a day when crucifixion was still a current method of execution, it would have been too familiar to need description and too horrible a thought to deserve elaboration.

The title on the cross, "JESUS OF NAZARETH, THE KING OF THE JEWS" (19), had a twofold significance. An inscription, of course, was usually hung over crucified criminals in order to inform the public of the reason for their execution. In this instance, it was used by Pilate as the vehicle for a sarcastic thrust at the Jews; for he was exhibiting this man, condemned to a criminal's death at the demand of His own national rulers, as their king! If Rome would thus treat their king, and if the Jewish priesthood concurred in valuing

Him so lightly, what were the rest of them worth? Small wonder that they protested, asking that the inscription be amended to state that the title was Jesus' claim, not the Roman verdict! Pilate refused to acquiesce to their demands, and in that refusal all of his sardonic hatred for the Jews was concentrated. He stubbornly objected to lifting the stigma which the death of Jesus placed upon the nation.

The other significance of this inscription was its ironic statement of truth. Though the concept of the kingdom of God is much less prominent in JOHN than in Matthew, the author put himself on record concerning the nature of the kingdom by quoting Jesus' own words. In the discourse with Nicodemus Jesus had said that the kingdom could not be entered except by those who experienced a spiritual rebirth (3:5), and He confirmed the essential spiritual character of the kingdom by saying to Pilate that it was "not of this world" (18:36). Jesus' claim to royalty was asserted in a new way and was supported by unusual methods. He demonstrated His sovereignty by dying, not by fighting; and the inscription on the cross was the laconic expression of that fact.

The division of the garments (23-25a) was not an exceptional deed of brutality. In any case of crucifixion, the garments of the victim became the property of the soldiery detailed for execution. The importance of the incident was that the soldiers gambled for the seamless tunic just as the prophetic psalm (Ps. 22) had predicted. Three times in this narrative the fulfillment of Scripture was mentioned, as if to make sure that the reader would understand that the event was connected with the Old Testament prophecy (24, 28, 36). The Synoptists did not suggest that the division of the garments was a fulfillment of prophecy.

The two paragraphs concerning Jesus' mother (25b-27) and the completion of His task (28-30) contain all of the words that Jesus spoke from the cross as John reported them. They represent the thought and action of Jesus in the last hour of His earthly life. Each word was significant because it denoted a different relation of Jesus to His work.

The utterance concerning His mother, "Woman, behold, thy son! . . . Behold, thy mother!" marked the discharge of His human obligations. Even at the cross, with the destiny of His person and calling at stake, He was not unmindful of His duty to His family. Perhaps the unbelief of His brethren (7:5) had created a rift in the family circle, and had alienated His brothers from Him. According to one theory not generally accepted, they were the children of Joseph by a former marriage, in which case He would be only a half brother, and His mother their stepmother.[4] Since probably there was no member of the family present to whom He could entrust her, He put her in the care of the beloved disciple, who alone of the Twelve appeared at the cross. The immediate response of this disciple was the proof of his loyalty.

"I thirst" betokened Jesus' deep participation in human suffering. He endured the terrible thirst that accompanied crucifixion as a token of His voluntary sharing in all human woe. The "vinegar" which was given to Him was the cheap sour wine which the common soldiers drank, sharp in taste and astringent in quality. Paradoxically enough, He who had offered to all men the water of life (4:14, 7:37, 38) died thirsting.

"It is finished," marked the achievement of perfection. Jesus died with a consciousness that His work was done, and that there was nothing left for Him to accomplish. The cry should not be interpreted as the last gasp of a defeated martyr,

---

4. This was the theory of Epiphanius, in the fourth century. See J. B. Mayor, in HDB, I, p. 320.

but as the shout of a triumphant victor. In His prayer in 17:4 He said, "I glorified thee on the earth, having accomplished the work which thou hast given me to do." His earthly mission was absolutely complete.

Two brief notes of comment on the language of verse 30 are pertinent. The word *bowed* can be translated "laid to rest." It occurs only this once in JOHN, but it was used once by Jesus as recorded by Matthew (8:20) and by Luke (9:58), where He said that "the Son of man hath not where to lay his head." As John said, "He came unto his own, and they that were his own received him not" (1:11). The only place where He could lay His head to rest was on the cross.

The second word in verse 30 worthy of note is, "he . . . gave up his spirit." It implies voluntary action, not deprivation. The fact that Jesus laid down His life of His own choice (10:11) goes far toward explaining the remarkable character of His death.

The removal of the body from the cross (31-37) was requested by the Jews, since leaving the bodies publicly suspended would be a breach of the Mosaic law and would defile the Passover. In accordance with the Roman custom, the executioners broke the legs of the victims prior to their removal from the cross. The purpose of this cruel deed was twofold. Either the shock and the pain would hasten death, or, if the victim survived, he would be crippled permanently, and so would be unable to engage in any further activities against the government. This episode was mentioned because of its importance as evidence for the actuality of Jesus' death. The executioners were experts who could tell the difference between death and a coma induced by pain and exhaustion. Since they refrained from breaking the legs of Jesus, they obviously regarded Him as dead. Furthermore, the piercing of His side by the soldier's spear with the resulting flow of blood (crassamentum) and water (serum) is certain proof that death had already taken place, since only blood would flow from a living body. If Jesus had not really died, it could not be said that He had been raised from the dead; and if He were a phantom, then death and resurrection alike would be meaningless to Him.

A careful consideration of the groups present at the crucifixion shows that the cross became the dividing line between belief and unbelief. Unbelief was at its height, since it had achieved its objective in destroying Jesus. Belief was at its lowest ebb, for it had been unable to stem the hostile tide that swept Jesus to His death. The distinction between the two is plainer than ever. On the side of unbelief were the Jewish high priests and rulers, Pilate, and the soldiers of the execution squad. On the other side were the women, including Jesus' mother, the beloved disciple, and possibly Nicodemus and Joseph of Arimathea who appeared later at the burial.

Each group was representative of the belief or unbelief of some class of person. The chief priests and Jews possessed the bitter and implacable unbelief of organized religionists who were actuated by jealousy, prejudice, self-aggrandizement, and self-interest. Their religion had lost its spontaneity and had become ritual which was defended rather than lived. Pilate embodied the unbelief of political expediency which was accompanied by no particular religious convictions — or by no convictions at all. He might have listened to Jesus more carefully had not his standing with Caesar been at stake, for he held no malicious grudge against Him. He might even have released Him if it had been expedient for his own interests. He did not, however, dare to oppose openly the priests and scribes who dominated Jerusalem. Pilate, in short, was the type of man who will believe, provided he does not have to sacrifice his reputation or personal convenience. The soldiers, rolling dice in a helmet at the foot of the cross to decide which of them should possess the meager belongings of the Crucified, were a picture of the callousness and indifference of unbelief. Jesus meant less to them than He did to Pilate; He was only an incident in a day's work, and a rather unimportant one at that. His sufferings and death evoked no interest from them. Unbelief, then, malicious, or selfish, or indifferent, appeared at its worst at the cross. Stripped of all polite disguise, it stood revealed in all its hideous rebellion against God.

Belief was manifested at the cross also. The women courageously took their stand nearby as a declaration of loyalty, though that loyalty seemed futile. The mother of Jesus, who had not been mentioned in the narrative since the account of the wedding at Cana, reappeared with the same faith and devotion that she showed when she said to the servants at the wedding, "Whatsoever he saith unto you, do it" (2:5). She could trust Him when she could not understand Him. Of Mary of Clopas, little or nothing is known. Mary Magdalene was one of the women who had traveled in Jesus' company and who had contributed to His support. Jesus had cured her of demon possession, according to Luke's Gospel (Luke 8:2, 3). Contrary to popular legend, there is no evidence that she had ever been a woman of ill fame. By these women the chief qualities of belief, loyalty, gratitude, and love, were exemplified. With them stood the unnamed disciple who had leaned on Jesus' breast and who had followed Him through the trial. His belief was rewarded by Jesus' confidence in Him, witnessed by the committal of His mother. In this case Jesus reversed the attitude predicated of Him in John 2:24: "Jesus did not trust himself unto them, for that he knew all men."

The Burial (19:38-42)

Although the account of the burial deserves separate treatment, it is closely related to the crucifixion by the thread of belief as explained above. Joseph of Arimathea and Nicodemus were Jewish noblemen, probably members of the Sanhedrin, and wealthy in their own right. Their eagerness to claim the body of Jesus is little short of surprising since by so doing they openly declared themselves as sympathizers with His cause. It is easy to belittle them as bringing spices for His burial when they should have stood up boldly for Him during His lifetime. Nicodemus, however, had once defended His rights before the council of the Pharisees (7:50-52). If Nicodemus and Joseph had been secret believers, the genuineness of their belief was proved by their open, though belated, act of loyalty. They dared to approach the sullen Pilate with their request for the body and they received it as a grant. Perhaps Pilate felt that he could afford to be generous after the crisis had passed.

The burial itself is important to the argument of JOHN since it added one more witness to the reality of Jesus' death. It is incredible that these two men should have handled Jesus' body without knowing whether his death were actual or not. Furthermore, they never would have committed it to the tomb if they had not been convinced that the breath of life had departed.

The method of burial was described as in accordance with the custom of the Jews.[5] The Jews did not embalm as the Egyptians did, by removing the soft organs of the body, and by drying the muscular tissues with preservatives. The corpse was washed (Acts 9:37), and swathed in bandage-like wrappings[6] from armpits to feet, in the folds of which spices were

---

5. T. Nicol, "Burial" in HDB, I, 331-333. Cf. B. F. Westcott, *op. cit.*, II, pp. 323, 324. "The process indicated is the simple wrapping of the dead body in swathes of linen cloth covered with thick layers of the aromatic preparation."

6. Greek: *othonia*—linen cloths, bandages. Used only in John 19:40, 20:5, 6, 7, and Luke 24:12, a disputed reading. In the LXX it means linen garments. Hippocrates and Aristophanes used the word of bandages. The parallel with Lazarus makes the latter meaning more probable.

placed (Matt. 27:59, Luke 23:53), and a cloth was wound around the head. John's use of "bound" (19:40) implies close wrapping, and comparison with the account of the burial of Lazarus in 11:44 confirms the implication. The tomb was Joseph's own (Matt. 27:60), which he had originally reserved for the use of his own family. Because evening was rapidly approaching when the feast day would begin, Joseph and Nicodemus chose this tomb as the burial place. Its close proximity to the place of execution eliminated the task of transporting the body any great distance, and Joseph's ownership would insure the comparative safety of Jesus' remains against vandalism or dishonor of any kind. Perhaps they intended to complete the burial after the Sabbath had closed, since the amount of spices which they had on hand seemed greater than could be used in so hasty an interment. At any rate, the body was tenderly and securely laid to rest, and the door was closed firmly by the stone which had been rolled against it.

The Resurrection (20:1-29)

The twentieth chapter of John is the climax of the book. The tragedy of unbelief which culminated in the cross would remain forever unresolved were there no resurrection, for evil would have triumphed over good and the heroic and vicarious death of Jesus would be at best a magnificent but futile gesture. In that event, faith in a good God would be irrational, the concept of a moral universe would be impossible, and stark pessimism would be the necessary philosophy of all humanity.

The Johannine account of the resurrection is remarkable for several reasons. It is compact, and tells the essential story in a surprisingly short compass. It is historical, for it connects spiritual meaning with events in space and time, and presents evidence which asserts the reality of the supernatural without employing the extravagant tales of apocryphal legend. It is personal and interprets the resurrection as it affected the intimate lives of certain of Jesus' disciples. It is coherent with the rest of the Gospel, for it summarizes by illustration the various effects of belief and brings that belief to its highest expression.

In order that the reader may see the content of the chapter at a glance, the mechanical analysis with derived topical outline is given instead of textual exposition as heretofore.

JOHN 20 — THE RESURRECTION

1 Now . . . | on the first day of the week
cometh Mary Magdalene
early,
while it was yet dark,
unto the tomb,
and seeth the stone taken away from the tomb.

2 She runneth therefore,
and cometh to Simon Peter,
| and to the other disciple / whom Jesus loved,
and saith unto them,
They have taken . . . the Lord
away
out of the tomb,
and we know not where they have laid him.

3 Peter therefore went forth,
and the other disciple,
and they went toward the tomb.

4 And they ran both together:
and the other disciple outran Peter,
and came first to the tomb;

5 and . . . he seeth the linen cloths lying;
stooping
and looking in,
yet entered he not in.

6 Simon Peter therefore also cometh,
following him,
and entered into the tomb;
and he beholdeth the linen cloths lying,

7   and the napkin / that was upon his head,
not lying with the linen cloths,
but rolled up in a place by itself.

8 Then entered in therefore the other disciple also,
who came first to the tomb,
and he saw,
and believed.

9 For as yet they knew not the scripture,
that he must rise again from the dead.

10 So the disciples went away again unto their own home.

11 But Mary was standing
without
at the tomb
weeping:
as she wept,
so . . . / she stooped
and looked into the tomb;

12 and she beholdeth two angels in white sitting,
one at the head,   where the body of Jesus had lain.
and one at the feet,

Paragraph I: DISCOVERY OF MATERIAL EVIDENCE

A. *The Open Tomb*

   1. The arrival of Mary

   2. The discovery of the open tomb
   3. The hasty return to Jerusalem
   4. The report to Simon Peter and the other disciple

   5. The conclusion: "They have taken away the Lord."

B. *The Grave Clothes*

   1. The response of Peter and the other disciple
   2. The race to the tomb

   3. The arrival of the other disciple

     a. "Saw" linen cloths

     b. Position outside

   4. The arrival of Peter
     a. Entrance into the tomb
     b. "Observed" cloths

   5. The entrance of the other disciple

     a. "Perceived" cloths
     b. Belief
       (Parenthetical explanation of ignorance of Scripture)

   6. The departure of the disciples

Paragraph II: DISCLOSURE OF THE LIVING LORD

A. *The Attitude of Mary*
   1. Lamentation—"wept"

   2. Investigation—"looked"
   3. Observation—"beholdeth two angels"
     a. Appearance of angels
     b. Position of angels

13 And they say unto her,
   Woman, why weepest thou?
 She saith unto them,
    Because they have taken away my Lord,
      and I know not where they have laid him.

14   When she had thus said,
 she turned herself back,
 and beholdeth Jesus standing,
 and knew not that it was Jesus.

15 Jesus saith unto her,
   | Woman, why weepest thou?
   | Whom seekest thou?
 She . . . saith unto him,
  supposing him to be the gardener,
    Sir, if thou hast borne him hence,
    tell me where thou hast laid him,
    and I will take him away.

16 Jesus saith unto her, Mary.
 She turneth herself,
    and saith unto him / in Hebrew, / Rabboni,
      which is to say, Teacher.

17 Jesus saith to her,
   | Touch me not;
   | for I am not yet ascended unto the Father:
   | but go unto my brethren,
   | and say to them,
     I ascend unto my Father,
       | and your Father,
       | and my God
       | and your God.

18 Mary Magdalene cometh
  and telleth the disciples,
    I have seen the Lord;
    and that he had said these things unto her.

19 | When therefore it was evening, on that day,
          the first day of the week,
  | and when the doors were shut
     | where the disciples were,
     | for fear of the Jews,
 Jesus came
 and stood in the midst,
 and saith unto them, Peace be unto you.

20 And when he had said this,
 he showed unto them | his hands
        | and his side.
 The disciples therefore were glad,
     when they saw the Lord.

4. Desperation (in answer)
   a. Question

   b. Answer
      (1) Deprivation
      (2) Disappointment
5. Frustration
   a. Attempted departure

   b. Failure to recognize Jesus
   c. Question
   d. Answer

      (1) False assumption of identity
      (2) Devotion

B. *The Revelation of Jesus*
   1. Salutation by name

   2. Recognition by title
   3. Adoration (inference from Jesus' subsequent language)
   4. Command of Jesus

   5. Comfort ("Not yet ascended")

   6. Commission

C. *The Transformation of Mary*

   1. Positive activity
   2. Testimony
      a. Of what she had seen
      b. Of what she had heard

Paragraph III: DEPRESSION OF DISCIPLES RELIEVED

A. *The Secret Meeting of the Disciples*
   1. Time: evening

   2. Atmosphere: fear

B. *The Arrival of Jesus among the Disciples*
   1. His presence: real
   2. His message: peace
   3. His demonstration of identity: wounds

C. *The Attitude of the Disciples: Changed to Gladness*

21 Jesus therefore said to them again,
                    Peace be unto you:
                            as the Father hath sent me,
                    even so send I you.

22 And   when he had said this,
        he breathed on them,
    and saith unto them,

23 | Receive ye the Holy Spirit:
    | whose soever sins ye forgive,
    | they are forgiven unto them;
    | whose soever sins ye retain,
    | they are retained.

24 But Thomas, . . . was not with them when Jesus came.
    | one of the twelve,
    | called Didymus,

25 The other disciples therefore said unto him,
                            We have seen the Lord.
    But he said unto them,
                    Except I shall see in his hands the print of tne nails,
                            and put my finger into the print of the nails,
                            and put my hand into his side,
            I will not believe.

26 And   after eight days again
        his disciples were within,
    and Thomas with them.
    Jesus cometh,
            the doors being shut,
        and stood in the midst,
    and said, Peace be unto you.

27 Then saith he to Thomas,
    | Reach hither thy finger,
    | and see my hands;
    | and reach hither thy hand,
    | and put it into my side:
    | and be not faithless,
    | but   believing.

28 Thomas answered
            and said unto him, My Lord and my God.

29 Jesus saith unto him,
    | Because thou hast seen me,
    | thou hast believed:
    | blessed are they that have not seen,
    | and yet have believed.

D. *The Commission to the Disciples*
1. A gift: peace
2. A command: to continue His mission

3. An enduement: The Holy Spirit
4. An authority: forgiveness

Paragraph IV: DOUBT DISPELLED

A. *Doubt Rampant*
1. Insufficient experience

2. Sufficient testimony

3. Demand for objective proof

B. *Doubt Refuted*

1. Resurrection power demonstrated

2. Reality of physical presence
3. Renewal of personal greeting
4. Reply to Thomas' challenge

5. Rebuke to Thomas' attitude

C. *Doubt Renounced*

1. Thomas' confession of faith

2. Jesus' evaluation of faith
   a. Belief on sight good
   b. Belief without sight better

Two topics which appear in the foregoing text deserve a
fuller treatment than the outline affords.

The Evidence of the Resurrection

So stupendous an event as the resurrection of Christ must
be confirmed by adequate evidence. Although its reality must
be received by faith, since unbelief will never of its own voli-
tion change its attitude, there are certain facts made clear in
this narrative which argue convincingly for the supernatural
restoration of Jesus to the world.

The first bit of evidence was the fact that the door of the
sepulchre was open. The rock hewn tombs in Palestine were
usually closed by a circular stone, weighing several tons, and
set in a slanting groove so that when the stone was released, it
would by its own weight roll into place over the door. Very
little strength would be required to close the door, but the
united effort of several men would be necessary to open it.
Since the stone was found rolled away, it must have been
moved by some powerful force and for a definite purpose.

Who would have moved it? The women, who were the
earliest visitors at the grave did not expect to find it rolled
away, and they were incapable of moving it themselves. If
Jesus' disciples had done it that they might take His body, they
did so without the knowledge of the women, Peter or the unnamed disciple. The latter two came running to the tomb when
they were informed it had been opened. They would hardly
have wasted that energy if they had known the facts in advance.
The enemies of Jesus were not responsible; for it was wholly
to their interest to keep the body where it was. John did not
say directly how the stone was moved; but he left the impression in the mind of the reader that it was done by divine intervention.

A second witness was the appearance of the grave clothes.
When the unnamed disciple came to the tomb and peered into
the dark interior, he probably could see little. The sun was not

high on the horizon; he would have to stand in his own light in order to look through the narrow doorway; and his eyes would not have been adjusted to the darkness within. The white outline of the grave clothes would be perceptible against the blackness of the interior, and so it was recorded that he "saw" them. Perhaps he assumed that if the clothes were in position the body was also there. It would have been practically impossible to extract the body from its wrappings and to leave them in good order. The probability is that any clever grave robber would have taken body, grave clothes and all. Consequently, he reasoned, the women were mistaken. Seeing the open door, they had jumped to the conclusion that the body had been taken away, while actually it was still there.

These meditations of the unnamed disciple were disturbed by Peter, who by this time had joined him, and had entered the tomb. Apparently it was not Peter's comments but his silence that induced his companion finally to enter, where he found Peter gazing intently at the grave clothes. Not only had they been left in the tomb, but they were still neatly folded. The head cloth in particular was rolled up just as if Jesus' head were still in it. The other disciple at once "saw"—perceived the significance of the fact—"and believed" (8). The tomb had not been opened to let Jesus out, but to let in the disciples. Transformed by the resurrection, He had passed through the grave clothes, leaving like an outworn chrysalis the cerements of the tomb for the vestments of glory.

The personal appearances of Jesus afforded direct evidence of His resurrection. They cannot be explained on the basis of hallucination, since the disciples neither expected nor believed that He would rise. Impersonation will not account for it, because His followers met in a locked room to which only members of their own company were admitted. In each instance which the author records the physical reality of Jesus was stressed. Mary saw, heard, and touched Him; the disciples recognized Him; and Thomas, who had demanded tangible

proof of the testimony of his friends, was convinced. If it be
objected that the whole record is improbable, and therefore
untrue, it is still necessary to account for the motives which
produced such a story, and for the initial evidence which made
it convincing to the first believers. There can be no doubt that
the Christians of the first century, including the author of this
Gospel, believed in the physical return of Jesus from death.
The simplest solution for the problem is to accept the resurrection as a fact.

The Effect of the Resurrection

Although it was necessary for John's purpose to demonstrate
the fact of the resurrection so that he might induce belief in
his hearers, it was equally imperative that he should describe
its effect on those who witnessed it. The mere chronicle of the
event, however wonderful that might be, would have no value
unless the acceptance of its actuality affected personal character. In selecting the material to be presented, John stressed
the change which was produced in the lives of the witnesses.
Five groups or individuals were mentioned in this chapter:
Mary Magdalene, who may have represented the women;
Peter; the unnamed disciple, who was doubtless John himself;
the ten or eleven disciples as a group; and Thomas.

Mary was the picture of frustrated devotion. Her love for
Jesus was emphasized particularly by John. She was apparently the leader of the women who went to the tomb to
anoint the body early on the first day of the week. Their neg-
lect to consider how they would remove the stone showed that
they were so taken up with their errand of love that they overlooked one of the most important problems in the execution of
it. Mary's agitation over finding the stone rolled away, her
hurried summons to Peter and John, and her uncontrollable
grief as she watched at the tomb, all indicate the depth of her
emotion. Life had lost its meaning for her when Jesus died because she had lost the object of her gratitude and affection.

Jesus' resurrection changed her futile tears into active effort. The mourner became a missionary as Jesus commissioned her to go to His disciples with the message that He had risen.

Peter was not given great prominence in the account, but the little said of him is significant. He ran to the tomb; and it is safe to say that he would not have run unless he had a deep concern for Jesus. The last reference to him prior to the twentieth chapter was the denial, though repentance followed quickly upon his failure, as the Synoptics relate (Matt. 26:75). It was, however, too late for Peter to express his sorrow to Jesus, and Jesus' death, as far as he knew, permanently removed any possibility of adjustment. Peter was left carrying the burden of an unforgiven sin. The resurrection meant for him the assurance of forgiveness and restoration to fellowship with his Lord.

John, the disciple who leaned on Jesus' breast at the last supper, and who regarded Him as his best friend, was left desolate after the crucifixion. Though he had not the bitterness of regret that Peter did, the gap in his life must have been wide. Like Peter, he ran to the tomb, prompted by the desire to ascertain what had happened to the body, and perhaps because he was dimly hopeful that by some good fortune Jesus might manifest Himself again. His discernment was keener than Peter's, for "he saw, and believed" (20:8). Later the sundered friendship was restored when Jesus returned.

The disciples as a group were oppressed by the emotion of fear. Primarily they dreaded the Jewish rulers, who had sent Jesus to His death and might be waiting to deal with them in similar fashion. They had not left Jerusalem, perhaps because they felt that remaining quietly in the city would make them less conspicuous than sudden flight would, and they met behind closed doors lest their presence should be known. The resurrection changed their fear into courage, so that on the day of Pentecost and afterward "with great power gave the apostles their witness of the resurrection of the Lord Jesus: and great grace was upon them all" (Acts 4:33).

Thomas was a living demonstration of the power of Christ to dispel doubt. He was naturally of a pessimistic temperament as his previous utterances showed (11:16, 14:5), and his doubt seems to have been the product of his pessimism rather than lack of confidence in Jesus Himself. After all, he knew that Jesus had died, and he could say, "The worst has happened just as I said it would." Jesus volunteered to submit to the very test that Thomas had demanded. The fact that He knew what Thomas had said when He was not present was convincing proof of His supernatural knowledge, and His willingness to accept Thomas on his own terms was a marvel of condescension and compassion. It is unthinkable that Thomas did actually put Jesus' body to the test. All his unbelief vanished as he worshipped. For a Jew to salute another man, however he might revere him, as "Lord and God" (28) could only mean that he had come to the point of worshipping Him as deity. The resurrection made the difference between the skepticism of despair and the worship which brings certainty.

Thus belief in a risen Christ made a mourner into a missionary, a penitent into a preacher, the bereaved friend into an apostle of love, a timid and shrinking coterie of disciples into the fearless heralds of a new movement, and a doubter into a confessor. With the confession of Thomas, JOHN reached the high peak of belief: faith can rise no higher than when it avows Jesus of Nazareth to be its Lord and God.

The main narrative of the Gospel closes with verses 30 and 31, which have already been treated as the key to the book. They echo Jesus' word to Thomas, "Become not unbelieving, but believing."[7]

---

7. John 20:27b—original translation.

THE EPILOGUE

THE EPILOGUE

A. The Manifestation of Jesus
B. The Invitation of Jesus
C. A New Motivation and Occupation
D. The Final Expectation

CHAPTER X

The Epilogue

21:1-25

THE twenty-first chapter of John is separated from the main body of the Gospel by the key, and in some respects it seems to be an afterthought because the preceding text has already brought the reader to a full and final declaration of faith. The Epilogue, however, is unmistakably genuine, and it is an integral part of the main narrative. Perhaps John wrote it later than the first part of his book; but there is no textual evidence that the rest of the Gospel was ever circulated without it, nor that it was added by an editor. The use of the Epilogue is fully consonant with the Johannine procedure of illustrating and enforcing a principle by recounting an historic event.

The purpose of the Epilogue is to show how the belief which the disciples had achieved should be applied. The witness of the risen Lord to His followers had been completed, and they were ready to undertake the responsibilities of discipleship. Consequently, the last chapter of the Gospel opens the door to the future and shows how belief should be translated into terms of daily activity.

The Manifestation of Jesus (21:1-8)

The Epilogue as a whole centers around one manifestation of Jesus to His disciples by the lake of Galilee. The group present at the lake were seven in number, and should probably be regarded as the loyal core of the apostolic band. Five of them are named; the identity of the other two is unknown. If they were Andrew and Philip, who have been mentioned previously in the Gospel, there was a close correspondence between this group and the one that constituted the earliest disciples of Jesus. Simon, Nathanael, Andrew and Philip were among His first followers, and if the unnamed disciple of 1:40 were John, it is likely that James joined them soon afterwards. Thomas was not included in the original list, but he was one of those named by the author. Whether the continuity of this group can be established from the first or not, they had just shared the experiences of the Passion Week and had travelled together back to Galilee.

The last week in Jerusalem had been a trying and confusing period in the lives of these men. In the space of a few days they had received more teaching from Jesus than their immature spiritual state could assimilate; they had seen their hopes of an outward kingdom shattered; one of their own number had betrayed Jesus to the chief priests, and all of them had forsaken Him as He went to the cross. In two or three hours they had been reduced from the position of disciples of an honored and popular teacher to that of the hunted partisans of a discredited impostor. Then, in addition to all this, came the resurrection, with the startling appearances and the unmistakable proof that Jesus had risen.

With these occurrences fresh in their memories, the disciples withdrew to Galilee. In Jerusalem they had been in a strange city where unnerving events had followed each other with dizzy rapidity. Perhaps they questioned whether these events were real, or whether they had been dreaming. Galilee, however, was the same. The familiar haunts, the sight of the fishing boats rocking gently on the lake, the smell of the fish, and the pressing need of food and occupation brought them to a crisis. They could not afford to mope over vanished hopes or to speculate idly on what might have been. Peter, spokesman for the group as usual, said, "I go a fishing" (3), and the rest assented. Practical action was the best cure for their mystification and disappointment.

There is no reason to believe that Simon's proposal was sinful, but it was dangerous. Jesus had trained these men for something besides fishing. Considering the tremendous upheaval through which their minds had passed, their action was quite excusable since they sought to forget their perplexities in the rugged joy of hard work. They might, however, in concentrating on their livelihood forget the life of which Jesus had spoken, and they needed to be recalled to it.

The manifestation of Jesus was, then, a call to a new reality. Just as He had once before given them a large catch of fish when He summoned them to become His disciples (Luke 5: 1 11), so He repeated the miracle under similar circumstances. At dawn, after a night of fruitless toil, a voice hailed them from the shore: "Boys, you haven't anything to eat, have you?"[1] The question implied a knowledge that they had no results, and that the questioner was interested. Perhaps they thought that he was a buyer from one of the nearby cities who had come to view their catch, and they replied, "No." Then the voice came again: "Cast the net on the right side of the boat, and ye shall find" (6). Such procedure was unorthodox in fishing, but the men were desperate enough to try anything. When they cast the net, they were rewarded with a catch so great that they could not put it into the boat. Instantly John grasped what had happened, as he had done when he saw the grave clothes. "It is the Lord," he said. This time the manifestation had not occurred in the strange surroundings of Jerusalem, under circumstances so unusual as to make them wonder whether it were all a dream or not. The risen Lord demonstrated His power in their own familiar Galilee, while they were engaged in their own occupation. There could be no doubt about the voice, nor about the fish, nor about His presence. The resur-

---

1. Original translation of 21:5.

rection reality fitted into the pattern of their everyday experience.

The Invitation of Jesus (21:9-14)

The invitation of Jesus to eat was a call to the resumption of that fellowship which His death had broken. If they had previously doubted their own senses or His identity on the occasions when He appeared to them as a group, they could do so no longer, "knowing that it was the Lord" (12). Doubtless they had eaten in this fashion many times beside the lake. His return to them would renew the continuity of their life with Him; and the fact that He ate with them would strengthen the conviction that He was really before them. Peter must have been especially impressed by this, for he referred to it later in his preaching (Acts 10:41). The invitation of Jesus was designed to show that personal contact with Him was possible after the resurrection.

A New Motivation and Occupation (21:15-17)

Although Jesus had already appeared to Peter privately,[2] on which occasion He may well have restored Peter to His fellowship, Jesus' dealing with him at this time reinstated him publicly before the other disciples, and also conveyed Jesus' desire for a new motive in service. Peter's eagerness to see Jesus, as evinced by his hurried departure from the boat when John said, "It is the Lord" (7), was in itself a testimony to his devotion; but Jesus wanted him to declare himself unmistakably.

The threefold question: "Lovest thou me?" searched Peter's deepest motives. The shift of the verb in the Greek text has been noted by all expositors of this passage. Twice, in his initial question, Jesus said, "Peter, do you love me?" The verb employed there is *agapao,* the same as the one used of *love* in 3:16, which speaks of the love of God. When Peter answered,

---

2. Mark 16:7, Luke 24:34, I Cor. 15:5.

he used another verb, *phileo,* which implies friendship or fondness. In the third question, Jesus used Peter's own word which implied that He doubted the genuineness of Peter's profession. This interpretation gives point to the statement that "Peter was grieved because he said unto him the third time, Lovest thou me?" (17) Peter was not upset because Jesus questioned him three times, but because on the third occurrence Jesus challenged his sincerity.

The reality of the distinction between these two words has been disputed[3] on two grounds. First, the conversation between Jesus and Peter, though recorded in Greek, probably was carried on in Aramaic. The contention is that in Aramaic no such differentiation occurs, for there is only one word for *love,* and in the Syriac (Aramaic) version the same word is used to render both Greek words.

Again, the two words at times are used interchangeably in this Gospel. Both represent God's love for men, *agapao* in 14:23, 17:23, *phileo* in 16:27. Both are employed to describe the Father's love for the Son, as *agapao* in 3:35, or 17:23, 24, 26, and *phileo* in 5:20, and they also denote Jesus' love for men: *agapao* in 11:5, *phileo* in 11:3. This latter instance is striking. Since both verbs apply to Lazarus, a distinction between them cannot be pressed. Lastly, both indicate the love of men for Jesus: *agapao* in 14:15, 21, 23, 24, 28, and *phileo* in 16:27.

To the first objection the answer may be given that Greek is more flexible than Aramaic, and that the use of a single word for all degrees and types of love may signify the poverty of Aramaic rather than confusion in Greek. In replying to the second objection, one may say that the frequent interchange of terms as exact synonyms does not mean that they are absolute equivalents, but only that they may be used as approxi-

---

3. J. H. Bernard, *op. cit.,* II, pp. 702-704. See also John A. Scott, "The Words for 'Love' in John 21:15ff.", *The Classical Weekly,* 40 (1946) 8, pp. 60, 61. Scott states that there is no real difference between *agapao* and *phileo.*

mately equivalent in many cases. It is true that *agapao* is a more dignified term, while *phileo* connotes mainly emotional warmth and intensity. Both are to be distinguished from *erao*, which is never used in the New Testament, and which invariably means physical love.

In any case, Jesus was seeking to probe Peter's inmost purpose in following Him. The desire for personal success, eminence, achievement, reward, or even the relatively unselfish motive of doing something for needy humanity was not enough. Only a complete love for Christ would be sufficient to carry him and his fellow-disciples through the careers which awaited them in the future. Peter's response undoubtedly was sincere. He had learned by this time that he could not trust himself, but he was penitent and willing to obey.

The new occupation which Jesus offered to Peter was expressed in the command which he repeated three times in reply to Peter's avowal of love.

> Feed my lambs (15)
> Tend my sheep (16)
> Feed my sheep (17)

Jesus did not reprimand Peter for returning to fishing, but He did want him to understand that fishing was not to be the main business of life. These commands are linked with the discourse of the tenth chapter, where Jesus spoke of the "sheep" whom He had come to save at the cost of His own life (10:15), to whom He opened a door of safety and satisfaction (10:7), and whom, as "other sheep" outside of Israel's fold, He must reclaim. He was asking Peter and, through him, the others, to take up the task assigned to them.

The two verbs in the three commands, "Feed" (15, 17) and "Tend" (16) have slightly different meanings. "Feed" means to supply with food, or to take to pasture. "Tend" includes all the care a shepherd would give to his sheep.

The words for sheep differ also. The first (15) is *lamb*
(*arnion*); the second (16) and third (17) denote *sheep* in general (*probatia*). All classes of believers are represented by
these two groups, whether the small lambs or the grown sheep.
There is an echo of this teaching in I Peter 5:2-4:

> Tend the flock of God which is among you, exercising the
> oversight, not of constraint, but willingly, according to the
> will of God; nor yet for filthy lucre, but of a ready mind;
> neither as lording it over the charge allotted to you, but
> making yourselves ensamples to the flock. And when the chief
> Shepherd shall be manifested, ye shall receive the crown of
> glory that fadeth not away.

Peter's own words complete the interpretation of Jesus' charge
to him.

The Final Expectation (21:18-23)

In assigning to Peter his new occupation Jesus made a prediction concerning the future. "When thou shalt be old, . . .
another shall gird thee, and carry thee whither thou wouldest
not" (18). The writer added his comment that Jesus thus
described the manner of Peter's death, which implied that his
fate was already known to the readers of the Gospel.

With characteristic impulsiveness Peter then turned to Jesus
and asked regarding the author of the Gospel, "Lord, and what
shall this man do?" (21) Jesus' reply, "If I will that he tarry
till I come, what is that to thee?" (22) indicated that the next
milepost in His program was His return. The condition, "If I
will that he tarry till I come," intimated that probably the time
of His return would be beyond the average span of life that
any of the disciples could expect. Nevertheless it was the ultimate objective for this present era. The work of the cross was
done, and the crown was yet to come. His coming would be a
time of definite reward and for the fulfillment of the divine
purpose.

With this aim in view, Jesus left with the disciples His last call to faith: "Follow thou me" (22). The use of the second person singular in the pronoun emphasized its personal force; it was not a mass invitation but an individual summons. Naturally the question would rise: If Jesus were asking these men to follow Him, where was He going? Quite plainly He was on the march toward the kingdom of which He had spoken to Pilate (18:36) and He enjoined the disciples to fall in line. Action, not speculation was His command.

The explanation that Jesus had not promised that the beloved disciple should never die was inserted to counteract false rumor that had become current. Unauthentic tradition was in circulation even at the time when the Gospels were written, and called for correction. This conscious attempt to discriminate between truth and exaggerated rumor confirms the authenticity of this Gospel.

Thus the Fourth Gospel concludes with the note of active faith. Having brought its reader to the realization of what belief is and of how it grows, it leaves him, like Peter, with a challenge to put that belief into action. In this way the fulfillment of the purpose of JOHN becomes the responsibility of the individual believer.

Part III

THE TOPICAL ANALYSIS
OF THE GOSPEL

CHAPTER XI

Topical Studies

THE frequent recurrence of certain themes and phrases in the Fourth Gospel leads to the obvious conclusion that the author desired to emphasize them. Some of these repetitions appear in the terms of his vocabulary, such as *belief, life, light, witness, work,* and *world.* Others are lists or classes of events or methods of presentation of his message, such as discourses, interviews or miracles. No attempt will be made within these pages to give a complete account of all possible topics in JOHN, but selected items will be treated because of their significance for the main theme of belief. In some instances where the topic already has been incorporated in the textual analysis, a diagram with critical notes will take the place of a more extended discussion.

The Authorship of the Gospel

Although the four Gospels give no explicit statements concerning their origin, they cannot accurately be called anonymous. The identity of their authors must have been known to the public for whom the writings were first designed. The incidental allusions to the writer which appear in the Fourth Gospel may be regarded as evidence that the authorship was no mystery to the generation in which it was produced, but that it was taken for granted.

The student of the twentieth century, however, is in a less advantageous position for deciding the question of authorship because he cannot call upon the witness of men who were contemporary with the writings. He is dependent upon such facts as may have been transmitted from antiquity and upon such deductions as may be drawn from the text itself. Unfortunately he cannot always be certain that the traditions held by the Fathers were founded on any more definite knowledge than he can derive from the basic documents. Tradition may be correct, and should never be rejected unless there is good reason for disbelieving it, but it is subject to alteration and corruption through accident or design. The evidence which the account contains stands or falls with it. If the narrative is correct, the facts in it constitute first class evidence of its authorship and composition. If it is untrue, neither the Gospel nor any implication to be drawn from it is of any significance. For this reason, many scholars place a higher value upon internal evidence than upon external attestation, since it is not so easily subject to the influence of current opinion.

In keeping with the foregoing principle, and with the inductive nature of this analytic study, internal evidence will be given first consideration.

The last two verses of the Gospel (21:24,25) form a postscript which may have been appended either by the amanuensis whom the author employed or by some of his close associates. The language indicates that "we," possibly the elders of the church in which this Gospel first was circulated, vouched for the truthfulness and authenticity of its contents.

It is possible that the verb "we know" might be rendered as a singular, not as a plural. In the uncial manuscripts of the Greek Gospels all letters were capitals and there were no spaces between the words. The word *oidamen* translated "we know," could have been *oida men* meaning, "I, for my part, know." If that were the case, the endorsement of the writer would emanate from some one person, quite likely his amanuensis, who would be his contemporary and who could represent the view of the church as a whole.

Whatever may be the interpretation of these two verses, two deductions may be drawn from them: the person or persons signified by the "I" or "we" professed knowledge of the truthfulness of the author, and that he or they identified him with the unnamed beloved disciple of the immediately preceding context: "This is the disciple that beareth witness of these things, and wrote these things" (21:24). The pronoun "this" referred back to "that disciple" of whom Jesus spoke to Peter (23) and who was present with Peter and the other disciples at the draught of fishes at the lake of Galilee. He must have been one of the last survivors of the apostolic band, for the story had been circulated "that he should not die" (23). There would have been no object in recording this statement for the public if the life of "that disciple" had not overlapped their generation sufficiently to make the rumor convincing. The author was assuredly known to the first readers by reputation at least.

Two clues to his identity may be derived from the passage as a whole. He was one of a group of seven men who went fishing together. Three were mentioned by name: Simon Peter, Thomas, and Nathanael. The remaining four were the two sons of Zebedee and the two who were unnamed. The one "whom Jesus loved" must have been one of the last four. Again, verse twenty positively identified him with the beloved disciple who leaned on Jesus' breast at the last supper (13:23). He belonged to the Twelve, and was one of the more intimate circle associated with Jesus.

These two clues explain some of the peculiarities of this Gospel. If the author belonged to the small coterie who followed Jesus, it is easy to see how he could have had access to knowledge that the majority of the others might not have possessed. He may have been present with Jesus on occasions when they were absent, and so may have heard teachings which Jesus did not give publicly.

A reconstruction of some of these activities is possible. The beloved disciple was originally a convert of John the Baptist who transferred his allegiance to Jesus on John's recommendation (1:37). He was probably in Jesus' company at the wedding at Cana (2:11), in Samaria at the interview with the woman at the well (4:8, 27), at the feeding of the five thousand (6:3), in Jerusalem at the Feast of Tabernacles (9:2), and with the band who went with Jesus to Bethany for the raising of Lazarus (11:12,16). Since he was included in the Twelve, he was an eyewitness of most of the episodes recounted in JOHN—a conclusion which the vivid details of this Gospel corroborate.

The thirteenth chapter alluded to him as an actor in the story which he told. He reclined on Jesus' breast at the supper (13:23), and at the request of Simon Peter asked Jesus who the traitor would be (13:24,25). He listened to the discourse that followed, but took no part in the questioning of Jesus. After the betrayal he followed Jesus back to Jerusalem and to the house of the high priest, where he obtained entrance because he was known there (18:15). He witnessed the hearing, and gained admittance for Peter also. He may have been present at the hearing before Pilate, though he was not mentioned specifically in the account. At the cross he reappeared, and Jesus there committed to him His mother, Mary. He left the scene of the crucifixion early in order to take Mary to his home. He was not present at the burial, but in company with Peter visited the tomb at the request of the women, "saw, and believed" (20:8).

If this disciple was as important as these references indicate, it is strange that he should have remained nameless. He was well known to Peter and to others, so that his anonymity was not caused by obscurity, unimportance, or lack of recognition. The only admissible reason for the omission of his name is that he himself suppressed it; but why should he have done so?

There are various solutions for this problem. Perhaps he was conforming to type. Although the other Gospels were attributed to men who enjoyed considerable prominence in the church of their day, not one mentions his own name as author.

The writer of the Fourth Gospel may have followed this precedent.

Possibly persecution had begun, for the hints concerning the hatred of the world given in the farewell discourse (15:18-20) may have been emphasized because of their immediate applicability to the time when JOHN was written. Peter had already suffered a violent death, as had others of the apostolic company, and the surviving member who wrote these memoirs may have refrained from declaring his identity to the public because he wished to end his days in peace.

Beside the facts concerning the author which have been recounted above, there are others which are implicit in the content and style. He was acquainted with the topography of Palestine, with the cycle of Jewish feasts, and with the prevalent attitudes of Judaism in the time of Jesus. He was a man of poetic temperament, yet not lacking in virility nor incapable of appreciating reasoning. The selection of historical information in the Gospel was screened through an experience of Christ that was both mature and fervent.

The Fourth Gospel, then, owed its origin to a contemporary of Jesus who associated with Him on intimate terms and who was present with Him at most of the major crises of His life. This person took care to record such events as had not been previously committed to writing, or else he narrated them in a new way and from a different standpoint. His main objective in writing was the development of faith. He can hardly have been other than John, the son of Zebedee. His inclusion in the inner circle, his companionship with Simon Peter, the total absence of any reference to the sons of Zebedee in the main body of the Gospel as compared to the frequent allusion to them in the Synoptics, and the strong possibility that he should be regarded as one of them in the narrative of the Epilogue all point in this direction. There is no more likely candidate for the place of "the disciple whom Jesus loved."

Certain facts tend to corroborate this conclusion. The one disciple associated with Peter in the book of Acts was John. It seems improbable that Peter should have changed associates in the few days between the resurrection and Pentecost. The picture of these two is more coherent if Peter and John were consistently close friends from the days of Jesus' ministry until the dispersion for their world mission compelled them to separate.

Jesus' committal of Mary to the beloved disciple is more easily understandable if he were John. According to Matthew's narrative, one of the women who witnessed the crucifixion was the mother of the sons of Zebedee (Matt. 27:56). A comparison with John 19:25 and Mark 15:40 establishes with a high degree of certainty that she was Salome, the sister of Jesus' mother. John was, therefore, the first cousin of Jesus and nephew of Mary. As the nearest male relative who was a believer, it would be natural for John to undertake the care of his aunt.

One more tenuous piece of evidence is worth mentioning, though by itself it is far from conclusive. In II Peter 1:16-18 the writer says:

> For we did not follow cunningly devised fables, when we made known unto you the power and coming of our Lord Jesus Christ, but we were eyewitnesses of his majesty. For he received from God the Father honor and glory, when there was borne such a voice to him by the Majestic Glory, This is my beloved Son, in whom I am well pleased: and this voice we ourselves heard borne out of heaven, when we were with him in the holy mount.

Three times in this context the glory of Christ is mentioned. The writer, who spoke of the transfiguration, was greatly impressed by the radiance and power of Christ on that occasion. JOHN seems to make a reference to the same event in 1:14: "We beheld his glory, glory as of the only begotten from the Father. . . ." If the Fourth Gospel was written by the son of

Zebedee and Second Peter by Peter, the stress of this word "glory" gains in significance, since these men were the only two survivors of the persecution of Herod who lived to transmit to the church the memories of that notable experience with Jesus.[1]

Thus the internal evidence of the Gospel points backward to an origin among the closest associates of Jesus. Tradition may not be infallible, but no more acceptable hypothesis has been invented to account for the authorship than the historic belief that this Gospel owed its genesis to John, the son of Zebedee.[2]

The Vocabulary

The vocabulary of the Fourth Gospel is so distinctive that it is instantly identifiable wherever it is quoted. Certain characteristics mark it as "Johannine."

First of all, it is limited. The words that express the main concepts of spiritual truth are relatively few in number. Out of seventy-five terms that are used most frequently in JOHN, not more than thirty-five occur so often that they are important; and the number may be reduced even more if roots rather than words are counted, and if some synonyms are regarded as being exact. Each of these words was in common use, was in itself a simple concept, and yet was invested with a profundity of meaning that would almost demand a separate essay.

Because these words were constantly used, the vocabulary of JOHN is repetitious. Consequently the emphasis of thought is heightened, for the recurring nouns and verbs produce a symphonic style. Unlike Paul, who proceeded from propo-

---

1. The Petrine authorship of II Peter has been widely denied by critical scholars; but the statement under discussion was certainly ascribed to Peter at an early date, irrespective of this question.

2. For a thorough discussion of the external evidence from a conservative standpoint, see Theodor Zahn, *Introduction to the New Testament.* (Translated from the Third German Edition . . . under the direction and supervision of M. W. Jacobus . . . New York: Charles Scribner's Sons, 1909) III, pp. 174-206.

sition to proposition by a close chain of reasoning, John began with a central theme which he developed by interrelating it with other kindred themes. These he interwove as a skillful musician elaborates a dominant melody with variations to create a symphony. For example, the Prologue says:

> In him was life,
> and the life was the light of men.
> And the light shineth in the darkness;
> and the darkness apprehended it not. (1:4, 5)

Each of these three terms, "life," "light," "darkness," can be traced as a separate theme throughout the Gospel, but in this passage they are linked together to indicate the identity of the principle of light and the source of spiritual life in Christ; and to show the contrast of these two with the surrounding darkness which could not triumph over Him.

Again, many of the common Johannine terms are symbolic. "Life," "light," "darkness," "work," "world," some uses of "word," "believe," "flesh," "hour," are all either figurative or possess a special technical meaning. "Life" (*zoe*) generally refers to spiritual life, not to physical vitality or career, and in nearly half of its occurrences is coupled with the adjective "eternal" (*aionios*). "Light" (*phos*) almost invariably means spiritual illumination proceeding from Jesus Himself. "World" (*kosmos*) is the system of human life that is opposed to the will and purpose of God, though in 1:29 and 3:16 it refers to the world of living men. The words have to be defined in terms of their peculiar Johannine usage if they are to be rightly understood.

In keeping with the main theme of the Gospel, the characteristic words may be classified as (1) terms relating to faith, (2) terms relating to conflict, and (3) terms relating to spiritual response and achievement.

Belief is the central concept in the Gospel of John. It is expressed by the word "believe" (*pisteuo*) which is repeated ninety-eight times. Curiously enough, the corresponding noun "faith" (*pistis*) does not occur once. The word has a progressive meaning, which can be determined by its use in the context. For instance, John 2:11 says that Jesus' disciples believed on Him, while again 20:8 says that the "other disciple also . . . saw and believed." If he had believed on Jesus on the former of these occasions, why should the assertion be repeated that he "believed" (or "came to belief") at the time of the resurrection? The belief at the wedding of Cana meant that the disciples accepted Jesus as a worker of genuine miracles, who merited their confidence in His powers. The belief at the resurrection indicated a wholehearted surrender, evoked by the conviction that Jesus had really risen from the dead.

The basis for this faith is the concept of witness. Both noun and verb occur in JOHN, the noun "witness" (*marturia*) thirteen times, the verb "bear witness" or "testify" (*martureo*) thirty-three times. This witness concerns chiefly the claims of Christ. Seven distinct witnesses are listed: Christ Himself (5:31, 8:14), John the Baptist (5:33, 1:19), the works (5:36, 10:25), the Father (5:37), the Scriptures (5:39), the Spirit (15:26), and the disciples (15:27).

Witness, however, is meaningful only when it is regarded as true. "Truth" (*aletheia*) is used twenty-five times in the Gospel, and its cognate adjectives, "true" (*alethes*) and "real" (*alethinos*), appear fourteen and nine times respectively. The adverb "truly," "indeed," or "verily," (*alethos*) occurs ten times. All refer to actuality or verity. The message of Christ is truth (1:14), the manner of worship must be truth (4:23), freedom is found in truth (8:32), and Jesus Himself is the Truth (14:6). Truth in JOHN means not only a quality, but the reality supporting all certainty. The adjective *alethinos* translated "true" in 1:9, 4:23, 37, 6:32, 7:28, 8:16, 15:1, 17:3, 19:35, means "true" not in the sense of opposite to lying, as *does alethes;* but in the sense of original or real, as opposed to imitation or illusion. Thus John 17:3 means "the only real God," the only God who actually is God, rather than the only truthful God. The use of these related terms throughout the Gospel makes a latent appeal to reality in contrast to speculation or fancy.

The plot is maintained by the use of three pairs of words which by their very contrast imply an undercurrent of conflict. The first pair appear early in the Prologue, "light" and "darkness." "Light" (*phos*) represents the illuminating revelation of God that comes from Him and leads to Him. Jesus claimed light as a title when He said, "I am the light of the world" (8: 12), and throughout the Gospel the concept of light is attached to His ministry.

"Darkness" (*skotia*) is used eight times in JOHN, six times in the First Epistle of John, and only twice elsewhere in the New Testament. The force of the word is qualitative, generally figurative in meaning, and it refers either to bewilderment or to evil. Another word derived from the same root (*skotos*) which is also translated "darkness" is customarily literal and concrete. It appears once in 3:19 and many times in other New Testament books.

The passage in the Prologue, "the light shineth in the darkness, and the darkness overcame it not" (R.V. margin) is the first hint of the conflict between the righteousness of God and the sin of man. Through the contrasting use of these figurative expressions, which represent spiritual illumination on the one hand and moral confusion on the other, the ethical tension of JOHN is consistently maintained.

The second pair of contrasting terms which carry forward the plot, "flesh" (*sarx*) and "spirit" (*pneuma*) are differentiated in two ways. Jesus first distinguished between the visible and the invisible man by saying in 3:6: "That which is born of the flesh is flesh; and that which is born of the Spirit is spirit." On another occasion He used "spirit" and "flesh" to denote respectively inner reality and outward appearance: "It is the spirit that giveth life; the flesh profiteth nothing: the words that I have spoken unto you are spirit, and are life"

(6:63). "Spirit" was used also by Jesus to define God (4:24), and in sixteen of its twenty-four occurrences in the Gospel it applies to the Holy Spirit. Consequently the cumulative emphasis of "spirit" is on the supernatural element in experience, while "flesh" pertains to the nonspiritual aspect of human life.

The third pair of words depict belief and unbelief through the emotions of "love" and "hate." In 12:25 they are applied to man's attitude to his own life and personality; and in 15:19, they are descriptive of the contrasting attitudes of the world: its love toward those that belong to it, and its hatred toward those that do not. The spirit of love which obtained between Christ and the Father is the secret of the cohesiveness of spiritual life within the Christian society. *Miseo*, "hate," denotes the division between the Christian and the world. Six of the eleven passages containing *miseo* refer to the opposition between the world and Christ, and in some of the others the opposition is implied. Belief and unbelief are inevitably divisive; and produce radical and irreconcilable conflict.

A third group of terms consists of words which portray spiritual response and achievement. The chief of these is "believe," which has already been discussed. Two others are connected with it. One is "follow" (*akoloutheo*), which describes the outward expression of belief. The men who were convinced of Jesus' truthfulness were ready to commit themselves to Him in action. He asked directly for this response (1:43, 21:19), and He received it from those who became His disciples (1:37). The parable of the good shepherd stresses "follow" as the word that pictures the normal relation of the sheep to the shepherd (10:4, 5, 27). In 13:36, 37 Jesus extended its meaning to include ultimate destiny. The word is not exclusively Johannine; it is used similarly by the Synoptics.

The other term connected with "believe" is "take" or "receive" (*lambano*) which means an aggressive rather than a passive reception. The first usage in 1:12 equates it with belief: "But as many as received him, to them gave he the right to become children of God, even to them that believe on his name." Five times it is used of receiving or accepting witness (3:11, 32, 33; 5:34, 43), and three times of the Holy Spirit (7:39, 14:17, 20:22). A parallel is drawn between rejecting Christ and "receiving not his sayings" (12:48); and "receiving his words" is equivalent to discipleship (17:8).

"Receive" is one of the simplest words in any language, for the act of taking is common to all men at all times. Achievement in the spiritual life consists of appropriating God's free offer of truth through His Son as an historic personality and through His Spirit as a pervasive presence.

One of the greatest results of belief is knowledge. Two words were used to express this concept. *Oida,* translated "know" in the Revised Version, means holding a fact as an acceptable mental datum, or taking it for granted. This word occurs eighty-four times in the text of Nestle's Greek Testament, and in three variant readings in 8:56, 14:4, and 14:7. *Ginosko,* usually translated "know," but sometimes "perceive" or "understand," is used fifty-six times in the same text, and appears in one variant reading in 14:7. In some of the passages there is little difference between the words, and one might ask whether the two were not employed indifferently for the sake of variety.

The true distinction, however, between the two words appears in the passages where they are used together. In 7:27, "Howbeit we know (*oidamen*) this man whence he is: but when the Christ cometh, no one knoweth (*ginoskei*) whence he is," the former verb means that the speakers were sure of the place of Jesus' origin, but that when the Messiah comes, no one will realize or understand His origin. John 8:55 is similar in meaning: "Ye have not known (*egnokate*) him: but I know (*oida*) him . . . " Jesus was suggesting that His hearers had not become acquainted with the Father, who was for Him an accepted fact of knowledge. The words to Peter in 13:7, "What I do thou knowest (*oidas*) not now; but thou

shalt understand (*gnosei*) hereafter," charged him with misunderstanding of the footwashing, but promised an interpretation of that meaning at a later time. In 14:7, "If ye had
known (*egnokeite*) me, ye would have known (*edeite*) my
Father also," Jesus implied that, if the disciples had come to a
thorough experiential knowledge of His person, the Father
would have seemed less remote from them. Peter's reply to
Jesus' question in 21:17, "Lord, thou knowest (*oidas*) all
things; thou knowest (*ginoskeis*) that I love thee," is the clearest illustration of all. Peter ascribed full knowledge of everything to Jesus, and then declared that He must have a full
realization or perception of His disciple's love. A fair conclusion, then, is that the distinction between the two words is
subtle, but real.

Of the two Greek words, *ginosko* is more often associated
with belief as might be expected. Progressive realization of
truth is the logical result of faith, whereas the cognition of individual facts is acquired by tradition or by investigation.
The one exception to the almost invariable coupling of *ginosko*
with belief is the confession of the Samaritans: "Now we
believe, not because of thy speaking: for we have heard for
ourselves, and know (*oidamen*) that this is indeed the Savior
of the world" (4:42). The Samaritans made knowledge the
reason for believing and treated it as a fixed premise of truth.
In the same chapter, however, the example of the nobleman
reversed the order of knowing and believing by the use of the
other word (*ginosko*). The author says, "The man believed
the word that Jesus spake unto him, and he went his way . . .
So the father knew (*egno*) that it was at that hour in which
Jesus said unto him, Thy son liveth: and himself believed . . ."
(4:50, 53). One stage of belief brought the perception of
truth which was followed by a further growth in belief.

Other examples of the relation of belief and knowledge
(*ginosko*) may be found in 6:69, 7:17, 8:31, 32, 10:14,
10:27, 10:38, and 17:8. Several expressions are treated as

THE DISTRIBUTION OF VERBS OF KNOWLEDGE IN JOHN

SECTION	KNOW: (Intuitive-*oida*)		KNOW: (Progressive-*ginosko*)	
PROLOGUE 1:1-18		(0)	1:10	(1)
PERIOD OF CONSIDERATION 1:19-4:54	1:26, 31, 33 2:9, 9 3:2, 8,11 4:10, 22, 22, 25, 32, 42	(14)	1:48 2:24, 25 3:10 4:1, 53	(6)
PERIOD OF CONTROVERSY 5:1-6:71	5:13, 32 6:6, 42, 61, 64	(6)	5:6, 42 6:15, 69	(4)
PERIOD OF CONFLICT 7:1-11:53	7:15, 27, 28, 28, 28, 29 8:14, 14, 19, 19, 19, 37, 55, 55, 55, 56* 9:12, 20, 21, 21, 24, 25, 25, 29, 29, 30, 31 10:4, 5 11:22, 24, 42, 49	(32)	7:17, 26, 27, 49, 51 8:27, 28, 32, 43, 52, 55 10:6, 14, 14, 15, 15, 27, 38, 38	(19)
PERIOD OF CRISIS 11:54-12:36a	12:35	(1)	11:57 12:9, 16	(3)
PERIOD OF CONFERENCE 12:36b-17:26	12:50 13:1, 3, 7, 11, 17, 18 14:4, 4*, 5, 5, 7* 15:15, 21 16:18, 30, 30	(16)	13:7, 12, 28, 35 14:7, 7*, 7, 9, 17, 17, 20, 31 15:18 16:3, 19 17:3, 7, 8, 23, 25, 25, 25	(21)
PERIOD OF CONSUMMATION 18:1-20:31	18:2, 4, 21 19:10, 28, 35 20:2, 9, 13, 14	(10)	19:4	(1)
EPILOGUE 21:1-25	21:4, 12, 15, 16, 17, 24	(6)	21:17	(1)
	TOTAL	85	TOTAL	56

*Variant Readings:
8:56—rejected
14:4—rejected
14:7—disputed, but prob-
ably correct

14:7—rejected

equivalent to belief: "to will to do his will" (7:17), to "abide in my word" (8:31), to be "my sheep" (10:14), to "hear" the shepherd's voice (10:27). In one of these instances the order is reversed, and belief follows knowledge (17:8). The consensus of these passages is that faith introduces the Christian to a new realm of experience in which he begins to apprehend spiritual truth.

The accompanying chart affords a complete survey of the occurrences of these two words in the Fourth Gospel.

The Signs

The signs in JOHN have already been discussed partially in connection with the key to the book. The attached diagram is designed to place before the reader a graphic picture of their relation to the structure of the Gospel. The first two signs belonged to the Period of Consideration. In both of them belief was the direct result of Jesus' work. The next three occurred in the Period of Controversy; and each affected a different section of Jesus' public. The healing of the man at the pool involved a single person, the feeding of the five thousand was witnessed by the largest assemblage of people recorded in the Gospels, and the walking on the water was a private manifestation to the disciples. The first two of these miracles was productive of controversy between Jesus and His enemies. The last two of the seven evoked the clearest affirmation of belief and unbelief to be found in the entire story of JOHN.

Although John asserted that the seven signs were selected from a much larger number known to him, he did not exaggerate their importance. He never presented Jesus as a magician who displayed His powers for advertising purposes, but he used these marvels to confirm or illustrate the nature of Jesus' teaching and claims. The miracles turn the attention of the reader to the One who performed them rather to themselves.

THE SIGNS IN JOHN

	Reference	Sign	Belief	Unbelief
C O N S I D E R A T I O N	(1) 2:1-11	*Water Changed to Wine* Quality	Disciples believed 2:11	
	(2) 4:46-54	*The Healing of the Nobleman's Son* Space	Man believed word 4:50 Man and household believed 4:53	
C O N T R O V E R S Y	(3) 5:1-18	*The Healing of the Man at the Pool* Time	Belief implied by action 5:9	Reaction of Jews 5:18
	(4) 6:1-14	*The Feeding of the Five Thousand* Quantity	Acknowledgment of Jesus as prophet 6:14	Departure of many 6:66
	(5) 6:16-21	*The Walking on the Water* Nature	Willing to receive Him into boat 6:21	
C O N F L I C T	(6) 9:1-41	*The Healing of the Blind Man* Misfortune	Progressive Belief 9:11, 17, 33, 38	Reaction of Pharisees 9:16, 24, 29, 40, 41
	(7) 11:1-44	*The Raising of Lazarus* Death	Martha—11:27 Jews—11:45 12:11	Plot of Pharisees 11:53

The truth of miracles is inseparably connected with the personality of Christ. None of these deeds was performed for selfish benefit, nor did Jesus emphasize them particularly. He healed as casually as He ate, whenever there was need. The character of His person does not depend upon the display of supernatural powers, but the signs are the logical expression of deity in action, and corroborate John's central message of the incarnation.

The Symbols

JOHN is usually regarded as the most mystical of the Gospels, and its critics have often said that it is more poetic than historical. The many symbols which it contains are not used extravagantly, but were employed by Christ Himself to depict various aspects of His ministry. Such symbols are: light, darkness, life, water, bread, a door, a shepherd, a vine. All these objects are general in character and universally familiar. Because Jesus applied many of them to Himself (with the exception of darkness), they became personalized parables.

The following chart illustrates how these symbols may be diagrammed with reference to the text and organization of JOHN.

The Interviews

There are no less than twenty-seven interviews between Jesus and some person or group in the Gospel of John. Unlike the witnesses and the signs, the interviews were not confined to the public ministry, but were distributed evenly throughout the book.

The pattern of the interviews is quite uniform. On each occasion, someone was brought into contact with Jesus; Jesus made an inquiry or comment revelatory of the other person's character; and the resultant effect was either belief or unbelief. The conversations were not all of the same length, for some occupied nearly an entire chapter, while others were compressed into a sentence or two. Each incident, however, made some important addition to the total growth of personal belief.

THE SYMBOLS IN JOHN: DISTRIBUTION AND CONTENT

SYMBOL	PERIOD	REFERENCE	CONTENT
Light	*Prologue*	1:4 1:5 1:7 1:8, 8 1:9	Light of men Illumined darkness Witnessed by John the Baptist Distinguished from John The real light
	Period of Consideration	3:19, 19 3:20, 20 3:21	Hated by men Avoided by evil men Sought by doers of truth
	Period of Controversy	(5:35)	Not applicable as general symbol
	Period of Conflict	8:12 :12 9:5 11:9 11:10	"I am the light of the world" Realm of Jesus' followers Repetition of 8:12 Reference to physical light Certainty the result of light
	Period of Crisis	12:35 12:35 12:36, 36, 36 }	Light temporarily manifested Command to take advantage of light
	Period of Conference	12:46	Essentially repetition of 9:5
	Period of Consummation		None
	Epilogue		None

The types of people whom Jesus engaged in conversation were varied and inclusive. Among them were fishermen, beggars, noblemen, priests, teachers, Jews and Samaritans. A few of these, like Nicodemus, were eager to learn from Jesus, but many, like Pilate, were indifferent to His invitations.

The conditions under which the interviews took place were also diverse. There were public and private discussions. Jesus talked with the Samaritan woman at midday; Nicodemus called on Him by night. Most people He met casually; some met Him under constraint. Almost every interview, however, was connected with a specific human problem which was either pressed by Jesus' questioner, or else was discovered by Jesus as the conversation proceeded. The picture drawn by these contacts presented Him as the universal physician of souls, and would be applicable to modern situations.

These interviews, with few exceptions such as those with Mary (2:1-11, centering on verse 4) and the disciples (4:27-38), resulted in immediate acceptance or rejection of His testimony. They were the barometers by which the rise and fall of the popular reaction to Jesus would be measured. The fluctuation of the tension between belief and unbelief was thus expressed by situations that personalized all of His teaching, and that translated the meaning of the incarnation into human experience.

The following chart lists the chief interviews in the Gospel, and summarizes the content and significance of each in relation to the plot.

INTERVIEWS IN THE GOSPEL OF JOHN

SEC.	NO.	REF.	PERSON	SUBJECT	BELIEF	UNBELIEF
I	1	1:35-42	Simon Peter	Introduction	Believed	
	2	1:43-51	Nathanael	Introduction	Believed	
	3	2:1-11	Mary	Hour not come		
	4	2:13-22	Jews	Signs		
	5	2:23-3:15	Nicodemus	New Birth	Believed (?)	
	6	4:1-26	Samaritan woman	Water of Life	Believed	
	7	4:27-38	Disciples	Father's Will		
	8	4:46-54	Nobleman	Sickness of son	Believed	
II	9	5:1-17	Man at pool	Healing	Believed (?)	Question of Pharisees
	10	5:19-46	Jews	Claims		Rejection
	11	6:22-59	Jews (multitude)	Bread of Life	Partial belief	Strife
	12	6:60-70	Disciples	Words-spirit	Declaration of Peter	Departure of many
III	13	7:1-13	Brethren	Visit to feast		Scorn
	14	7:14-24	Jews	Teaching		Misunderstanding
	15	8:12-59	Jews	Claims		Stoning attempted
	16	9:7, 35-38	Blind man	Relation to Jesus	Confession	
	17	10:1-39	Jews	Shepherd		Stoning attempted
	18	11:17-45	Mary and Martha	Death of Lazarus	Confession	
IV	19	12:20-50	Multitude	Death	Secret belief	Open unbelief
V	20	13:1-16:33	Disciples	Farewell	Professed loyalty	
	21	17:1-26	Father	Report of work		
VI	22	18:19-23	High Priest	Charges		Rejection
	23	18:28-19:6	Pilate	Charges		Compromise
	24	20:11-18	Mary Magdalene		Joy	
	25	20:19-23	Disciples		Gladness	
	26	20:26-29	Thomas	Reality	Confession	
VII	27	21:15-23	Peter	Love	Profession	

Bibliography

The following list is by no means exhaustive, but it includes the majority of the commentaries and reference works that the average reader will find helpful in the study of JOHN. Not all of the titles listed represent the viewpoint maintained in this book, and some of them should be read cautiously and critically. Those works that are predominantly conservative in character are marked with an asterisk (*).

Abbott, Edwin A. *Johannine Vocabulary.* Cambridge: The University Press, or London: Adam and Charles Black, 1905. Pp. xviii, 364.

—*Johannine Grammar*, Cambridge: The University Press, or London: Adam and Charles Black, 1906. Pp. xxvii, 687. Useful chiefly to students of Greek.

Bernard, J. H. *A Critical and Exegetical Commentary on the Gospel According to St. John.* Vols. II. In *International Critical Commentary,* Edited by A. H. McNeile. New York: Charles Scribner's Sons, 1929. Pp. clxxxviii, 740.

*Erdman, Charles R. *The Gospel of John: An Exposition.* Philadelphia: The Westminster Press, 1916. Pp. 178.

*Fisher, George P. *The Grounds of Theistic and Christian Belief.* Revised Edition. New York: Charles Scribner's Sons, 1909. See Ch. XI, "The Authorship of the Fourth Gospel," pp. 245-321.

*Gloag, Paton J. *Introduction to the Johannine Writings.* London: James Nisbet and Company, 1891. Pp. xiii, 440.

*Godet, Frederic. *Commentary on the Gospel of John.* Translated from the second French edition by Frances Crombie and M. D. Cusin. Three volumes. Edinburgh: T. & T. Clark, 1876-77.

*Hayes, Doremus A. *John and His Writings.* New York: The Methodist Book Concern, 1917. Pp. 371.

Lange, John Peter. *The Gospel According to John.* Translated from the German by Edward D. Yeomans and Evaline Moore, edited by Philip Schaff. New York: Scribner, Armstrong & Co., 1872. Pp. xiv, 654.

*Lightfoot, J. B. *Biblical Essays.* London: Macmillan & Co., 1893. Pp. xiv, 459. Excellent treatment of authorship.

Meyer, Heinrich. *Critical and Exegetical Handbook to the Gospel of John.* Translated from the fifth German edition by Wm. Urwick. New York: Funk & Wagnalls Co., 1884. Pp. 565.

*Milligan, William and Moulton, William F. *The Gospel of John* in *A Popular Commentary on the New Testament,* edited by Philip Schaff. Volume II. New York: Charles Scribner's Sons, 1880. Pp. xxvi, 577.

*Morgan, G. Campbell. *The Analyzed Bible: John.* New York: Fleming H. Revell Co., 1907. Pp. 237.

*—*The Gospel According to John.* New York: Fleming H. Revell Co., n.d. Pp. 333.

*Nunn, H. P. V. *The Son of Zebedee.* London: Society for Promoting Christian Knowledge, 1927. Pp. ix, 150.

Plummer, Alfred. *The Gospel According to John* in *Cambridge Greek Testament.* Cambridge: University Press, 1896. Pp. lxiv, 382.

—*The Gospel According to St. John* in *The Cambridge Bible.* Cambridge: University Press, 1912.

*Reith, George. *St. John's Gospel with Introduction and Notes,* in *Handbooks for Bible Classes and Private Students,* edited by Alexander Whyte and James Moffatt. Two Volumes. Edinburgh: T. & T. Clark, 1926.

*Robertson, Archibald T. *The Divinity of Christ in the Gospel of John.* New York: Fleming H. Revell Co., 1916. Pp. 172.

*—*The Fourth Gospel: The Epistle to the Hebrews.* Vol. V in *Word Pictures in the New Testament.* Nashville Tenn.: Sunday School Board of the Southern Baptist Convention, 1932. Pp. xxvii, 451.

*—*Epochs in the Life of the Apostle John.* New York: Fleming H. Revell Co., 1935. Pp. 253. A very comprehensive treatment of the life and works of John.

*Smith, P. V. *The Fourth Gospel: Its Historical Importance.* London: Society for Promoting Christian Knowledge, 1926. Pp. xi, 146.

Stanton, V. H. *The Gospels as Historical Documents.* Part IV: "The Fourth Gospel." Cambridge: University Press, 1920.

Stevens, George B. *The Johannine Theology.* New York: Charles Scribner's Sons, 1895. Pp. xiii, 387.

Streeter, B. H. *The Four Gospels.* New York: The Macmillan Co., 1925. See Part II, "The Fourth Gospel and Its Sources," pp. 361-482.

*Thiessen, Henry C. *Introduction to the New Testament.* Fourth Edition. Grand Rapids, Michigan: Wm. B. Eerdmans Publishing Co., 1948. Pp. 347.

*Griffith-Thomas, W. H. *The Apostle John: His Life and Writings.* Grand Rapids, Mich., Wm. B. Eerdmans Publishing Co., 1946. Pp. 372. Contains excellent homiletical outlines.

Watkins, H. W. *The Gospel According to John* in *The Handy Commentary,* edited by G. J. Ellicott. London: Cassell & Co., Ltd., n.d. Pp. 468.

*Westcott, Brooke Foss. *The Gospel According to St. John.* Two Volumes. London: John Murray, 1908. Pp. cxcvi, 283, 394. Probably the greatest single commentary on JOHN ever published.

*White, W. W. *Studies in the Gospel of John.* New York: Fleming P Revell Co., 1895. Pp. 130.

*Zahn, Theodor. *Introduction to the New Testament.* Translated from the third German edition under direction and supervision of M. W. Jacobus and C. S. Thayer. Three Volumes. Edinburgh: T. & T. Clark, 1909. See Vol. III, pp. viii, 539.

Index

319

Satan (see Devil)
Scriptures, 109, 110, 134
Second coming of Christ, 221
Shepherd, Good, 161-166
Signs, 28, 30, 31, 33, 34, 47, 83, 84, 97, 113, 116, 117, 152, 156, 170, 177, 218, 311, 312 (chart), 313
Simon, see Peter
Sleep (death), 173
Structure, 27, 49
Sin, or sins, 148, 232, 236
Sychar 47, 92
Synoptics or Synoptists, 34, 36, 41, 43, 45, 49, 68, 69, 79, 84 fn., 91, 97, 112, 122, 124, 162, 184, 185, 196, 197, 253, 254, 257 fn., 258, 266, 283, 301, 307

Temple, 47, 84, 105, 132, 138, 139, 142, 143, 151, 161, 166, 203, 226
Textual criticism, 120 fn., 137, 138, 152 fn., 154, 160 fn., 214 fn. 271 fn.
Thomas, 27, 173, 214-216, 219, 253, 278, 279, 281, 282, 284, 288, 299
Tiberias, Sea of, (see Galilee, Lake of), 48

Time, Reckoning of, 92, 114
Trinity, 239
Truth, 215, 262, 263, 305
Unbelief, 51, 53, 89-91, 123, 125, 129, 130, 143, 146, 151, 159, 160, 167, 177, 181, 183, 190, 193-196, 205, 256, 258, 264, 265, 269, 270, 272, 284, 307, 312
Unity, 248, 249
Upper Room, 203, 205, 254

Vine, 226-229
Virgin birth, 120, 121, 150
Vocabulary, 27-29, 51, 67, 131, 132 fn.[5], 135, 147, 175, 200, 211, 223, 235, 240, 241, 244, 245, 246, 247 fn., 248, 268, 290-292, 297. 303-311

Walking on water, 31, 34, 114, 115
Water, Living, 93, 94, 134, 135
Witness(es), 73, 74, 107-111, 150, 158, 230, 232, 271, 287, 297, 305
Word (incarnate), 39, 50, 53, 59-73, 195
Works, 108, 117, 169, 177, 218, 219, 297
World, 63, 67, 131, 222, 226, 230-233, 235, 237, 240, 297, 304